A HISTORY OF MODERN LIBYA

Second Edition

Dirk Vandewalle is one of only a handful of scholars who have made frequent visits to Libya over the last four decades. His formidable knowledge of the region is encapsulated in his history of Libya, which was first published in 2006. The book – based on original research and interviews with Libya's political elite – traces Libya's history back to the 1900s with a portrait of Libya's desert terrain, its peoples, and the personalities that shaped its development. It then examines the harrowing years of the Italian occupation in the early twentieth century, through the Sanusi monarchy and, thereafter, to the revolution of 1969 and the accession of Qadhafi. The chapters that follow analyze the economics and politics of Qadhafi's revolution, offering insights into the man and his ideology as reflected in his *Green Book*. In the wake of the civil war and Qadhafi's demise, the time is ripe for an updated edition of the history, which covers the years from 2005 to the present. These were the years when Libya finally came in from the cold after years of political and economic isolation. The agreement to give up the weapons of mass destruction program paved the way for improved relations with the West. By this time, however, Qadhafi had lost the support of his people and, despite attempts to liberalize the economy, real structural reform proved impossible. This, as Vandewalle contends in the preface to this new edition, coupled with tribal rivalries, regional divisions, and a general lack of unity, paved the way for revolution and civil war. In an epilogue, the author reflects on Qadhafi's premiership, *The Green Book*'s stateless society, and the legacy that Qadhafi leaves behind.

Dirk Vandewalle is Associate Professor of Government at Dartmouth College. He is the author of *Libya Since Independence: Oil and State-Building* (1998) and editor of *North Africa: Development and Reform in a Changing Global Economy* (1996) and *Qadhafi's Libya: 1969–1994* (1995).

A HISTORY OF MODERN LIBYA

Second Edition

DIRK VANDEWALLE

Dartmouth College

CAMBRIDGE UNIVERSITY PRESS

CAMBRIDGE UNIVERSITY PRESS
Cambridge, New York, Melbourne, Madrid, Cape Town,
Singapore, São Paulo, Delhi, Mexico City

Cambridge University Press
32 Avenue of the Americas, New York, NY 10013-2473, USA

www.cambridge.org
Information on this title: www.cambridge.org/9781107615748

© Cambridge University Press 2006, 2012

First published 2006
Second edition 2012

Printed in the United States of America

A catalog record for this publication is available from the British Library.

Library of Congress Cataloging in Publication data
Vandewalle, Dirk J.
A history of modern Libya / Dirk Vandewalle. – 2nd ed.
p.   cm.
Includes bibliographical references and index.
ISBN 978-1-107-01939-3 (hardback) – ISBN 978-1-107-61574-8 (paperback)
1. Libya – History – 1969–   2. Libya – Foreign relations – 1969–
3. Libya – Politics and government – 1969–   I. Title.
DT236.V35   2012
961.204–dc23   2011040931

ISBN 978-1-107-01939-3 Hardback
ISBN 978-1-107-61574-8 Paperback

Contents

Illustrations

Maps

Preface to the Second Edition

The uprising against the government of Mu'ammar al-Qadhafi that started in eastern Libya in February 2011 questioned many of the assumptions even seasoned observers of the country had made about the regime and about its durability. To many, the carapace of security organizations and other measures to protect the regime had long seemed unassailable. Yet, slightly over six months later, on the 1 September 2011 anniversary of Qadhafi's revolution, the Libyan leader was in hiding, and an international conference in Paris announced measures to provide international support to the Libyan opposition to help rebuild Libya. Seven weeks later, on 20 October, Qadhafi was dead. The willingness, by a population that had for more than four decades been cowered by the diktats of Qadhafi's revolution, to stand up for its rights seemed almost beyond belief. The surprise was even greater in light of internal developments in Libya since December 2003 when the government had agreed to hand over its weapons of mass destruction to the West and had embarked on a period of economic liberalization and reintegration into the international community that had seemingly provided a safety valve for the regime.

In the first edition of this book I covered developments in Libya roughly through 2005. In the conclusion to the final chapter I wrote about the challenges Libya would face as it moved toward becoming part of the international community once more. The assumption that underpinned much of the chapter's analysis was that Libya would somehow muddle through under Qadhafi, sustained by its oil revenues – but that serious economic reform would also entail political reform, something the regime was unlikely to allow (despite the entreaties of Saif al-Islam al-Qadhafi, the Libyan leader's son).

In retrospect, it is clear that none of Libya's essential political problems were seriously addressed between 2003 and the eruption of popular anger in 2011. This at least had come as no surprise. As I argued in the first edition, Qadhafi's self-styled revolution had become a self-reverential and

self-centered political experiment that would only change upon the death
or the replacement of its creator. Most observers and most Libyans therefore had resigned themselves to a prolonged period of muddling through,
aided by oil revenues that had once more dramatically increased by 2011.
The uprising, therefore, marked a clear, surprising break with politics – or
lack thereof – as usual in Libya.

When my editor, Marigold Acland, approached me to consider a second
edition of *A Modern History of Libya*, her request afforded me the chance
to not only bring the earlier volume up to date, but also to reflect in the
Epilogue on what I see as the larger theme of political and economic development in an exceptionally rich oil exporter whose ruler has squandered
much of that wealth in pursuit of a number of visions that to most Western
observers looked quixotic, if not incomprehensible. The major question, as
this book goes to press, is whether Libya's current and future rulers, now
facing the enormous tasks of state and nation building, will do better.

The Libya that I visited prior to 2003 and the Libya that had emerged by
the spring of 2011 – the period covered in the final chapter of this edition –
was, at least at the surface, very different. The agreement on WMDs, the
settlement of the Lockerbie claims, the reestablishment of more open trade
relations with the rest of the world, and the renewal of diplomatic relations with the United States all contributed in various ways to help change
the physical appearance of the country. Long an economic backwater as a
result of the economic and diplomatic sanctions by the international community, the return of international oil companies and the renewed influx
of oil money created virtually overnight a building boom the like of which
Libya had never experienced in its history. For a short while, aided by the
assurances by Saif al-Islam al-Qadhafi that Libya had turned a corner, it
seemed as if the country would finally embark on a path of development
relatively untainted by Qadhafi's earlier ideological preoccupations. When
Libya reestablished diplomatic relations with the United States and then
became its favored partner in the fight against Islamic radicalism in the
region, the country's newfound direction seemed confirmed.

In the concluding chapter of the first edition I had remarked that
"inexorably, the combination of economic necessity, generational turnover, and reintegration into the global economy will continue to change
Libya's political and economic life." When I wrote those words in 2006,
many close observers were cautiously optimistic about the country's
future. There were, however, some warning signs that little had structurally
changed in how the country was being governed. The events I describe in
the final chapter of this second edition, particularly the cult of personality

and the propaganda campaign to burnish Qadhafi's international image after 2005 – eagerly underwritten by a bevy of Western intellectuals and public figures – should have made us more aware of some of the immutable aspects of Libyan politics.

The uprising against the regime came at a point when Libya's fortunes looked somewhat promising. The regime seemed firmly entrenched once more, with ample oil revenues capable of lubricating the regime's extensive patronage mechanisms. As the battles along the *litoranea* in spring and early summer 2011 became stalemated, however, the vicious fighting by both Qadhafi's supporters and the rebels starkly exposed some of the old faultlines the regime's policies since 1969 has obscured but never obliterated: the lingering suspicion between the tribes, between the provinces, among Libyans generally, and the more general lack of national identity. Above all, as the country descended into a war of attrition, there were hints of the chaos to come – the result of first the monarchy's and then Qadhafi's unwillingness to create this sense of identity that could have transcended the primordial divisions within a country that was formed willy-nilly and *ex nihilo* six decades ago.

History has never been kind to modern Libya, and it will no doubt be equally unkind in the few months and years ahead. The civil war was only a harbinger of the equally daunting difficulties that lie ahead in whatever configuration post-conflict Libya emerges. Hopefully, as the reconstruction – or, perhaps more accurately, the construction, for the first time – of Libya as a political community with a truly national identity takes place, the sad shadows of the country's past can be erased. However, as I point out in the Epilogue to this book, the dual challenges of state and nation building will undoubtedly prove arduous in light of the tortuous political path the country has stumbled along since its independence.

London,
28 October 2011

Preface to the First Edition

This book is the result of almost three decades of observing and writing about Libya. In the process, countless individuals in a number of countries have talked to me and corresponded with me about Libya. Many of them I have acknowledged earlier in my *Libya Since Independence*. Since then, however, I have incurred additional debts to a number of others who kindly provided additional help and insights since the late 1990s. In no particular order, they include Dr. Saleh Ibrahim and Milad Saad Milad at the Academy of Higher Education in Tripoli; Ms. Salma al-Gaeer of the Academy of Higher Education and the Green Book Center; Youssef Sawani of the Green Book Center; Zahi Mogherbi of Gar Yunis University; Muhammad Siala, Secretary for International Cooperation; Mehdi Emberish, Secretary of Culture; Ahmed Jalala of the Academy of Graduate Studies; Engineer Jadalla al-Talhi, former Prime Minister and Foreign Minister of the Jamahiriyya; Abu Zayed Dorda, former Prime Minister and Minister of the Economy; Saif al-Islam al-Qadhafi; Salem al-Maiar and Tony Allan of the School of Oriental and African Studies in London; Ethan Chorin of the United States Liaison Office in Tripoli; Tarik Yousef of Georgetown University; David Mack at the Middle East Institute in Washington; Moncef Djaziri at the University of Geneva; and Saad al-Ghariani of the Academy of Higher Education in Tripoli.

A very special thanks to Rosemary Hollis of the Royal Institute of International Affairs in London. My gratitude as well to Robert Springborg and Arnold Luethold, who organized two conferences at, respectively, the London Middle East Centre (at the School of Oriental and African Studies) and the Geneva Centre for the Democratic Control of Armed Forces. Last but not least, my gratitude to Mustafa Ben Halim, Prime Minister of Libya during the monarchy, who agreed to meet in London in order to shed light on the tumultuous developments that took place during his tenure in office. A sabbatical leave from Dartmouth College allowed me to finish the manuscript. Marigold Acland and two anonymous readers for Cambridge

University Press provided insightful and thoughtful comments as the manuscript progressed.

Transliterations from the Arabic in this book use the classical Arabic spelling except where any attempt to do so would render names unintelligible to some readers – hence Tripoli rather than Tarabulus. For the transliteration of place names I have relied on *Gazetteer No. 41 – Libya* (June 1958) published by the United States Board on Geographic Names. The *ta marbuta*, however, when not in construct state, is rendered a and not ah as in the *Gazetteer*: Zuwara rather than Zuwarah. Arabic words familiar to a western audience – such as *ulama* and *sharia* – are written without diacritical marks. Unless in quotations from original sources – that, for example, render Jaghbub as Giarbub or Giarabub in official Italian documents – I have chosen to adopt the spelling used by the *Gazetteer*, with the caveat noted above.

The General People's Congress and Committee system (Libya's equivalent of a parliament and a cabinet) used a complex and confusing set of designations for its institutions and for those who represent it. The Secretary of the General People's Committee for Foreign Affairs is simply "the Foreign Minister" or "the Secretary of Foreign Affairs" in this book. The General Secretariat of the People's Bureau for Planning is simply "the Ministry of Planning."

A final note on sources: the literature on Libya is by now enormous, and of widely varying quality. In order to provide some guidance, and to keep the text manageable and accessible, readers will find in the bibliography and in the endnotes to each chapter references to some of what are, in my estimation, the most important works on Libya's modern history. Most, except for references to newspaper articles and Libyan documents, and excluding a handful of French sources, are in English. A more exhaustive bibliography, as well as references to additional Arabic sources, can be found in my *Libya Since Independence* and in specialized bibliographies of Libya. Just before going to press, the Centre for Libyan Studies in Oxford graciously provided me with the first three (of a projected eight) volumes of *Libya Between the Past and the Present* (in Arabic) by Dr. Muhammad Mugharyif [Mohamed Yousef Al-Magariaf]. They provide an extremely valuable overview of Libyan history, and include a collection of historical documents as well as previously unavailable pictures – some of which were provided, courtesy of the Centre for Libyan Studies, for this book. My sincere thanks to Youssef El-Megreisi for making them available.

A special thanks to Ian Martin who asked me to serve as his political advisor at the United Nations during its pre-assessment phase for Libyan post-conflict planning in Summer 2011. Finally, as a result of Libya's civil war, several people mentioned in this Preface have either been killed or have left the country. This second edition is dedicated to the memory of Dr. Salma al-Gaeer, a close and longtime friend, who unfortunately did not survive her country's civil war.

Chronology, 1900–2011

THE OTTOMAN AND ITALIAN PERIOD

1517	The Ottoman Empire occupies Cyrenaica.
1551	The Ottoman Empire occupies Tripoli.
1711	Ahmed Bey Qaramanli, the Ottoman governor of Tripoli, establishes the Qaramanli dynasty.
1803	The *Philiadelphia*, a United States frigate, is captured off Tripoli harbor.
1835	End of the Qaramanli dynasty; the Ottoman Empire re-occupies Tripolitania, Fazzan, and Cyrenaica during three campaigns of conquest.
1843	Muhammad Abd al-Wahhab al-Sanusi, founder of the Sanusiyya, establishes his headquarters in Cyrenaica.
1843	The Ottomans occupy Ghadames.
1855	The Sanusiyya moves its headquarters to Jaghbub.
1859	Muhammad al-Sanusi dies in Jaghbub.
1890	Anglo-French convention delineates British and Ottoman spheres of influence in North Africa.
1895	The Sanusiyya moves its headquarters to Kufra.
1902	Ahmad al-Shariff al-Sanusi becomes head of the Sanusiyya.
1908	The Young Turk revolt takes place in Constantinople, briefly raising hopes for political independence in Tripolitania.
1910	A French–Ottoman agreement settles the borders between Tripolitania, Algeria, and Tunisia.
26 September 1911	Italy sends the Ottoman sultan an ultimatum, announcing its intent to occupy Tripolitania and Cyrenaica.

5 November 1911	Italy announces the annexation of Tripolitania and Cyrenaica and does so formally on 25 February 1912.
October 1912	The Ottoman Empire and Italy sign an ambiguous agreement at Ouchy, Italy, claiming sovereignty while Constantinople refuses to renounce its claim.
1912	Ahmad al-Shariff assumes the leadership of resistance against the Italians in Cyrenaica.
March 1913	Sulayman Al-Baruni, a Berber leader from Tripolitania, and his followers, are defeated at the Battle of Asabaa by the Italians. Al-Baruni flees to Turkey.
1913	Italian forces attempt the occupation of Tripolitania, Cyrenaica, and Fazzan, but make little initial headway.
1915	The Italians suffer a defeat at the hand of Ramadan al-Suwayhli of Misrata, at the battle of Qasr Bu Hadi.
1915	Sulayman Al-Baruni returns from Istanbul to Libya as governor of Tripolitania.
1915	Ramadan al-Suwayhli and his followers form an independent republic at Misrata.
April 1917	Sayyid Idris al-Sanusi, now head of the Sanusiyya, signs the Akrama Agreement with Italy, which placed virtually all of Cyrenaica under Sanusi control.
18 October 1918	Italian–Turkish peace treaty gives Italy nominal control over Tripolitania and Cyrenaica.
October 1918	The defeated Ottoman Empire formally signs the Armistice agreements.
November 1918	Al-Baruni and Suwayhli formally declare Tripolitania independent, resulting in the creation of the Tripolitanian Republic.
1 June 1919	Italy recognizes, and issues statutes for, the Tripolitanian Republic.
October 1919	Separate statutes known as the Legge Fondamentale, for Cyrenaica and Tripolitania, accepted by Italy; each province to have its own parliament and local councils.
August 1920	Ramadan al-Suwayhli is killed in a battle with rival tribesmen who object to the Tripolitanian Republic.

October 1920	The al-Rajma Agreement between the Italians and the Sanusiyya confirms Sayyid Idris al-Sanusi as Amir of Cyrenaica.
November 1920	At the Gharyan conference Tripolitanian leaders attempt to forge a common agenda to press their demands vis-à-vis Italy.
28 July 1922	Representatives from the Gharyan conference offer the Amirate of Tripolitania to Sayyid Idris al-Sanusi.
October 1922	Benito Mussolini comes to power in Italy.
November 1922	Sayyid Idris accepts the Amirate of Tripolitania, and is now the recognized Amir of both Cyrenaica and Tripolitania.
December 1922	Sayyid Idris al-Sanusi leaves Cyrenaica for exile in Cairo where he will remain until after World War II.
1923	Umar al-Mukhtar organizes the resistance to the Italians in Cyrenaica after Sayyid Idris's exile to Cairo.
11 September 1931	Umar al-Mukhtar is captured by the Italians.
16 September 1931	Umar al-Mukhtar is executed.
June 1934	The Libyan–Sudan border is agreed upon between Great Britain and Italy.
March 1937	Mussolini visits Libya to inaugurate the Litoranea Libica and to have himself proclaimed Protector of Islam.
1938	Italy embarks upon grand-scale agricultural settlements in Libya.
August 1940	During a meeting in Cairo with Libyan exiles, Sayyid Idris al-Sanusi is authorized to negotiate with the British after the war for independence.
October–December 1942	Second battle of al-Alamein. As a result of the battles in Cyrenaica and western Egypt, the Italian settlers leave Cyrenaica and the Italians withdraw from Libya.
1943	The Allies' expulsion of Germany and Italy from North Africa leads to the creation of a British Military Administration in Tripolitania and Cyrenaica, and of a French Military Administration in Fazzan.

15 February 1947	Italy formally relinquishes its sovereignty over Libya.
6 March 1948	The Four Power Commission of Investigation arrives in Libya and finishes its work on 20 May.
15 September 1948	The United Nations General Assembly takes up the matter of Libyan independence.
10 May 1949	France and Great Britain publish the Bevin-Sforza plan, proposing ten-year trusteeships for the Libyan provinces. A resolution in support of the plan is defeated in the UN General Assembly.
June 1949	Cyrenaica creates an independent administration. Tripolitania, under British administration, creates municipal councils. Fazzan remains governed under French Military Administration.
21 November 1949	The United Nations General Assembly passes a resolution creating an "independent and sovereign state" of Libya, assigning to a future National Assembly the task of creating a provisional government of Libya.
25 November 1949	Libya's National Assembly, consisting of sixty selected members chosen equally from the three provinces – Tripolitania, Cyrenaica, and Fazzan – meets in Tripoli for the first time in order to prepare the country's constitution. It declares that Libya will be a federal state.
10 December 1949	The United Nations appoints Adrian Pelt as the UN Commissioner in Libya.
2 December 1950	Libya's National Assembly decides to create as soon as possible a United Kingdom of Libya and offers Idris al-Sanusi the throne.
4 December 1950	The National Assembly creates a Committee of the Constitution to prepare a draft constitution.
March 1951	Provincial governments are created in Tripolitania and Fazzan.
29 March 1951	Libya's National Assembly creates a provisional government.
10 September 1951	Discussions begin in the National Assembly on a draft constitution.

7 October 1951	Libya's Constitution is promulgated by the National Assembly.

THE LIBYAN MONARCHY

24 December 1951	The United Kingdom of Libya proclaims its independence and is headed by King Idris al-Sanusi.
19 February 1952	Libya holds its first general election. Political parties are banned in its aftermath.
25 March 1952	Libya's Parliament meets for the first time.
12 February 1953	Libya joins the Arab League.
26 July 1953	Libya signs a twenty-year military agreement with Great Britain.
9 September 1954	Libya signs a military agreement with the United States.
5 October 1955	Assassination of Ibrahim al-Shalhi, Councilor to King Idris, by Al-Shariff Bin al-Sayyid Muhi al-Din al-Sanusi, grandson of Sayyid Ahmad al-Shariff and cousin of King Idris.
1955	Libyan Petroleum Law comes into effect, also creating the country's Petroleum Commission.
24 May 1957	Mustafa Bin Halim resigns as Prime Minister.
1961	Amendments are added to the 1955 Libyan Petroleum Law.
25 October 1961	Libya's first oil shipment leaves from Marsa al-Burayqa [Brega].
1962	Libya joins the Organization of Petroleum Exporting Countries (OPEC).
January 1963	Re-establishment of Sanusi zuwaya (religious lodges).
April 1963	The federal arrangement is abandoned in favor of a unitary state.
May 1963	Libya launches its first five-year plan for economic and social development. Creation of a Ministry of Planning.
1963	First development plan from 1963 to 1968.
1965	Second set of amendments added to the 1955 Libyan Petroleum Law, followed by the creation of the Libyan National Oil Company.
April 1968	Creation of the Libyan Petroleum Company (LIPETCO).

| July 1968 | Libya announces that it will no longer award concession agreements, and that all future agreements will be awarded under joint ventures with LIPETCO. |

THE QADHAFI PERIOD

1 September 1969	A military coup, headed by Mu'ammar al-Qadhafi, overthrows the monarchy.
29 October 1969	The Libyan government demands the withdrawal of all British troops and the liquidation of its military bases.
14 November 1969	The first foreign banks and hospitals in Libya are nationalized.
28 November 1969	First major speech by Qadhafi on why representative democracy is unsuited to Libya.
11 December 1969	Proclamation of the new Provisional Constitutional Declaration.
27 December 1969	Libya, Egypt, and Sudan sign the Tripoli Charter.
28 March 1970	British forces are requested to evacuate Al-Adem Airbase.
5 May 1970	First colloquium of Libyan intellectuals and revolutionaries to debate the revolutionary orientations of the country.
16 June 1970	The last American troops evacuate Wheelus Airbase.
21 June 1970	Confiscation of Italian-owned properties announced.
5 July 1970	First major laws on the nationalization of the oil industry, initially limited to the nationalization of the internal distribution networks of Shell and Esso.
1 August 1970	The internal distribution networks of the remaining oil companies are nationalized.
28 September 1970	President Nasser of Egypt dies.
14 November 1970	Administrative reorganization: creation of governorates (*muhafadhat*) and municipalities (*baladiyyat*) or districts (*mudiriyyat*) to break down traditional tribal administrative boundaries.
December 1970	Nationalization of all banks.
14 January 1971	At Zawiya, Qadhafi announces the creation of Popular Congresses.

15 January 1971	Libyan Producers' Agreements announced.
17 April 1971	Libya, Egypt, and Syria agree to create the Union of Arab Republics, to officially come into effect on 1 January 1972.
5 June 1971	All foreign cultural centers, except that of France, are closed.
12 June 1971	Creation of the Arab Socialist Union (ASU).
15 October 1971	All Libyan insurance companies are nationalized.
28 October 1971	Creation of a commission by the Revolutionary Command Council to revise the country's legal system in conformity with Islamic law.
7 December 1971	British Petroleum nationalized.
28 March–7 April 1972	First national ASU congress in Tripoli.
12 April 1972	Abolition of the right to strike.
30 May 1972	The ASU adopts a law making all political activities outside the single party punishable by death.
4 August 1972	The United States reduces its embassy staff in Tripoli to fifteen members at Libya's request. The U.S. ambassador in Tripoli resigns.
November 1972	Qadhafi for the first time specifically proclaims sovereignty over the Gulf of Sirt.
16 April 1973	Qadhafi issues his Third Universal Theory and announces the popular revolution in a speech at Zuwara.
18 April 1973	Creation of the first popular committees.
2 June 1973	Popular committees take over the country's television and radio stations.
8 June 1973	Libya accuses the United States of infringing its 100-mile "restricted air zone" off the Mediterranean coast. Tripoli expels a U.S. diplomat for not having an Arabic passport.
11 June 1973	The popular committees take over education, agriculture, and culture in the country.
11 August 1973	The Libyan government nationalizes 51% of Occidental Petroleum.
1 September 1973	51% of all remaining foreign oil companies nationalized.

6 October 1973	Start of the Ramadan / Yom Kippur War, leading to the end of Qadhafi's unity plans with Egypt.
18 October 1973	The average price of Libyan crude oil jumps from $4.604 to $9.061 per barrel.
26 October 1973	Libya embargoes oil exports to the United States for its support of Israel.
1 January 1974	The price of Libyan crude jumps from roughly $9 per barrel to $15.768 per barrel.
11 February 1974	Libya nationalizes three U.S. oil companies: Texaco, the Libyan American Oil Company, and California Asiatic.
7 April 1974	Qadhafi resigns to devote himself to revolutionary activities, becoming the qa'id ath-thawra (Leader of the Revolution), but remains head of the armed forces. Abd as-Salam Jallud becomes head of state.
May 1974	Jallud visits the Soviet Union and concludes the first major Soviet–Libyan arms agreement.
6 September 1974	Reinvigoration of the popular revolution.
1974	Libya concludes its first Exploration and Production-Sharing Arrangements (EPSA I).
2 March 1975	Student demonstrations against the Qadhafi government in Benghazi.
27 April 1975	New statutes of the ASU announced.
13 August 1975	First major abortive coup against the Qadhafi regime, led by two Revolutionary Command Council (RCC) members.
26 August 1975	Creation of Revolutionary Courts.
3 September 1975	Three major "socialist" laws are announced, restricting real-estate speculation and imports of certain goods.
12 September 1975	The United States announces restrictions on strategic equipment purchased by Libya and restrictions on training of Libyans in the use of certain types of aircraft.
17 September 1975	Publication of the first of several essays in Al-Fajr al-Jadid that will eventually become *The Green Book*.
November 1975	First Basic People's Congresses created.

5–18 January 1976	The first General People's Congress (GPC) convenes; the ASU is abolished.
7 April 1976	The government puts down student demonstrations.
25 May 1976	Qadhafi announces the creation of special committees that will intensify the revolution. They will eventually become the Revolutionary Committees.
17 September 1976	Official publication of Democracy, the first volume of *The Green Book*.
13–24 November 1976	Second meeting of the General People's Congress.
4 February 1977	Libya is added to the United States Defense Department's list of potential enemies of the United States.
28 February 1977	Extraordinary GPC meeting at Sabha to ratify the declaration of People's Power.
2 March 1977	Sabha Declaration: the GPC special congress declares Libya a Jamahiriyya – a state managed directly by its citizens. The Declaration on the Authority of the People replaces the Provisional Constitutional Declaration of 11 December 1969.
3 July 1977	Major debate between Qadhafi and the *ulama* at Tripoli's Moulay Muhammad Mosque regarding the political and economic role of Islam in modern societies.
21–24 July 1977	Egyptian–Libyan border clashes.
6 November 1977	Establishment of the first Revolutionary Committee in Tripoli.
November 1977	Third GPC meeting. The second volume of *The Green Book – The Solution of the Economic Problem* – is published.
March 1978	Announcement of the elimination of private property.
6 May 1978	Promulgation of the *bayt li sakinihi* policy: "The house belongs to [those] who live in it."
1 September 1978	First calls for the separation of "the instruments of the revolution" and "the instruments of governing."

19 December 1978	Qadhafi resigns as Secretary General of the General People's Congress to dedicate himself to the intensification of the revolution.
December 1978	Intensification of the campaign to abolish all retail and private trading.
2 March 1979	Remaining Revolutionary Command Council members are relieved of their duties. The GPC issues "The Declaration on the Separation of Rule and Revolution," officially separating the "instruments of the revolution" and the "instruments of government."
1 June 1979	Publication of *The Social Basis of the Third Universal Theory*, the third part of *The Green Book*.
1 September 1979	Libyan embassies are converted into People's Bureaus. Announcement of the creation of Revolutionary Committees within the Libyan army.
2 December 1979	Attack on the U.S. embassy in Tripoli; the embassy is set on fire.
29 December 1979	Libya is put on the U.S. State Department's list of sponsors of state terrorism.
1979	Libya concludes its second Exploration and Production-Sharing Arrangements (EPSA II).
3 February 1980	Qadhafi calls for the physical liquidation of Libyan dissidents – "stray dogs" – living abroad.
15 February 1980	The U.S. embassy in Tripoli closes.
Spring through Fall 1980	First campaign spearheaded by the Revolutionary Committees to eliminate Libyan opponents – "stray dogs" – overseas.
March 1980	Elimination of private savings accounts.
16 May 1980	26 U.S. citizens expelled from Libya; the United States withdraws its two remaining diplomats.
2 September 1980	Libyan–Syrian union announced. Libya opens itself up to all Arabs and creates Arab passports.
6 May 1981	The United States closes the Libyan embassy in Washington.
12 May 1981	The right to maintain private practices for all professional occupations is abolished.

19 August 1981	Two Libyan aircraft downed by the United States over the Gulf of Sirt.
7 October 1981	Creation of the National Front for the Salvation of Libya, an opposition movement to Qadhafi.
4 November 1981	Exxon withdraws its operations from Libya.
10 March 1982	The United States bans all exports except food and medicine to Libya; the import of Libyan oil into the United States is prohibited.
13 December 1982	Qadhafi announces the replacement of the country's armed forces by a popular army.
January 1983	Mobil withdraws its operations from Libya.
June 1983	Second major Libyan invasion of Chad.
Spring 1984	New campaign against "stray dogs." Creation of state supermarkets.
17 April 1984	British policewoman Yvonne Fletcher is fatally shot by Libyan security personnel outside the Libyan embassy in London, leading to a rupture in British–Libyan relations.
July/September 1985	Libya expels large numbers of foreign laborers, in an effort to help balance the country's budget in the wake of lowered oil revenues.
15 November 1985	President Reagan bans the import of all refined petroleum products from Libya.
7 January 1986	The United States invokes the International Emergency Economic Powers Act, halting imports of all goods and services of Libyan origin. U.S. companies are prohibited from engaging in industrial or commercial contracts with Libya.
5 April 1986	A bomb explodes at a discotheque in West Berlin, killing three people.
15 April 1986	U.S. aerial attack on Tripoli and Benghazi. In its aftermath, officially organized demonstrations in Tripoli are lackluster. Qadhafi fails to make public addresses for several weeks. The European Union agrees to more restrictive visa policies for Libyan nationals.
6 May 1986	The leaders of the G7 countries vow to fight terrorism and single out Libya as a major perpetrator.

30 June 1986	The U.S. Treasury Department forces remaining U.S. oil companies to leave Libya but allows them to negotiate standstill agreements, retaining ownership for three years while allowing the Libyan National Oil Company to operate the fields.
February 1987	At the GPC meeting, criticism of the country's economic hardships paves the way for an attempted economic and political liberalization.
26 March 1987	Announcement of Libya's first *infitah* (economic liberalization).
23 May 1987	Qadhafi speech on industrial and agricultural reform.
1 September 1987	Qadhafi speech at the anniversary celebrations of the revolution, allowing the re-introduction of a private sector.
22 November 1987	The Revolutionary Committees are severely criticized at the thirteenth General People's Congress.
March 1988	Creation of the Ministry of Mass Mobilization and Revolutionary Orientation to limit and institutionalize the power of the revolutionary committees.
May 1988	Curtailment of the power of the Jamahiriyya's revolutionary courts. They are replaced by People's Courts.
12 June 1988	Adoption of the Great Green Charter of Human Rights.
21 December 1988	Pan Am flight 103 explodes over Lockerbie.
1988	Libya concludes its third Exploration and Production Sharing Arrangements (EPSA-III).
4 January 1989	U.S. fighter jets down two Libyan aircraft over the Gulf of Sirt.
1 September 1989	Libya agrees to submit the Aouzou dispute to the International Court of Justice.
19 September 1989	French airliner UTA 772 explodes over Niger.
15 November 1991	Libya is indicted by the United States and Great Britain in connection with the 1988 Lockerbie bombing of Pan Am 103. Two Libyans are charged with the bombing.
21 January 1992	The United Nations Security Council unanimously approves a resolution requiring Libya to

cooperate with investigations made by the United States and Great Britain in the Lockerbie incident by surrendering two of its citizens.

31 March 1992	The United Nations Security Council passes Resolution 748, asking Libya to turn over suspects in the Lockerbie and UTA cases.
15 April 1992	A boycott of commercial airflights into the Jamahiriyya, approved by the United Nations Security Council, takes effect.
11 November 1993	The UN passes Resolution 883, strengthening existing sanctions and freezing Libyan assets in foreign banks, as well as banning imports of spare parts for the country's oil industry.
3 February 1994	The International Court of Justice assigns the Aouzou strip to Chad, voiding Libya's claim to the disputed territory.
October 1994	Major rebellion by army units near Misrata are put down by units loyal to Qadhafi.
11 November 1994	The United Nations Security Council further extends its embargo against Libya.
5 August 1996	The United States adopts the Iran and Libya Sanctions Act that penalizes all firms (including foreign ones) that invest more than $40 million in the Libyan energy sector.
April 1998	Libya confirms that it will allow a trial of the Lockerbie defendants in a neutral country, operating under Scottish law.
24 August 1998	The United States and Great Britain agree to a trial in the Netherlands for the Lockerbie suspects.
27 August 1998	The United Nations Security Council passes Resolution 1192, promising to suspend economic sanctions if Libya turns over the Lockerbie suspects.
5 April 1999	Libya agrees to surrender the two Lockerbie suspects for trial in the Netherlands.
11 June 1999	Libyan and U.S. officials meet for the first time in eighteen years to discuss the UN sanctions.
September 1999	Libya organizes a special meeting of the Organization of African Unity in Sirt.

25 March 2000	U.S. State Department officials visit Libya to assess lifting the ban on travel into Libya.
3 May 2000	The Lockerbie trial opens.
31 January 2001	A panel of three judges finds one of the Libyan Lockerbie defendants guilty and acquits the other.
March 2003	The GPC adopts legislation to reform the Libyan economy.
June 2003	Dr. Shukri Ghanem is appointed as Prime Minister, in part to guide the economic reform efforts.
May 2003	Libya approaches Britain and the United States to discuss outstanding issues, including weapons of mass destruction. Libya makes an offer to the Lockerbie families for a settlement that ties compensation to the lifting of sanctions.
August 2003	Libya and the Lockerbie victims' families agree on a framework for compensation totaling $2.7 billion.
18 August 2003	Libya and the International Monetary Fund (IMF) conclude Article IV consultations.
12 September 2003	The UN Security Council votes to lift sanctions against Libya.
23 October 2003	The IMF issues Public Information Notice 03/125 following the conclusion of Article IV consultations.
19 December 2003	The Libyan government announces that the country will abandon its pursuit of weapons of mass destruction.
January 2004	The United States removes from Libya equipment and documents related to the country's nuclear and missile programs, and starts to destroy its chemical munitions.
9 January 2004	Libya agrees to pay additional compensation to the families of victims of a French UTA airliner that exploded in 1989 over Niger.
February 2004	Muhammad Al-Baradei, Director General of the International Atomic Energy Agency, arrives in Tripoli for discussions to dismantle Libya's nuclear program.
26 February 2004	President Bush issues an executive order that will allow American companies to begin negotiating a

	return to Libya. The order lifts the ban on travel to Libya.
March 2004	The National People's Congress discusses an additional number of measures meant to liberalize the Libyan economy.
April 2004	Qadhafi visits Brussels at the invitation of the European Union, his first trip outside the Middle East or Africa in fifteen years. Prime Minister Tony Blair visits Tripoli.
23 April 2004	A number of U.S. economic sanctions are lifted, allowing trade between Libya and the United States – except for specified goods – to proceed.
23 May 2004	Qadhafi walks out of the Arab summit in Tunis, arguing that its agenda is irrelevant.
June 2004	Libya and the United States re-establish diplomatic relations.
3 September 2004	Libya signs an agreement to compensate victims of the LaBelle discotheque ($35 million), to be paid out fully by 1 March 2005.
20 September 2004	The United States formally revokes its trade embargo against Libya.
11 October 2004	The European Union lifts its arms embargo against Libya.
January 2005	The Libyan National Oil Company announces the awarding of new exploration agreements for fifteen onshore and offshore blocks. U.S. companies obtain the majority of the new exploration licenses.
January 2005	At the Davos economic summit, Saif al-Islam al-Qadhafi announces further measures to liberalize the Libyan economy.
12 January 2005	Libya abolishes its People's Courts.
May 2005	Qadhafi convenes Sudanese representatives in Tripoli to help find a solution to the Darfur crisis.
May 2006	The United States restores full diplomatic relations with Libya.
February 2007	Creation of the Libyan Economic Development Board.

April 2007	John Negroponte, U.S. Deputy Secretary of State, visits Libya, but is snubbed by Qadhafi who instead meets with lower-ranking officials.
April 2007	Libya hosts talks on Darfur in Sirte.
July 2007	President Bush nominates Gene Cretz as ambassador to Libya. His appointment is held up until Libya pays further compensation for past terrorist incidents.
May 2008	The United States and Libya agree in principle on compensation settlements for Lockerbie, the La Belle discotheque bombing, and the 1989 UTA airliner.
14 August 2008	The United States and Libya conclude a comprehensive claims settlement in Tripoli, agreed to in principle in May. The agreement leads to normalization between the two countries.
August 2008	Saif al-Islam al-Qadhafi announces that he is withdrawing from politics.
September 2008	Secretary of State Condoleezza Rice visits Libya.
20 August 2009	Abd al-Baset al-Megrahi, the convicted Lockerbie bomber, is released by the Scottish government on compassionate grounds. Accompanied by Saif al-Islam al-Qadhafi, Megrahi returns to Tripoli where he is given a hero's welcome and meets with Colonel Qadhafi.
17 February 2011	The uprising against the Qadhafi regime starts in Benghazi after Fathi Tarbil, a human rights activist, is arrested.
21 February 2011	Diplomats at the Libyan mission to the United Nations side with the revolt.
26 February 2011	The United Nations Security Council imposes sanctions on Qadhafi and his family and refers Libya to the International Criminal Court. It also asks the International Criminal Court to investigate human rights abuses.
28 February 2011	The European Union approves sanctions, including an arms embargo and travel ban.
1 March 2011	The United Nations General Assembly unanimously suspends Libya's membership of the UN Human Rights Council.

5 March 2011	An interim national council meets in Benghazi and declares itself the sole representative of the Libyan people.
10 March 2011	France recognizes the Libyan National Council as the legitimate representative of the Libyan people.
16 March 2011	Loyalist forces are near Benghazi; Saif al-Islam al-Qadhafi declares that "Everything will be over in 48 hours."
17 March 2011	United Nations Security Resolution 1973 authorizes the establishment of a no-fly zone over Libya and allows additional measures to protect the lives of civilians.
19 March 2011	U.S.-led coalition air strikes commence and halt the advance of Qadhafi's forces on Benghazi.
28 March 2011	Qatar recognizes Libya's rebels as the legitimate representatives of the Libyan people.
29 March 2011	Convening of the London Conference, meant to create an international framework of assistance to the Libyan rebels.
31 March 2011	NATO takes over command of operations in Libya.
10 April 2011	Qadhafi accepts a roadmap to end the conflict after meeting with an African delegation headed by President Zuma of South Africa.
13 April 2011	First meeting of the Libya Contact Group in Doha, Qatar. Representatives from twenty-one countries as well as from the United Nations, the Arab League, NATO, the European Union, the Organisation of Islamic Conference, and the Cooperation Council for the Arab Gulf States discuss the situation in Libya. The African Union attends as an invitee.
25 April 2011	NATO strikes Bab al-Azziziya, Qadhafi's compound, in Tripoli.
30 April 2011	A NATO strike kills Qadhafi's youngest son, Saif al-Arab al-Qadhafi, and three grandchildren. Libyan Foreign Minister Musa Kusa defects and flees to Great Britain.
5 May 2011	Second meeting of the Libya Contact Group in Rome.
16 May 2011	Luis Moreno-Ocampo, the prosecutor of the International Criminal Court in The Hague, indicts Mu'ammar al-Qadhafi, Saif al-Islam al-Qadhafi, and Abdullah al-Sanusi for crimes against humanity.

30 May 2011	President Jacob Zuma of South Africa meets with Qadhafi to discuss a negotiated settlement to the civil war, hoping to revive the African Union's "roadmap."
1 June 2011	Russian Foreign Minister Sergei Lavrov repeats his criticism of NATO, arguing that the coalition's military operations exceeded the UNSC's mandate.
9 June 2011	Third meeting of the Libya Contact Group in Abu Dhabi.
15 June 2011	The Obama administration issues a statement that U.S. military actions in Libya do not amount to "hostilities" and as such the executive branch was not in violation of the War Powers Resolution.
15 June 2011	South African president Jacob Zuma condemns NATO operations in Libya, arguing that they extend beyond the mandate provided by UNSC 1973.
27 June 2011	The International Criminal Court issues arrest warrants for Mu'ammar al-Qadhafi, Saif al-Islam al-Qadhafi, and Abdullah al-Sanusi for crimes against humanity.
29 June 2011	France acknowledges that it has provided the Libyan rebels with weapons; Russia argues that France committed a violation of UN Resolution 1970, which imposes a weapons embargo on Libya.
15 July 2011	At the fourth Libya Contact Group meeting in Istanbul, the United States announces its formal recognition of Libya's National Transitional Council as the country's legitimate government.
20 July 2011	French foreign minister Alain Juppé states that Qadhafi will be allowed to stay in Libya once the conflict is ended, provided that "he very clearly steps aside from Libyan political life." Juppé's statement mirrors a similar one made on 16 July by American diplomats in Tunis to Libyan regime officials, subject to Libyan rebels' agreement.
21 July 2011	Libyan opposition leader Mustafa Abdel Jalil states that Qadhafi could potentially remain in Libya as part of a negotiated settlement.
23 July 2011	Libyan prime minister Al-Baghdadi al-Mahmoudi declines all offers of negotiations that would put restrictions on Mu'ammar al-Qadhafi.

28 July 2011	Abdul Fatih Younes, the Libya rebels' military commander, is killed, exposing a number of faultlines among the TNC and within eastern Libya in its wake.
8 August 2011	In the aftermath of Younes's killing, the Libyan rebels dissolve the TNC cabinet.
18 August 2011	The rebels take control of the Zawiya's oil refinery.
20 August 2011	Rebel forces enter Tripoli.
1 September 2011	At an international conference in Paris, on the forty-second anniversary of Qadhafi's 1969 revolution, world leaders gather to consolidate international support for a post-Qadhafi Libya.
October 2011	Final civil war battles for Bani Walid and Sirt.
20 October 2011	Mu'ammar al-Qadhafi is killed in Sirt.
21 October 2011	NATO announces that it will cease operations in Libya on 31 October.
23 October 2011	Libya's Transitional National Council issues the country's Declaration of Liberation in Benghazi.
27 October 2011	The United National Security Council votes unanimously to end its authorization of the foreign military intervention in Libya on 31 October 2011.

Acronyms

AAN	*Annuaire de l'Afrique du Nord*
ASU	Arab Socialist Union
BMA	British Military Administration
BPC	Basic People's Congress
CYDEF	Cyrenaican Defense Force
FBIS	*Foreign Broadcast Information Service* (Near East and South Asia) (transcription service provided by US government)
GPC	General People's Congress
IBRD	International Bank of Reconstruction and Development
JR	*Al-Jarida Al-Rasmiyya* – Libyan newspaper
LNOC	Libyan National Oil Company
NFSL	National Front for the Salvation of Libya
RCC	Revolutionary Command Council
SQ	*As-Sijil Al-Qawmi bayanat wa ahadith al-aqid Mu'ammar al-Qadhafi* – collected speeches and pronouncements by Mu'ammar al-Qadhafi
ZA	*Al-Zahf Al-Akhdar* – newspaper of the Revolutionary Committees

Introduction: Libya, the enigmatic oil state

The history of Libya in the twentieth century represents, even by Middle Eastern standards, an extraordinary odyssey: from Ottoman backwater to Italian colony; from conservative monarchy to revolutionary regime; from rags to riches; and from brinkmanship to a grudging and still unfolding statesmanship. For most of the century, the inhabitants of the three provinces that became incorporated into the United Kingdom of Libya in 1951 – Tripolitania, Cyrenaica, and Fazzan – stood on the sidelines as a succession of foreign and local rulers and interests shaped their country. Excluded from involvement with the colonial machinery during the Italian occupation (1911–1942), marginalized politically during the monarchy (1951–1969), and subject to a homegrown version of socialism after the military coup in 1969, Libyans share a tumultuous history of statebuilding that continues to leave them perplexed even today.

Perhaps it is more accurate to observe that the people of Libya became witnesses to a political and economic phenomenon that has often been observed in oil exporters throughout the Middle East: the attempt by their rulers, with the aid of extensive oil revenues, to avoid the process of statebuilding that normally includes the steady expansion of the administrative reach of the state, as well as a growing incorporation of local citizens in that process. Indeed, in Libya even today, it remains problematic to consider its people truly as citizens. Despite his rhetoric to the contrary, their current ruler continues to view them more or less as his personal subjects, and he has done little to help create confidence in the more impersonal institutions of a modern state. To that extent, the Qadhafi regime shows a remarkable continuity with the monarchy that preceded it, and has created a political system that will face considerable challenges in the future.

How, and why, Libya's rulers chose to pursue what I refer to in this book as statelessness – the avoidance of creating a modern state – forms its intellectual Leitmotiv. In order to address its multiple dimensions, I raise a number of more fundamental questions that throw light on the political, social, and economic history of modern Libya: about the role of oil in the development of the country, and about the weight and legacies of history in the relationships between the local population and its rulers. Simultaneously, I attempt to trace the impact of Arab nationalism and Islam on Libya's development, to discern the precise impact of petroleum revenues on social stratification and on development, and to gauge the changing roles of individuals and primordial loyalties in a society that became rapidly and inexorably incorporated within the global economy. Finally, I also investigate the interaction between a traditional society and an incomplete state whose survival and economic fortunes are overwhelmingly determined by unimpeded access to the global economy.

The two central features in the development of Libya after its independence in 1951 have been oil, and the revenues its sales generated. It freed first the monarchy, and then the Qadhafi regime, from many of the burdens other countries faced during their state-building history – burdens that, in all countries, shape the political, economic, and social relationships between rulers and ruled. Perhaps the most important freedom is that in an oil exporter like Libya, rulers face few burdens of taxation or accountability that can limit their actions. Libya's rulers, starting very soon after independence, seemingly had the luxury to construct the contours of their political community without undue political or economic constraints. What truly makes Libya a political anomaly, however, is that it chose to follow a path – at first, during the monarchy as a policy of benign neglect, then in a more deliberate fashion after the 1969 coup – that systematically reduced and severely limited the construction of a modern state and its institutions.

In a century when the growing power of the state has constituted one of the few shared political traits across the world, Libya's rulers questioned its validity – and then acted upon that conviction to circumscribe its influence. The idea that oil riches can be used to transform rapidly and irrevocably – or, in this case, halt or reverse – the social and political structures of local societies is of course not unique to the Libyan leadership. For a variety of reasons, at least rhetorical lip service to the "ethos of the tribe" as an alternative to modern state institutions has lingered on far into the twentieth century within several oil exporters in the Middle East. What has been unique once more in Libya after independence in 1951 has been the attempt to extend on a national scale – but very selectively – the kind of primordial structures and relationships that had not really been present in the country since it became exposed to the wider world during the Italian colonial period.

It is important to understand that, from the creation of the monarchy onward, there existed in Libya a tension between the pursuit and maintenance of an earlier form of political community – based on family and tribe – and the exigencies of a modern state that could potentially obliterate the relevance of such primordial ties in favor of the more impersonal relations of modern economic life. Particularly after 1969, the rhetoric and flamboyance of the regime obscured a more profound and unique process by which it attempted to avoid the burdens of extending the mechanisms of a modern state. Instead, it enunciated a vision of statelessness that was carefully wrapped in a cloak of nostalgia for earlier times when family and tribe provided solidarity, equity, and egalitarianism. In the end, of course, the pursuit of that vision proved contradictory and impossible. Much of Libya's current attempt to reintegrate itself into the international community proves how futile and costly those attempts at trying to avoid modern state structures have been.

Perhaps the more important question, however, is what made the very notion of statelessness so attractive in a country that was willy-nilly being rapidly dragged into the global economy? To most readers, this wish to maintain a stateless, essentially pre-bureaucratic society will strike them as archaic and naive – particularly in light of a hydrocarbon state's intimate reliance on exposure to the international economy. What then explains its continued pursuit in the country's political life since independence? To understand this anomaly, one must understand how – starting with the retreat of the Ottoman Empire from the country in the early part of the twentieth century – a multilayered set of factors promoted the idea among Libya's rulers that statelessness was both possible and desirable, while oil created the permissive and enabling environment to act upon that conviction.

One reason the nostalgia for a pre-burcaucratic community resonated so strongly throughout Libya's modern history was undoubtedly the memories of the country's first traumatic encounter with the notion of modern statehood during the Italian colonial period, described in Chapter 2. The construction of what the Italians referred to as their "Fourth Shore" left a heavy legacy of political exclusion and brutal subjugation of the local population that, until today, continues to provide a focus for the country's collective memories. The uprising against the Italians collapsed in 1931 when Umar al-Mukhtar, a Cyrenaican *shaykb* and Libya's enduring national hero, was captured and hanged by the fascists. Libya's first exposure to modern statehood under the Italians had been uniformly deleterious, and left few of its future leaders with a taste for a unified, strong state.

Italy's defeat in World War II effectively put an end to further Italian ambitions for its Libyan territories. In the aftermath of the war – which had destroyed a substantial part of the country's existing infrastructure – the Great Powers at the United Nations, after considerable wrangling, decided to create the United Kingdom of Libya in 1951. As king of the new nation, they settled upon Idris al-Sanusi, the heir to a religious movement in Cyrenaica that had provided much of the resistance against the Italians. As described in Chapter 3, the newly created kingdom faced a number of complex challenges. The United Kingdom of Libya in 1951 presented – as had once been argued about Italy itself during the nineteenth century – little more than a geographical expression. The three provinces that made up the newly created country lacked most of the ingredients necessary for the creation of modern statehood: its citizens possessed no sense of national identity, and the newly created state barely managed to raise enough revenues to maintain even the most rudimentary state institutions, or – the sine qua non of modern states – the monopoly of coercive power. Citizens from Tripolitania, Cyrenaica, and Fazzan reluctantly agreed to the creation of the Sanusi monarchy out of fear of the imposition of United Nations' trusteeships that would have meant further foreign tutelage.

The country and its new ruler thus faced the simultaneous challenges of creating a political community and a modern state. This difficult task – headed by a monarch who himself showed no real interest in ruling the three provinces as a unified political community – was exacerbated from the start by the inflows of capital that Great Britain and the United States extended in return for the rent of military bases. It allowed the king to avoid flexing the young state's institutional muscles and to postpone the process of building a state that could attract the attention of its newly minted citizens across the three provinces. Indeed, in 1952 he summarily – allegedly on British advice – canceled the first and only multi-party elections the country has known until today.

The discovery of oil in 1959 further and forever changed the country's fortunes, but in highly unexpected and unforeseen ways. It provided Idris al-Sanusi with an even greater and inordinate power to shape the country's political and economic life – or, as it happened, to avoid doing so. The relative wealth now in the country's coffers could seemingly help compensate for the weaknesses of the state. It could be used for strengthening family and tribal alliances in support of the monarchy while leaving most of the state's underdeveloped economic and political structures unattended. Since existing social groups had weakly developed collective interests, the king found it easy to obliterate their collective identities by means of spending oil revenues. The power of the purse, and the emergence of a patrimonial political system, allowed Idris al-Sanusi to further weaken the few organized groups that existed within the country's civil society. The monarchy thus started Libya on the road of political exclusion of its citizens, and of a profound de-politicization, that continue to characterize it today.

My central argument, traced throughout Libya's emergence as an independent country in the twentieth century, is that a number of interlocking factors extended this lopsided and incomplete nature of local state-building: the legacy of the Italian period; the sudden arrival of enormous revenues that accrued directly to the country's rulers without, in the process, creating adequate checks and balances; the political exclusion of the Libyan population; the lingering attraction of tribe and family that seemingly provided acceptable alternatives to the notion of state; and the eagerness of the country's rulers not to perfect that state for their own ideological and often predatory purposes. Chapters 2 and 3 explore the emergence of some of these factors during the Italian colonial period and during the monarchy, while the subsequent chapters concentrate on the years since 1969 when the military coup took place. The years covered in Chapters 2 and 3 deserve closer attention in understanding Libya's modern history, not only because they have been relatively uninvestigated but also because they set in motion the processes of political exclusion and suspicion of the structures of the modern state that then informed, and were extended, by the revolutionary government.

To many readers of this book, Libya will primarily be identified with the regime of Mu'ammar al-Qadhafi, and with the decades of spectacular internal and foreign policies his self-styled revolutionary regime pursued. The inordinate attention that has been lavished on the current Libyan leader, and on his actions since 1969, is perhaps unavoidable. He has dominated the country's political life for three-and-a-half decades, and for the largest part of the country's existence as an independent nation. Yet many of the current regime's past actions – its insistence on self-reliance, its pursuit of statelessness that seemed so hopelessly anachronistic, its antagonism to the West, and the use of terrorism as a foreign policy tool – must be understood against the backdrop of the earlier chapters.

For over three decades, after its self-proclaimed revolution in 1969, the rhetoric and brinkmanship of the Libyan leadership partly obscured what transpired inside the country. Much of the West's attention, fueled by an inexhaustible media appetite for the Libyan leader's often eccentric behavior, ignored the more profound contradictions and difficulties Qadhafi's attempt at pursuing statelessness engendered. The focus on

Qadhafi – unfortunately often expressed in a manner that added little to our understanding – was not wholly misplaced however. For the Libyan leader has intimately controlled his country's political system and its inter-action with the international community, to a degree only highly authori-tarian systems permit.

In addition, Qadhafi's Jamahiriyya – his neologism meant to convey statelessness, a system in which the people govern themselves without the apparatuses of a modern state – proved to be full of contradictions. For example, until his conversion to pan-African unity, Qadhafi claimed to represent the future of pan-Arabism and Arab nationalism in the Middle East. Yet Libya remained forever too inconsequential a player on the regional political scene to pursue and implement such ambitions, and the Libyan leader's exhortations for Arab unity were routinely dismissed with derision and scorn in the Arab world and the West alike. In the same vein, although the Libyan leader is an austere and devout Muslim, his vision of Islam is both deeply personal and idiosyncratic. Also, in theory, all power in the Jamahiriyya belongs to the people, but organized opposition is expressly forbidden. The Green Book, Qadhafi's ideological primer to his self-styled revolution, asserts that the country's citizens directly manage its political and economic life, but Libya even today remains an exclusionary political system whose decision-making process has been restricted to a small cadre of advisors and confidantes, and where economic decisions are similarly outside popular purview or devoid of any means of checks and balances. Finally, Qadhafi, while decrying the structures of modern state-hood, has also denounced primordial tribal and family ties as antiquated remnants unsuitable to a Jamahiriyya. At the same time, evidence suggests that the Libyan leader increasingly relied on them for his own physical survival as the revolutionary aspects of his rule started to falter by the early to mid-1990s.

For analytical purposes, as his revolution waxed and waned, Qadhafi's years in power can be subdivided into four more or less distinct periods.

The first (Chapter 4) concerns the early years of the revolution, when the regime attempted to consolidate itself, and expended a great amount of political energy to mobilize Libya's society on behalf of its revolution. After imitating the mobilizational efforts of his hero, President Gamal Abdul Nasser of Egypt, the Libyan leader quickly discovered the limits of polit-ical persuasion. The revolutionary regime had to adjust to the fact that, the rhetoric of statelessness notwithstanding, oil exporters have little choice but to rely on active state intervention in their economies – albeit in a unique fashion. The first four years of the regime can thus essentially be considered as a period of stocktaking for the young revolutionaries, during which Qadhafi in somewhat gingerly fashion tested the limits of the country's emerging political system.

His disappointment, combined with the inflow of massive oil revenues after 1973, led to the more spectacular economic and political experiments that constitute the focus of Chapter 4. The long decade between 1973 and early 1986 forever became the hallmark of Qadhafi's Libya. In a spectacular set of reforms, based on the philosophy contained in his Green Book, the Libyan leader transformed or obliterated many of the country's economic and political structures. He did so while emphasizing that Libya could do without a set of state structures that, at least in his estimation, prevented citizens from running their daily lives. Simultaneously, however, the Libyan state became even more an overwhelmingly powerful economic agent in the country. Rather than engaging in regulation, however, it engaged in a kind of wholesale management that left little room for fine-tuning its economy. This shortcut hinted at the much more fundamental weaknesses of a state that, at least superficially, looked strong. As part of its efforts at political mobilization, the regime ratcheted up its rhetoric against the West but, temporarily, still refrained from engaging wholesale in terrorist activities.

The political and economic experiments continued until the mid-1980s when a growing combination of economic hardship, confrontation with the West, and inefficient economic management started to take its toll on the country. The outcome of Libya's first attempt to adjust to these challenges, and to reform politically and economically, is described in Chapter 6. It focuses, in part, on what occurs in an oil exporter like Libya after long periods of neglect of the local economy, and after years of unwillingness to regulate and diversify the economy. It details furthermore Libya's inability to reform when the country encountered a financial crisis, and it delineates its leader's impotence to refashion the existing social contracts with his country's citizens that had often grown into extensive entitlements during periods of high oil revenues. In Libya, the economic hardships proved particularly severe because of the constraints upon the country's economy resulting from a combination of US and multilateral sanctions, and because of the growing diplomatic isolation of the country. While the regime managed to postpone meaningful reform for a decade longer and became the last great spender of petrodollars during the decade, there were the first indications that the revolution had reached its limits and that a slow process of institutionalization and bureaucratization was finally starting to take place.

Chapter 7 provides the capstone to the analysis of Libya's pursuit of statelessness and of Qadhafi's attempts to foment revolutionary upheaval. It analyzes the regime's decision to put an end to its foreign adventures and to attempt to reform its economy once more. Focusing on the remarkable set of adjustments and compromises the Jamahiriyya embarked upon starting in mid-1999, the chapter demonstrates how, even in countries where personal rule and tightly controlled patrimonial systems prevail, their leadership is ultimately subjected to conditions, international developments, and internal adjustments they must, willy-nilly, come to terms with. Eventually, all revolutionary regimes start to institutionalize, and Libya proved no exception. The country's "everlasting revolution" in retrospect has not been unique. It did not escape the inexorable pull toward greater bureaucratization, efficiency, and pragmatism, when faced with the onslaught of internal economic and political difficulties, generational renewal, and fewer international economic and diplomatic options. Careful observers of Libya had noted the beginning of this emerging pragmatism almost a decade before its government announced in December 2003 that it would abandon its pursuit of weapons of mass destruction.[1] When the announcement came, however, it marked the formal acceptance – commented on by the Libyan leader and his entourage alike – that the country's revolutionary pursuits and methods had become impossible. But it would take the 2011 uprising and the country's subsequent civil war to bring home the message of how impossible Qadhafi's self-styled revolution had become.

In writing the history of an oil exporter, it is always tempting to blame the course of events simply on the pernicious impact of oil on the country's political and economic structures and fate. Certainly, oil in Libya created the permissive environment: the monarchy could never have practiced its policies of benign neglect except for oil revenues, and the Qadhafi government could not have experimented with statelessness without them. Such an analysis, however, reduces or obliterates the impact countless individuals could have – and did have – in determining the outcome of the different layers of state-building (or lack thereof), as described in this book, during crucial turning points in the country's history. While oil may have made political experimentation possible, whatever decisions the country's rulers made were motivated by personal considerations, and tempered by a number of social, cultural, and religious restraints that resonated within Libya at large: codes of conduct, customs, cultural norms, and a collection of traditions that informally helped to determine the behavior of the country's rulers – who very often were anxious to portray their policies as falling within those understood traditions and norms.

In retrospect, it is perhaps facile to say that Libya until now has not been served well by its leaders – but that is to ignore the difficult circumstances under which they had to take decisions in incremental fashion, often with few alternatives, when faced by an often indifferent or hostile set of superpowers and by an apathetic society, and when trying to survive both physically and politically. Much of what the following chapters portray focuses in part on the struggles both regimes – but particularly the revolutionary one – experienced as they attempted to create and recreate social bases of support for their policies during the country's economic boom-and-bust cycles.

Blaming everything on oil also draws attention away from the often agonizing struggles individuals – leaders as much as ordinary citizens – and social groups in Libya experienced as they tried simultaneously to embark upon (or hold in abeyance) a process of western-inspired modernization while devising ways to hold a weak state together as it was torn between modernity and an often artificially maintained tradition. It is ultimately this struggle in Libya – traditional and often insular internally, but intricately and unavoidably linked to the larger international economy and community – that forms the inevitable backdrop to its history.

While the title of this book is *A History of Modern Libya*, it can perhaps more accurately be described as a social and political economy study of the country. Many of its organizing ideas derive from the institutional literature that sociologists, economists, and political scientists have used since the mid-1980s. In that literature, the attention to individuals and social groups has sometimes been minimized for the sake of discerning broader structural patterns and developments. As previously mentioned, Libya's history, however, cannot be properly understood without careful attention to a collection of individuals, tribes, families, and assorted other social groups that helped to determine the outcome and shape of the country's historical path. Indeed, while in political systems like Libya oil seemingly invokes an uncommon passivity among the population, its rulers nevertheless – very much precisely because of the informal and de-institutionalized form of the country's political life – spend inordinate amounts of time shaping and managing political coalitions they need for their survival. I have attempted, particularly where they constitute a crucial factor, to bring these individuals and groups into focus against the backdrop of the larger history of the country.

It is my hope, as Libya starts to rejoin the international community in the wake of the 2011 civil war, that its own scholars will once more contribute to writing their country's history, unencumbered by the political

or ideological constraints of the past.[2] Much of what this book analyzes –
from Libya's earlier encounter with the West to its development under the
monarchy in particular – remains either terra incognita to the country's
own academic community, or has been left unexplored because its exam-
ination proved incompatible with ideological considerations during the
Qadhafi period. Until those local voices help to rewrite Libyan history in
a more full and comprehensive manner in the wake of the civil war, this
book hopefully provides a careful and critical interpretation of the country's emergence and development in the twentieth century.

"A tract which is wholly sand . . ." Herodotus

More than two millennia after Herodotus described the empty vastness of the Libyan desert, the German explorer Gustav Nachtigal set out in February 1869 from Tripoli toward Fazzan, and beyond, on a trip to the ruler of Bornu. His camel – burdened on one side with a "red velvety chair of state" and on the other side by a crate of "lifesize portraits of King William, Queen Augusta, and the Crown Prince" – followed a wide arc east of Tripoli across the desert to southern Murzuq and Qatrun. Throughout his travels, Nachtigal ably summarized much of what was known of the Ottoman provinces of Tripolitania, Cyrenaica, and Fazzan at the time – the three immense pieces of territory that would eventually constitute modern-day Libya.[1]

Nachtigal's presence was not entirely fortuitous. Germany and Italy were slowly developing an interest in what Britain and France at the time considered a combination of forbidding and economically uninteresting territories. Within little more than a decade after France's seizure of Tunisia in 1881, however, Cyrenaica, Tripolitania, and Fazzan became the only territories in North Africa left unclaimed by a European power. By that time, the scramble to delineate the borders of the remaining Ottoman possessions in North Africa had already started in earnest.

For most Europeans in the nineteenth century, the territories Nachtigal ventured across were – except for the exoticism the caravan trade conjured up in the popular mind – known primarily for their earlier, more illustrious history. Besides occasional traveler accounts like Nachtigal's, little was known about their more recent past or about the forbidding hinterlands. The remnants of that earlier history – the magnificent Greek, Roman, and Byzantine ruins of Sabratha, Leptis Magna, Cyrene, Appolonia, and dozens of other cities and temples – lay clustered like a string of faded pearls along the Mediterranean. For much of the subsequent centuries, the history of Tripolitania, Cyrenaica, and Fazzan was one of separateness, until they eventually belonged as a whole to the Sublime Porte. Conquerors – until

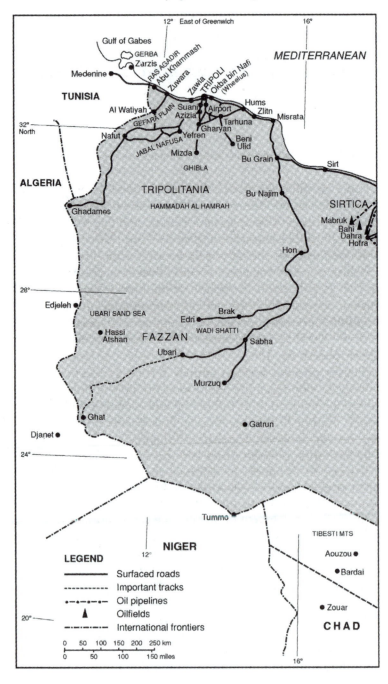

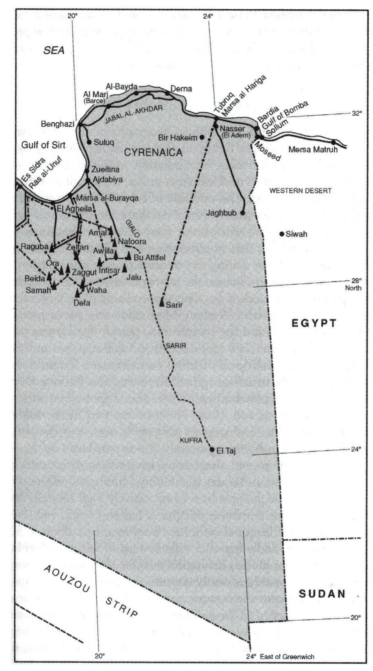

Map 1. General map of Libya

the arrival of the second Ottoman occupation in 1835 – were mostly content to establish their presence along the coastal areas of Cyrenaica and Tripolitania, leaving Fazzan and the hinterland of the two northern provinces untouched.

Undoubtedly, the physical and human geography of the territories that eventually became a unified Libya in the twentieth century, played an important role in maintaining the isolation and the diversity of its constituent parts – a reality that would continue to bedevil its rulers even after independence in 1951. The vast bulk of Libya's 680,000 square miles (1,761, 132 sq. km) is located within the Sahara. At the time Nachtigal ventured south, less than 1% of the enormous area was suitable for agriculture – a condition that would remain virtually unchanged, despite Italian agricultural efforts during the colonial period, until Libyan independence in 1951.[2] In Tripolitania, the Jafara plain west of Tripoli allowed for some pastoralists who eked out a precarious living on its dry soil. Only in the Jabal al-Gharb (the Western Mountain) was more permanent cultivation possible beyond the coastal strip, permitting farmers to grow some cereals and olives. East of Tripoli, the Sahil stretches out toward the Gulf of Sirt, the traditional dividing point between Tripolitania and Cyrenaica. Here more sustained agriculture took place, feeding the population of the areas's coastal cities of Zuwara, Tripoli, Suq al-Jum'ah, Tajura, Misrata, Khums and Zlitn. The southern part of the Sahil then slowly gives way to the Dahar plain that spills over into the desert of Fazzan. Here only transhumant pastoralism was possible.

In Cyrenaica, remote and desolate in its interior, some settlements extended into the Jabal al-Akhdar (the Green Mountains) where consistent cultivation is made possible by a comparatively high rainfall. Beyond the coastline's cities of Ajdabiya, Benghazi, Tukra, Derna, and Tubruq, the desert extends for hundreds of miles, merging eventually into Sudan. Only where water could be found in sufficient quantities, as in Jaghbub or Kufra, was permanent human habitation possible. Fazzan, to the south of Tripolitania, is a vast inland sandy depression. Except for its important role as a transit route for the caravan trade, it was of little consequence to its northern neighbors. Disregarding its permanent settlements at Murzuq, Sabha, and Brak, that facilitated the caravan trade between sub-Saharan Africa and the Mediterranean, only scattered bands of tribesmen roamed the desert.[3] Physical contact or economic interaction between Fazzan and its northern neighbors remained sporadic and limited, well into the twentieth century.

The disparities and low levels of sustained interaction between the three provinces were exacerbated by the physical characteristics of the landscape. The enormous distances – the central coast along the Gulf of Sirt alone measures more than 800 miles (1,287 km) as the crow flies – and a formidable 300-mile-long (483 km) stretch of desert that reaches the Mediterranean and separates Tripolitania from Cyrenaica between Ajdabiya and Misrata scattered and isolated villages and towns on both sides of the sandy divide. Hundreds of miles of rocky or sandy desert separate Fazzan from the coastal settlements of Tripolitania. As a measure of the difficulty of transportation and to provide a sense of the isolation and forbidding nature of the terrain, traveling times for caravans were often expressed in terms of weeks or months of travel. Furthermore, the separate histories of the three provinces, as well as the absence of incentives for greater economic interaction within essentially self-contained local economies, had added to distinct outlooks and orientations among the citizens of each territory over the centuries. Tripolitania's cultural traditions and economy were largely oriented toward the western part of the Maghreb (North Africa) with whom it shared its Roman history. As a result of its colonization by the Greeks, Cyrenaica's equivalents were largely those of countries east of its still undefined borders. Fazzan remained a small, semi-nomadic and economically barely self-sufficient society that, except for the caravan trade, interacted overwhelmingly with sub-Saharan Africa.

Rudimentary estimates put the population of the three territories combined at less than 1 million throughout the nineteenth century.[4] Tripoli, at the time of Nachtigal's travels, contained roughly 60,000– 70,000 people; Benghazi less than half that amount. The estimates made by travelers and by Ottoman and western officials stationed in Tripoli varied widely. This reflected the difficulty of counting a population that was still in part and occasionally nomadic, depending on weather conditions and available labor. It also reflected the fact that throughout the nineteenth century, important population fluctuations took place, linked to epidemics, plagues, and famines that swept periodically across the area.[5]

Early twentieth-century figures estimated that less than one-fifth of eastern Libya lived in urban areas or in oases – a figure that had likely remained unchanged from previous centuries. Tripolitania was by far the most populated area, containing an estimated two-thirds of the population, while in Fazzan by the mid nineteenth century an estimated 30,000–50,000 people lived.[6] With the exception of a few thousand Tuaregs around Ghat and

Ghadames, and Jewish, Christian, black, and *Kulughli* (descendants of
Ottomans and natives) minorities in the more urbanized areas along the
coast, the two main population groups were Berbers and Arabs – the latter
the descendants of seventh-century invaders and of later invasions of the
Banu Sulaym and Banu Hilal.⁷ By the nineteenth century a considerable
amount of intermarriage between the two groups had occurred, although
the Berbers of central Tripolitania and particularly of Jabal Nafusa had
managed to hold onto their own language and traditions. Both Berbers
and Arabs belonged to an intricate network of families, tribes, and tribal
lineages, guided by local shaykhs, and relied on tribal networks for economic purposes as well as for identification.

THE OTTOMAN PERIOD AND THE SANUSIYYA

The seeming timelessness of daily life described by Nachtigal within each
territory belied the fact, however, that Tripolitania, Cyrenaica, and Fazzan
had, since the sixteenth century, slowly but inexorably been drawn into
the larger world around them. In 1517 and 1551, respectively, the Ottoman
Empire occupied Cyrenaica and Tripoli, thus providing a balance, at least
temporarily, to the interests of the European naval powers who had started
to scour the southern shores of the Mediterranean. Ottoman control initially restricted itself mostly to the principal towns of both territories, with
only occasional and half-hearted forays into the hinterland to collect taxes.
Their control on the whole proved slight and nominal. Until the early
part of the nineteenth century, the Sublime Porte restricted its presence
and activities as long as the annual tribute and formal allegiance to the
sultan were paid. Beyond this, the Sublime Porte left its provinces to their
own devices in organizing their affairs. In 1711, when the Ottoman governor of Tripoli – Ahmed Bey Qaramanli – established his own dynasty,
and started conducting his own diplomatic relations with the European
powers, it provoked little reaction from Constantinople which eventually
granted Ahmed Bey a *firman* (decree by the sultan) confirming his position
in Tripolitania. The Qaramanli dynasty ruled part of what became known
as the Barbary Coast until 1835, its acts of piracy and buccaneering involving the North African city-state for the first time with the United States in
a dispute in 1803 over a captured vessel, the *Philadelphia*, and its crew.

During the Qaramanli period, however, the Ottoman Empire had
started to review its earlier *laissez-faire* attitude toward its remaining North
African possessions, worried by the resentment and enmity Qaramanli foreign policy had generated among the outside powers, as well as by lingering

revolts as the increasingly rapacious dynasty attempted to extend taxation internally. Constantinople had also become sufficiently preoccupied with French and British expansionist policies in neighboring countries to reconsider its earlier policy of benign neglect. The French occupation of Algeria in 1831, the resultant loss of a part of its empire, and France's emerging interest in the Sahara and in areas on the southern fringe of the Sublime Porte's Libyan possessions, were telltale signs to Constantinople that a scramble for territory was in the making. At the same time, Great Britain was starting to exert pressure from the east and southeast, expanding and solidifying its presence in Egypt and Sudan.

In any case, at the start of the second Ottoman occupation in 1835, the borders between Tripolitania, Fazzan, and Cyrenaica and the surrounding territories coveted by the European powers remained undefined, *resnullius*. Their delineation would form a steady source of friction between Constantinople and the European powers for the remainder of the nineteenth century. Each confrontation would demonstrate how the Ottomans steadily lost the political will and military power to settle the disputes to their advantage. They proved unable or unwilling to protect their own political interests, to concern themselves with issues of sovereignty, or to protect the economic interests of the territories against the Europeans. Between 1835 and 1911, thirty-three Ottoman representatives ruled the territories, the high number indicative of the difficulty the Sublime Porte had in finding officials willing to devote their careers to managing territories that had consistently proven rebellious, difficult to govern, and economically of little importance to Constantinople. By the time the Anglo-French convention was signed in 1890 – defining British and Ottoman spheres of influence in North Africa – and the 1910 agreement that settled French–Ottoman contentions on the borders between Tripolitania, Algeria, and Tunisia, power and diplomatic initiative had shifted forever in Europe's favor.

In an effort to project an image of strength as the encroachments at the fringes of its dependencies took place, the empire attempted to assert its military power internally. In a set of three campaigns of conquest – two of which lasted for roughly twenty years – the Sublime Porte sought to extend its control systematically throughout Cyrenaica, Fazzan, and Tripolitania after 1835. Despite the sultan's nominal position as spiritual leader of Libya's Muslims, however, this second Ottoman occupation – much like the previous Qaramanli policies – provoked considerable opposition within the provinces the empire's armies were attempting to subjugate. Its attempts to extend bureaucratic control – and more importantly taxation – into the

hinterland met with equally great resistance from organized tribal affilia-
tions in Fazzan (headed by Abd al-Jalil Saif al-Nasr of the Awlad Sulayman
tribe) and other tribal, berber groups in the Jabal Nafusa area. Eventually
the Ottoman Empire succeeded, defeating the Awlad Sulayman in 1842
and occupying berber Ghadames the following year. The bloody conquest
of western Libya and Fazzan lasted twenty-four years, making enduring
heroes of Saif al-Nasr and other resistance figures who would become early
revered figures for future Libyan nationalists.

Throughout the remainder of the century, the Ottomans maintained
a presence even in the most remote parts of the re-conquered territories,
building for that purpose new forts in Ghadames in 1862, and in Ghat
in 1875. They stationed numerous small garrisons at distant oases, and,
by 1909, extended their military occupation into Tibesti in modern-day
Chad. These represented, perhaps belatedly and often in what amounted
to little more than a symbolic gesture, attempts to establish their claims
vis-à-vis the local inhabitants and the European powers alike. Efforts to
implement conscription campaigns among the local population never
proved entirely successful, although, by the end of Ottoman presence in the
country, a small army of locals commanded by Ottoman officers had been
established. At the same time, a number of Tripolitanian and Cyrenaican
families joined forces with the Ottomans in their effort to extend their
administration and to extend trade and commerce, providing a nucleus of
"grand families" whose economic and political influence would survive the
colonial period.

While the Sublime Porte was concentrating its efforts on the rebellion in
Tripolitania and Fazzan, and on establishing some bureaucratic and commercial presence, Cyrenaica by the mid nineteenth century had become
home to a religious movement that would prove of equal, if not greater,
importance for the political future of a unified Libya.[8] The Sanusiyya,
named after its founder, Sayyid Muhammad ibn Ali al-Sanusi, was a
purifying, revivalist Islamic movement whose task consisted of "remind-
ing the negligent, teaching the ignorant, and guiding him who has gone
astray."[9] Like those of Muhammad Abd al-Wahhab in Saudi Arabia, Sayyid
Muhammad's teachings were meant to remove what he considered to be
unacceptable accretions to Islam, and to return its adherents to a more pristine, scriptural form of the religion. The Grand Sanusi, as he was known,
had studied in Fes and Mecca, and established a number of religious lodges
(*zuwaya*) that provided focal points for persuading local tribes to join his
muslim fraternity. By the time the Ottomans occupied Ghadames in 1843,
the Grand Sanusi had settled in Cyrenaica, and the same year established

the *zawiya al-bayda* (the White Monastery) in the Jabal al-Akhdar region. Relying on adherents – known as brothers *(Ikhwan)* to propagate his vision, the Sanusiyya movement rapidly built a network of *zuwaya* in Cyrenaica and eventually beyond into Tripolitania and within the neighboring territories of Darfur, Wadai, and Bornu. The movement's inner core of support, however, continued to reside among the Cyrenaican tribes.

Perhaps not surprisingly, the Sanusiyya doctrine, with its emphasis on a purifying, ascetic practice of Islam that provided solidarity and support, resonated within the tribal ethos of Cyrenaica, which at the time was still a remote country where nomadic and semi-nomadic tribes of Arab descent roamed. It was to these tribes that Muhammad al-Sanusi brought a rudimentary structure of governance – through tax collection, by providing social services to the tribes, and by maintaining peace among them – and a sense of identification. The movement met with little resistance from the Ottomans who remained preoccupied with their reconquest in Tripolitania and Fazzan, and who viewed the Sanusiyya's opposition to the French with favor. The religious movement steadily expanded – particularly under the leadership of the Grand Sanusi's son Muhammad al-Mahdi – into western Egypt, into modern Chad and beyond but, significantly, found few adherents among the more cosmopolitan Tripolitanians. Faced with increasing hostility from France, the movement retreated ever further into the southern reaches of Cyrenaica's hinterland, moving its headquarters away from the coastal area to Jaghbub in 1855 (where the Grand Sanusi died in 1859) and to Kufra in 1895. Upon the death of Muhammad al-Mahdi in 1902, Ahmad al-Shariff – the son of one of al-Mahdi's brothers – was appointed as new head of the movement as al-Mahdi's own sons (including the future king of Libya, Idris al-Sanusi) were minors at the time.

At each point the Sanusiyya provided not only religious sustenance and guidance, but also controlled local pilgrimage routes and was able to safeguard alternative trade routes – particularly the Wadai road, which proved important as the European nations started to undermine traditional trans-Saharan commerce. In this fashion, it provided a rudimentary, unshaped form of social, political, and economic organization that would, in due time, crystallize within Cyrenaica into the nucleus of an opposition movement to the Italian invasion. During the last decade of the nineteenth century and the first decade of the twentieth century, however, the Sanusiyya found itself preoccupied with France whose encroachments threatened some of the areas under the Order's control. Desperate for reinforcements to oppose the French, the Sanusi leadership appealed to the Ottomans but were rebuffed. In a cruel twist of fate, Ahmad al-Shariff then approached the Italians via their embassy in Cairo. Italy, anxious to maintain good relations with the Order and equally intent on checking French activity in southern Cyrenaica and Chad, promptly delivered a cache of weapons to the Sanusi tribal forces – weapons the movement would later use against the Italians themselves.

EUROPEAN INTRUSIONS AND THE YOUNG TURK REVOLT

By the mid nineteenth century, the fate of the trans-Saharan caravan routes assumed more immediate urgency for the local inhabitants and the Ottoman Empire alike. Some of them in use since pre-Roman times, caravan routes connected sub-Saharan Africa and Mediterranean ports, enriching both sedentary and nomadic populations en route. Tripoli in particular, gateway to three great trade routes into Central Africa, relied on access to maintain its position as a leading trading and merchant town. From Tripoli and Benghazi an assortment of manufactured goods from Europe and North Africa traveled south, bringing in return a combination of feathers, ivory, gold, and, most importantly, slaves. By the mid nineteenth century, half of all slaves brought from sub-Saharan Africa to the coast were transported through Tripolitania, Cyrenaica, and Fazzan.[10] Tripolitania's and Cyrenaica's foreign trade was mainly, in descending order, with Malta, Great Britain, Turkey, France, and Italy.

As the European penetration of Africa started in earnest, however, several of the traditional routes were disturbed and shifted either westwards or southwards to take advantage of more secure river-steamer routes and railway connections to Atlantic Ocean ports. This undermining of trans-Saharan commerce was heightened when the European powers prohibited the selling of slaves, its most lucrative activity. Although the Sanusi had earlier in the century been able to open an alternative route that ran from Benghazi into Wadai – albeit eventually stretching out the arduous journey to seventy and sometimes ninety days – which would be maintained until the early decades of the twentieth century, the curtailment and diversion of the trans-Saharan trade eventually proved economically disastrous for the merchant towns like Tripoli and Benghazi, and provoked considerable local resentment against the Ottomans who did little to halt the deterioration of the trade routes.

The European interference with, and infringement upon, the caravan trade provided only one telltale indication of growing British and French influence. By 1850, France under Napoleon III had started a policy of expansion in Africa that would steadily bring it into conflict with the

Ottomans for the remainder of the century. The struggle to delineate borders between French and Ottoman possessions in North Africa and into sub-Saharan Africa, added to by similar difficulties with the British over borders with Egypt and Sudan, steadily increased pressure on the Sublime Porte to defend territories it had once ruled in a cavalier fashion. Partly with the aid of the Sanusi in Cyrenaica, the Ottomans by the beginning of the twentieth century had managed to preserve the core of the three territories of Cyrenaica, Tripolitania, and Fazzan under their control – even if, in the diplomatic struggles with the European powers, they had lost considerable border areas. For the first time, and with some modifications to follow during the colonial period, the borders and territory of what would eventually be called Libya had emerged as an identifiable territorial unit.[11] In retrospect, this preservation of territorial unity was perhaps the most notable legacy the Ottoman Empire left to Cyrenaica, Tripolitania, and Fazzan.

Neither Great Britain nor France, however, had colonial ambitions in regard to the provinces themselves. It was Italy, in the throes of state consolidation and growing colonial ambitions after the unification of the country in 1861, that steadily sought to increase its presence in Libya and to claim the territories for itself. By the end of 1881, after the seizure of Tunisia by France, Cyrenaica, Tripolitania, and Fazzan remained the only areas in North Africa left unclaimed by any of the European powers, and Italy had started the diplomatic campaign that would allow it to bring the areas under its control. A *rapprochement politique* with France, promising an Italian hands-off policy in Tunisia in return for a French equivalent regarding Tripolitania, Cyrenaica, and Fazzan, removed one major obstacle. Similar diplomatic initiatives with Germany (1887), with Austria and Britain (1902), and with Russia (1909) further prepared Italy's eventual road for annexation.[12] Italy's Banco di Roma meanwhile had started a "peaceful penetration" at the end of the nineteenth century, steadily expanding its control over the territory's commerce, light industry, agriculture, shipping, and trade, by establishing branches in Tripoli, Benghazi, Zlitn, Khums, and Misrata. Indeed, alleged Ottoman interference with Italian commercial ventures would form one of Italy's rationales for military intervention in 1911.

The Young Turk revolt in Constantinople in 1908 provoked mixed reactions within the provinces, and led to a decade of turmoil that would not reach its apotheosis until after the Italian invasion in 1911. As Italian interest in Cyrenaica and Tripolitania – and to a much lesser extent Fazzan – had become palpable, local citizens were not oblivious to what the Italian pressures would likely mean for the independence of the provinces. Although religion remained a strong bond between them and the Sublime Porte, and although there was little evidence of separatist sentiment throughout the three territories, many were critical of the actions of the Ottomans vis-à-vis Italy and the European powers. This was in part because they considered that the Porte's often reactive, rather than proactive, policies made the loss of their independence at the hands of the Italians more likely. The reformist Young Turk movement in Istanbul in the first decade of the century therefore was watched with some weariness. There was little open affection for the Turks in light of their administration of the territories since 1835 – but a reformed leadership in Istanbul, local people hoped, would perhaps keep a check on Italy. Representatives from Cyrenaica, Tripolitania, and Fazzan participated in the Young Turk Parliament in Istanbul in 1908, but they returned home disappointed. Italian occupation now seemed all but inevitable.

THE OTTOMAN LEGACY

In retrospect, the Ottoman legacy for the three provinces that later became amalgamated into a single country under the Italians proved double-edged. The Sublime Porte had managed to create some embryonic bureaucratic and military structures, and, willy-nilly, had brought some geographical unity to the country. Its policy allowing the Sanusiyya to act in a semi-autonomous fashion created a regional focus of leadership within Cyrenaica that would prove important for the country's future during the colonial period and at independence. Some of the local administrators it recruited in Tripolitania would emerge as leaders of a brief flowering of reform and political activism that led to the creation of the Tripolitanian Republic in 1918. But economic stagnation had steadily spread within the provinces after a brief flowering in the 1850s. This was due in part to the loss of the caravan trade – something a joint Ottoman– Sanusi initiative could perhaps have prevented – but also to the fact that Constantinople proved little interested and was ultimately unable to invest in the economic future of the country. The Banco di Roma's commercial penetration at the expense of the Ottomans had provided a small but telltale indication of Ottoman neglect and of the empire's growing commercial and financial powerlessness.

Ultimately, however, the most deleterious impact for what was to follow in the history of Cyrenaica, Tripolitania, and Fazzan was the inability or unwillingness of the Porte to help create a common identity, beyond the mantle of Islam, among the people it governed. Constantinople had only imperfectly managed to install an administrative apparatus that governed the territories' tribes, despite their defeat during the military campaigns. It had possessed the military capability to prevent internal opposition to its rule but, within the hinterland where formal equalities of kinship within a tribal system were maintained, the Ottoman administration's authority was never fully implemented. Indeed, one could argue that, as described in Chapter 2, the Tripolitanian Republic in 1918 would fail not only because of Italy's local policies as a colonial power – but also because tribal, local, and, at best, regional political identity continued to dominate the landscape at the expense of a truly developed provincial identity.

As the remainder of this book will show, in Libya the focus and rationale for a national identity would only materialize, intermittently and temporarily, when an outside threat appeared imminent. The stark bifurcation at the beginning of the twentieth century between an economically self-sufficient tribal hinterland and a small urbanized population, the inability to conceive of an integrated territory, and the inclination of local tribes to pursue autonomy would, for almost thirty years, be suspended as Libya became Italy's Fourth Shore. It is this struggle, however, between essentially inward-looking citizens and local elites, and the ambitions of the cosmopolitan conqueror, that would form the backdrop to Libya's history during the disastrous decades of the Italian colonial period – disastrous because, among other factors, Libya's first encounter with a modern European state would reinforce local perceptions that statehood itself was at best a mixed blessing. This imperfect understanding of modern statehood would come to haunt Libya and its citizens far into the future.

CHAPTER 2

Italy's Fourth Shore and decolonization, 1911–1950

When it invaded the remaining Ottoman North African possessions in 1911, unified Italy had existed for exactly fifty years. Since the 1870s, its politicians had slowly prepared local and international opinion for its eventual colonial oversight of Tripolitxania, Cyrenaica, and Fazzan. In doing so, it had been aided by a persuasive imperialist lobby that had touted Italy's progress into Somalia, Eritrea – and now potentially *Libia* – as Italy's version of manifest destiny, providing commercial opportunities, trade, and an outlet for the nation's industrial goods and its perennial surplus population. In addition, the failure to annex Ethiopia in 1896 had strengthened the country's resolve to claim Libya as a necessary bulwark – the poet Gabriele d'Annunzio's lyrical Fourth Shore – to protect its strategic security in the Mediterranean and its growing shipping trade, and to project its Great Power aspirations.

THE ITALIAN OCCUPATION, 1911–1923

Italy seized upon alleged Ottoman hostility to its economic activities in Libya as a *casus belli*, sending an ultimatum to the sultan on 26 September 1911 that included its intention to occupy Tripolitania and Cyrenaica. A seaborne invasion the following month allowed Italy to occupy the major coastal cities – Tripoli, Benghazi, Darna, Ilums, and Tubruq – where they were met by a number of small but determined Ottoman garrisons. These had been augmented by the local population who, while not favorable to the sultan, still considered him as their "commander of the faithful." The Italian government announced the annexation of the two provinces on 5 November 1911 and formally annexed them on 25 February 1912, but these were largely empty gestures. For despite the introduction of the latest new weapons from Europe – including airplanes and airships – and the presence of 115,000 troops by April 1912, the war reached an impasse by the Spring of 1912. Although the total of Ottoman and local forces constituted

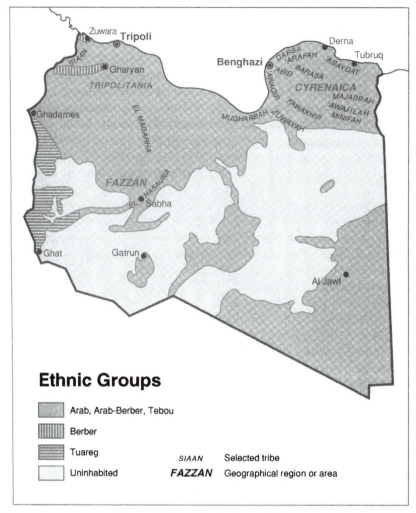

Map 2. Ethnic and tribal map of Libya

only one-fifth of the Italian presence, the difficult terrain and Italy's inexperience had brought the campaigns to a standstill.[1]

Under international pressure, the two sides at Ouchy (near Lausanne) signed a peace treaty in October 1912. The treaty, however, was ambiguous: the Sublime Porte did not relinquish its sovereignty over Tripoli while Italy rested its own claims to sovereignty on Italian law. The ambiguity was important for future events, for it meant, in effect, that the local population still considered the sultan as its spiritual and political leader. As the stalemate continued throughout 1912, the Italians held on to little more than enclaves along the Mediterranean coast. Even the largest of these – Tripoli – barely extended ten miles into the hinterland.[2]

In 1913, the Italian advance in Tripolitania proceeded, made distinctly easier than in Cyrenaica by the more open terrain. In addition, Tripolitanians in the coastal cities showed little inclination to fight, in part because they lacked an organized leadership. Some prominent families, including the Muntasirs, supported the Italians, hoping to protect their economic fortunes. Sulayman Al-Baruni, who had represented the berber areas around Jabal Nafusa at the Young Turk meeting in 1908, attempted to rally the Berbers to fight for their independence, but the effort failed when they were defeated in March 1913. In its aftermath, Al-Baruni fled to Turkey where he became a senator in the Ottoman Parliament.

In Cyrenaica, the resistance to the Italian invasion proved stronger, centered around the Sanusi Order. Despite his hesitations – and earlier requests for help from the Italians – Sayyid Ahmad al-Shariff in 1912 assumed the leadership of the resistance, vowing to continue the war as the sultan's representative.[3] This not only provided a focus for military opposition to the Italians, but it simultaneously turned the Sanusiyya into an emerging political movement within Cyrenaica. The Italians – as did other European powers in their own colonies – were subsequently to depict the war as one pitting religious fanatics (with their calls for *jihad*), consisting of perennially war-like Bedouin, against their efforts at colonization. In effect, resistance in Cyrenaica and Tripolitania was neither based purely on religious grounds or on identification with the sultan in Constantinople, nor exclusively Bedouin. It was almost by default that the struggle against the Italians, particularly in Cyrenaica, would be fought by a religious Islamic order that relied overwhelmingly on tribal support.[4]

When the Italians attacked Cyrenaica in 1913 and intensified their hold on the coastal area between Benghazi and Darna, the Sanusiyya was unable to offer formal resistance. Instead, it readily adapted its tribal support to a guerrilla-style warfare that suited both its tribal constituencies and the difficult terrain on which the battles with the Italians took place.[5] In Fazzan, the withdrawal of the Turkish garrisons by 1913 had led to a power vacuum that France eagerly sought to fill, leading to a struggle with the Italians. As Italy attempted to rebuff the French incursions, its campaigns against the local tribes failed – due in part to local resistance, but also to the necessity of diverting Italian forces toward the country's involvement in World War I. By the end of 1915, the Italian position in Libya had steadily deteriorated, reducing their forces' hold once more to Tripolitania's and Cyrenaica's coastal cities. In April that year they suffered a heavy defeat when one of their supposed allies, Ramadan al-Suwayhli of Misrata, defeated an Italian column at the battle of Qasr Bu Hadi.[6]

The Italian withdrawal and preoccupation with the war in Europe provoked a temporary flowering of political activity in Tripolitania and Cyrenaica. The first stirrings of Arab nationalism were wafting across the area, inspired in part by political circles in Tunisia and Egypt. In Tripolitania, the young Egyptian nationalist Abd al-Rahman Azzam Bey – who would later become the first secretary general of the Arab League – became advisor to al-Suwayhili. Together with Sulayman Al-Baruni, Ahmad al-Murayyid of Tarhuna and Abd al-Nabi Bilkhayr of Warfalla, al-Suwayhli created what was known as the Tripolitanian Republic in 1918 after a number of earlier attempts at consolidating power in Tripolitania.[7] Although the Tripolitarian Republic was soon to collapse because of dis-agreements among rival factions and because of Italian pressures, it consti-tuted at the time the first attempt at a republican form of government in the Arab world.

In Cyrenaica, Ahmad al-Shariff, who had been pressured by the Ottomans to attack British forces in Egypt, abdicated his leadership of the Sanusi Order to his cousin, Sayyid Idris al-Sanusi, a grandson of the Grand Sanusi and the son of al-Mahdi al-Sanusi. Idris, a scholarly indi-vidual whose entire life would be marked by a reluctance to engage in politics, opposed the campaign against the British. He brought about a rapprochement with them, creating a tacit alliance that would last for half a century. This also gave the Sanusi Order *de facto* diplomatic sta-tus, enabling it to speak on behalf of the Cyrenaican Bedouin. Eager to find a compromise, Sayyid Idris in July 1916 opened negotiations with the Italians, the British acting as intermediaries. It resulted in a peace treaty – the Akrama Agreement of April 1917 – that effectively put all of Cyrenaica, except for the coastal strip, under Sanusi control. Unfortunately, relations between Suwayhli of Tripolitania and the Sanusi Order were acrimonious. A Sanusi attempt to extend its power into eastern Tripolitania had resulted in a pitched battle near Bani Walid, forcing the Sanusis to withdraw back into Cyrenaica. Although the incident itself was not significant, it made cooperation between the two provinces even more problematic – a fact that would come to haunt them in the two coming decades when joint resistance against the Italians was needed.

When the Ottoman Empire signed the Armistice agreements in October 1918, Italy had already been promised sovereignty over Libya by the

European powers at the April 1915 Pact of London. The country, however, faced grave economic, social, and political difficulties at home, and proved reluctant to use military force to extend its power in Libya. As a result, the Italians temporarily acquiesced to British patronage of the Sanusiyya and to the relative autonomy of the Sanusi Order in Cyrenaica. Italy also issued separate statutes for the Tripolitanian Republic and Cyrenaica in June and October 1919 – the *Legge Fondamentale* – hoping to reach political compromises that would make its physical presence less burdensome financially and militarily. Under the statutes, each province was to have its own Parliament and governing councils. Libyans were promised the right to a special Libyan-Italian citizenship, were exempted from military conscription, and could only be taxed by the locally elected Parliament. Italy's *Legge Fondamentale* were in effect remarkably liberal, providing considerable and broad powers to the local leaders, and went well beyond concessions made in neighboring countries to local nationalist groups.

Although the stipulations of the statutes were warmly received by both provinces – Al-Baruni and Idris both visited Rome to join celebrations of their promulgation – they were never seriously put to the test. The Cyreniacan Parliament met five times – until it was abolished in 1923 – but consisted almost exclusively of tribal shaykhs, leaving the towns and the Italians themselves barely represented. Moreover, the shaykhs, aware of the weakness of the Italians at the time, refused them all but a limited economic role in the province. In October 1920, new negotiations between Cyrenaica and Italy took place, resulting in the Accord of al-Rajma. Idris al-Sanusi was granted the title of Amir of Cyrenaica, allowing him to administer autonomously the oases around Kufra, Jalu, Jaghbub, Awjila and Ajdabiya. He was given a monthly stipend, and Italy agreed to police and administer the regions under Sanusi control. In return, Sayyid Idris promised to help implement the stipulations of the *Legge Fondamentale* and to disband the Cyrenaican military units operated by the Sanusi-allied tribes. The latter, however, never happened and, by the end of 1921, relations between the two sides had once more deteriorated. The interlude between the end of World War I and the arrival of Italian fascism, however, had legitimated the status of the Amirate of Cyrenaica as a virtually autonomous region, and consolidated the leadership of the Sanusis within it.

In Tripolitania, parliamentary elections were never held. In the wake of the creation of the Tripolitanian Republic, the province descended into a virtual civil war linked to personal feuds among its leaders, to arguments over administrative appointments, and to Ramadan al-Suwayhli's attempt to extend the Republic's authority across the entire territory. When he was killed in battle in August 1920, the province descended further into chaos, forcing much of the berber population to flee to the coast, where they enjoyed Italian protection. Although the Italians attempted to mediate between the warring sides, it was not until the appointment of Idris al-Sanusi as Amir of Cyrenaica later that year that the Tripolitanian leadership began to realize how the perpetual internal discord was weakening the province's chances of wringing concessions for its own form of autonomy from Italy.

To overcome the existing impasse, Tripolitania's leaders met in Gharyan in November 1920 to settle their differences.[8] By that time, relations between the Arab tribes and the Berbers had substantially deteriorated. Pointedly, the berber leader Al-Baruni refused to attend the conference, despite being offered the leadership of whatever collective body was created. The delegates to the Gharyan conference resolved to appoint a single leader to rule the province, and established a Council of the Association for National Reform (or Central Reform Board) that traveled to Italy to press its demands. They also met in January 1922 with a representative of Sayyid Idris in Sirt, and thereafter called upon him to extend the Sanusi Amirate of Cyrenaica into Tripolitania, presenting him with a formal document for that purpose on 28 July 1922.[9] After considerable hesitation and consultation with the Cyrenaican Bedouin tribes – for they would be forced to face the brunt of any fighting with the Italians, who were likely to object – Idris accepted the request in November. The appointment, however, placed the Amir in a delicate situation. His advisors were divided on the matter. The Italians also conveyed to him, as he had expected, that any such action would be considered a breach of the al-Rajma Agreement that had delivered a level of autonomy to Cyrenaica. The Italians clearly understood that the unification of the two provinces would be disastrous for their interests.

Sayyid Idris, finding no solution to the dilemma, and realizing that a compromise with the increasingly intransigent Italians appeared remote – Mussolini had come to power in October 1922 – went into exile in Egypt in December that year. In retrospect, his fears of an Italian reaction were preempted, for, by the time he left, relations between Italy and the two provinces had started to change considerably. Giuseppe Volpi, the Italian governor appointed to Tripolitania in July 1921, had almost single-handedly started a reconquest of Tripolitania, imposing martial law, and negating all the stipulations of the *Legge Fondamentale* agreements between Italy and the province. The result was that, by the time Mussolini came to power, northern Tripolitania's occupation was well under way – helped along by internecine warfare between Berbers and Arabs. Whatever resistance still existed had effectively been contained as well. As a result, the hoped-for unification of Cyrenaica and Tripolitania under a single amir had become a lost dream – an outcome both sides would soon ruefully reflect upon. The Tripolitanian Republic had failed to unite Tripolitania, and the Sirt meeting, despite an outward appearance of unity, masked the deep divisions and distrust that persisted between the two northern provinces of Libya.

FASCISM AND THE ITALIAN SETTLER COLONY

By the end of 1922, the only effective Libyan resistance to the Italians left was concentrated in the Cyrenaican hinterlands, where the Sanusiyya held sway over its tribal affiliates. In Tripolitania and Fazzan, the *riconquista* had proceeded swiftly, putting Italy in control of most of the population, coastal area, and countryside by the end of 1924. In the eastern province, however, Italy's modern and well-equipped army – consisting increasingly of Eritrean conscripts – faced resistance from tribes who continued their guerrilla warfare tactics to oppose the colonizers. Shaykh Rida, Sayyid Idris's brother and his successor when the amir went into exile, commanded a force of tribal irregulars containing an estimated 2,000 to 6,000 men that initially kept the Italians at bay. In December 1925, however, an agreement between Great Britain and Italy firmly established the latter's sovereignty over Jaghbub and Kufra. This immensely complicated the efforts of the tribal guerrillas as the Italians, in the wake of the agreement, constructed a 186-mile (300-km) barbed wire fence along the border, patrolled by aircraft and armored cars, making it virtually impossible for the guerrillas to slip back and forth into British-controlled territory between battles. Sanusi *zuwaya* were closed and their estates confiscated. Shaykh Rida was captured in January 1928 and banished to Sicily.

His leadership position was taken up by Sayyid Umar al-Mukhtar, a tribal shaykh who had once fought with Ahmad al-Shariff and then joined Sayyid Idris in exile in Cairo, where he resided until 1923. Educated at Sanusi zuwaya in Zanzur and Jaghbub, al-Mukhtar later that year returned to Cyrenaica. For nearly eight years he led bands of Bedouin guerrillas in an increasingly bitter and unequal war against fascist Italy.

The campaigns, supervised by Italy's Commander-in-Chief in Libya, General Rodolfo Graziani, brought enormous devastation to the country, forcibly moved a large percentage of Cyrenaica's population into Italian concentration camps, and decimated local livestock.[10] It was, by any standard, a brutal and unsparing campaign of subjugation. Estimates of overall

Figure 1. Omar al-Mukhtar. Cyrenaican tribal shaykh who spearheaded the rebellion against the Italian invaders. Libya's enduring national hero.

deaths among the Libyan population as a whole vary considerably, but one reliable source estimates that the number of deaths, from all causes except natural ones, from 1912 to 1943, were between 250,000 and 300,000, from a population that stood at between 800,000 and 1 million at the time.[11] Most of these occurred during the fascist period when, by execution alone, an estimated 12,000 Cyrenaicans died in 1930 and in 1931.[12] Kufra was seized in January 1931, the Italians pursuing and strafing the Bedouin as they fled into the desert.[13] In the end, on 11 September 1931, Umar al-Mukhtar himself was captured. Graziani, on vacation in Italy, hurriedly returned to Libya and oversaw a summary trial that led to the public hanging of Libya's everlasting national hero five days later at Suluq, in the presence of 20,000 forcibly assembled Bedouin and notables.

His death marked the end of any organized resistance to Italy's colonial intentions. However, what those intentions were – or how they should be achieved – was not always clear. The fascist government clearly assigned great ideological importance to the *riconquista*, replacing Volpi with Emilio de Bono in 1925 – de Bono having been one of the leaders of the

March on Rome that had brought Mussolini to power. Italian poets like Gabriele d'Annuncio and Giovanni Pascoli portrayed the colonial enter-prise in terms that were meant to stir the national imagination: Italy bring-ing peace and enlightenment to *Tripoli Latina*, and as an expression of the proletariat's political awakening and resettlement in the country's Fourth Shore. Behind the rhetoric and lyricism, however, a more pragmatic real-ity asserted itself. Italian leaders realized that despite their own country's growing industrial power, colonial agriculture seemed more appropriate for Libya, but the limited amount of soil that could be cultivated proved extremely capital-intensive. Libya was also overwhelmingly portrayed and perceived as a potential outlet for the country's surplus population, who had few skills but constituted an abundant supply of cheap and available labor.

From the beginning, therefore, Italy put high faith in agricultural cul-tivation and regeneration in its Fourth Shore. Until the fascist policy of "demographic colonization" was implemented, however, settlement colon-ization in Libya proceeded slowly, mainly financed by north Italian capital that favored large estates. Between 1914 and 1929 roughly 180,000 acres of agricultural land were brought into production for Italian settlement.[14] Although much of Italy's initial investment in its colony included utilities and public works, the focus of investments changed rapidly as the Fascists adopted a set of more intense, state-sponsored and subsidized programs that were meant to settle individual Italian peasant families on their own, small individual farms.[15] In line with this fascist vision of self-sufficiency, each family property became the unit of settlement, self-contained and providing its own labor. This policy had already become accentuated dur-ing the 1930s, but it was not until 1938, under Marshal Italo Bablo, that Italy embarked upon a number of grand-scale settlement experiments that brought 20,000 Italians – the sailing of the *Ventimila* – in one fell swoop to prepared family farms in Cyrenaica and Tripolitania. This was followed by another 12,000 in 1939 when "Libia" as the two northern provinces were now known, became an integral part of metropolitan Italy.

Between 1936 and 1942 Italy would spend two-thirds of its investment in Libya on land reclamation and agricultural development, in anticipa-tion of further settlement. Except for the large estates in Tripolitania, the overwhelming majority of the Italian settlers consisted of poor, landless peasants and of an urban proletariat that was attracted by the chance of becoming property owners, within twenty years, of the initially state-owned and state-subsidized farms. By 1940, 225,000 hectares (495,000 acres) were in production and 110,000 Italian settlers had arrived.[16] Libya now possessed a basic modern infrastructure including public utilities and ports, a coastal highway – the Litoranea Libica inaugurated by Mussolini in 1937 – that connected Tunisia with Egypt, and an estimated 6,000 Italian families settled on their own farms. Compared to 1911, the country had achieved a level of material development that was impressive, particularly in view of the difficult physical conditions the Italians often faced. Though the achievements had continuously necessitated heavy expenditures Italy found difficult to support, there were nevertheless further plans for an estimated 100,000 settlers by 1942 and – with the eternal optimism of contemporary colonialism – for half a million by the 1960s.

From the native population's viewpoint, the colonial presence looked decidedly dismal. Except for some occasional labor, Libyans had been systematically excluded from the country's progress and investments. As one observer noted: "All Libya was now Italian, a land for Italians."[17] Despite the palliative of the *Cittadinanza Italiana Speciale* that bestowed a special form of citizenship upon some Libyans, most of the population was excluded from the country's economic, political, and administrative life except at the very lowest level. Displaced or prevented from engaging in productive farming, with reduced livestock, and with little chance for improvement, the Libyans belittled whatever few efforts Italy made to improve the fortunes of the local population. Beyond the agricultural sector, local handicrafts faced increasingly unequal competition from Italian imports that often survived only because of official subsidies. Official fascist colonial policy simply excluded the local population wherever and whenever it could.

The impact of Italy's colonialism was even more pernicious for Libyan society. In the process of subjugating the Cyrenaican tribes, the Italians had in effect pursued policies that substantially weakened the power of the Sanusiyya as an organizational and political force. Many of its leaders and their followers were in exile; an estimated 14,000 Libyans lived in Egypt, mostly in impoverished conditions, divorced from the familiar life they had known in the desert. The traditional tribal assemblies on which the Sanusi Order relied had been abolished, and the powers of the shaykhs decimated. In Tripolitania and in Cyrenaican coastal cities, Libyans became a cheap supply of menial labor, forced to become low wage earners in a cash economy over which they had no control.[18] Substantial Libyan exile communities existed in Syria, Chad, Sudan, Tunisia, and Algeria. Certainly nothing was done under the circumstances to prepare the population within Libya for any form of self-government. For Libyans, their perception of their first encounter with the mechanisms of a modern state was that of an authoritarian and domineering administration that could be used, seemingly unchecked, to subjugate and often dispossess them. In contrast, the ethos of the tribe, with its promises of egalitarianism and inclusion would – as subsequent events were to show – not surprisingly remain firmly lodged as a positive factor in the imagination of many Libyans.

WORLD WAR II, ITALY'S DEFEAT, AND THE GREAT POWER
DELIBERATIONS

At the dawn of World War II, just as Italy's dreams of implementing its Fourth Shore seemed a possibility, the country's fortunes started to decline dramatically and irrevocably. By 1940, neither Libya nor any of Italy's other African possessions had become important outlets for the country's industrial goods or for trade. The estimated 300,000 Italians living in Africa by that time constituted less than the average annual natural increase of population in metropolitan Italy in the years leading up to World War II.[19] In Libya, an estimated 40,000 Italian settlers lived in Cyrenaica in 1941; another 70,000 were in Tripolitania, of whom half lived in Tripoli itself.[20] Whatever plans or hopes existed to turn Libyans slowly into (admittedly second-class) citizens of Italy and to consolidate Italy's position in Libya – hence Mussolini's symbolically important gesture of having himself ordained as the Protector of Islam in Tripoli in 1937 – started to crumble when the country joined World War II in June 1940 as an ally of a then seemingly undefeatable Nazi Germany.

Much of the history of Libya during World War II is encapsulated in the celebrated military campaigns that took place among the foreign belligerents, followed by the turning of the tide in favor of the Allied powers after the second battle of al-Alamein in late 1942, and the slow but inexorable expulsion of German and Italian troops from North Africa. The British war effort in North Africa, and the Italian and German evacuation of North Africa, were matched by the advance of the Free French Forces under General Leclerc from French Equatorial Africa and led to the establishment of a British Military Administration (BMA) in Tripolitania and Cyrenaica and a French Military Administration in Fazzan after the country's final conquest by the Allies in 1943.[21] Damage to the country as a result of the battles was substantial. Much of the Italian infrastructure was destroyed, especially in Cyrenaica. Benghazi alone had been subject to more than 1,000 air raids. The Italian colonists in Cyrenaica had been evacuated from the province in November and December of 1942, leaving behind abandoned fields and farmhouses in the Jabal al-Akhdar, amidst

Figure 2. Benito Mussolini is ceremonially presented with the Sword of Islam during his visit to Libya in 1937.

the rubble of war. The land was quickly taken over by returning nomads and their herds.

Just before the war, building upon the slender threads of cooperation that reached back to the 1920s when Sayyid Idris had been offered the Amirate of Tripolitania, a delegation of fifty-one Libyan exiles from both northern provinces had met in Alexandria in 1939 to define a course of action. Several of Tripolitania's representatives at the time proved reluctant to choose sides between support for the Allied or the Axis Powers – afraid in part that throwing their lot in with the British would strengthen the position of the Sanusis and of Cyrenaica at their expense; Sayyid Idris, however, unequivocally declared himself in favor of siding with the British, arguing strategically that if the British won, Libya could hope to wring concessions from them; if they lost, Libya at worst faced a *status quo ante* under continued Italian tutelage. When the group met again in Cairo in August 1940, Sayyid Idris prevailed and both provinces decided to support the British side, proclaiming for that purpose a Sanusi Amirate over Cyrenaica and Tripolitania. The delegates also empowered Sayyid Idris to conclude agreements with the British for eventual independence in return for support for their cause. A Libyan Arab Force, consisting of five infantry battalions of volunteers, was created to support the British war effort – even though their role remained limited (except for one engagement near Benghazi) to support and gendarmerie duties.[22]

The Italians, having initially encouraged them, had of course not been unaware of the nationalist pressures building throughout North Africa and in Libya in the years leading up to World War II. They had hoped, however, that the settler presence would be able to contain such sentiments in Libya. Italy's propaganda had always stressed that it was not an imperialist nation like the other European countries, but a poor proletarian nation seeking an outlet for its surplus population. Mussolini ceremoniously appointed himself as the Protector of Islam to symbolize the confluence of Italian and Libyan interests. But the bloody campaigns and subjugation in the 1920s and 1930s, and Italy's defeat during the war, had forever destroyed those fictions.

It was those memories, and the defeat of the Italians at al-Alamein, that fueled efforts by the Cyrenaicans and by the Sanusi exiles in Egypt to discern British intentions for the post-World-War-II period. When the Tripolitanians pressured Sayyid Idris into wringing guarantees of post-war independence from Great Britain, however, the British Foreign Secretary, Anthony Eden, in January 1942 promised that under no circumstances would the Sanusi of Cyrenaica come under Italian domination again. Eden's singular attention to Cyrenaica was interpreted by the Tripolitanians either as an attempt by Britain itself to assume an oversight role in the country's post-war future or, worse, to recognize the Sanusi leadership as representing both territories' interests after the war. The two provinces had little choice, however, but to await the end of the hostilities and an international settlement of their fate. They were given a BMA "care and maintenance" status, administered according to the 1907 Hague Convention, until the end of 1949. Fazzan similarly was subject to French Military Administration, and would remain so until independence in 1951.

After the defeat of Italy, under the relative freedom of the British and French administrations, a multitude of political interests, most often at cross-purposes, developed concerning the future of Cyrenaica, Tripolitania, and Fazzan. The first set of these developed within the provinces themselves. In Cyrenaica, political allegiance and any discussion of the province's future naturally converged around the Sanusis who enjoyed the confidence of the British. In 1946, after the creation of the Sanusi-dominated National Congress, the Cyrenaicans began to lay the groundwork for self-government. Although considerably less so than in Tripolitania, ideas of nationalism had started to infiltrate the political ideas of a younger generation whose views were expressed through the Cyrenaican branch of the Umar al-Mukhtar club, soon renamed the National Association of Cyrenaica. Although the Association stuck loyally to the broader Sanusi program, it was clear that its members were not opposed to a larger, more inclusive political union for the provinces.

In Tripolitania – traditionally more cosmopolitan and urbane – a much richer stew of political groupings developed under the relative freedom of the BMA, inspired by ideas of Arab nationalism that accompanied the return of its exiles from several Arab countries. With the memories of the earlier Tripolitanian Republic still lingering, Tripolitanians proved more progressive and more unity-minded than their Cyrenaican counterparts. Politics within the province, however, remained marked by infighting among a number of factions and families. Tripolitania also possessed a sizeable minority of about 40,000 Italians whose interests needed to be considered and, unlike Cyrenaica, had not been promised that it would not revert back to a post-fascist Italy. By 1947, Tripolitania had roughly a half-dozen political parties whose self-proclaimed memberships ranged from a few dozen to several thousand. Irrespective of their differences, they all agreed upon independence for the country, unity of all three provinces, and membership in the Arab League.[23] Not surprisingly, however, the major dividing issue among the different parties concerned the role the

Sanusis would play in the future of the country – an obstacle that continued to bedevil them as the future of the country was soon to be taken up
by the United Nations.

The second set of interests in Cyrenaica, Tripolitania, and Fazzan were
those of the Great Powers – Britain and France, the United States and the
Soviet Union – after World War II. Italy, despite its defeat in the war, still
held legal sovereignty over Libya, a claim it reasserted after the war ended.
Without real consultation of the three provinces, the Four Powers agreed
that Italy would need to relinquish this sovereignty – accomplished on 15
February 1947 – but then proved unable to agree on how the territories
should be disposed of, each power proposing a different solution. The matter was finally referred to a Four Power Commission that arrived in Libya
in early 1948. By that time, the positions of Cyrenaica and Tripolitania
had hardened considerably. The western province still declared itself overwhelmingly in favor of unity. In Cyrenaica political consensus had become
represented by a single political party, the National Congress, that wanted
independence under a Sanusi government. Only under Sanusi rule would
it consider unity with Tripolitania. In Fazzan, almost half of the population
pronounced itself in favor of continued French administration, and beyond
that few political opinions existed. In its report the Commission noted the
nearly universal appeal of independence – but cryptically remarked as well
on the dire social, economic, and political conditions in the provinces.

Although the United States and the Soviet Union initially showed relatively little direct interest in Libya's fate, Cold War considerations steadily intruded upon the unfolding diplomatic wrangling. After three years
of virtual diplomatic deadlock, the Libyan matter was passed on to the
United Nations General Assembly on 15 September 1948.[24] The infighting
continued, now clearly and directly colored by issues surrounding Cold
War interests. Neither France nor Great Britain initially would support
attempts to create a united Libya during some of the United Nations committee debates.[25] France in particular was anxious to hold on to Fazzan.
Trying to pre-empt a United Nations decision, the two administering powers signed the Bevin-Sforza plan, published on 10 May 1949, proposing
ten-year trusteeships for France in Fazzan, for Great Britain in Cyrenaica,
and for Italy in Tripolitania. Violent demonstrations in Cyrenaica and
Tripolitania – supported vocally by Soviet and Arab protests – indicated
internal opposition to such a disposition of the provinces. The Bevin-
Sforza plan, however, made possible what had on several previous occasions eluded the Tripolitanians and Cyrenaicans: a united stance after
decades of irresolution and disagreement.

A resolution based on the Bevin-Sforza plan was defeated in the United Nations General Assembly, and the Libyan issue was referred to its Fall 1949 session. By that time, the general sentiment among the Four Powers and within the General Assembly had decidedly shifted from earlier proposals – like Bevin-Sforza – that were based on trusteeships for the provinces, to suggestions for actual independence. When the General Assembly met again in September 1949, Britain had already unilaterally decided to grant Cyrenaica self-government under the leadership of Sayyid Idris. Despite British protestations that this would not prejudice further United Nations' decisions, it effectively meant that if independence were to granted to the provinces, it would necessarily propel Sayyid Idris into a privileged position – and protect British and western interests. In February 1950, France followed suit, setting up a transitional government in Fazzan and creating a Representative Assembly for the province. By that time, the General Assembly had started to draft a resolution to decide upon the means and timing of Libyan independence as a unified country. On 21 November 1949, the resolution on Libyan independence was adopted, stipulating the country would become independent no later than 1 January 1952. Shortly afterwards, on 10 December 1949, Dr. Adrian Pelt was appointed as United Nations' Commissioner in Libya to supervise the transition process and the resolution's implementation.

After years of competing claims and interests, and internal and international wrangling, Libya finally achieved its independence on 24 December 1951. What prompted the change from earlier Great Power suggestions for trusteeships to independence once Bevin-Sforza had been rejected remains in part a matter of conjecture, but the shift was clearly influenced by unfolding larger political and economic concerns.[26] Great Britain and the United States seemingly concluded, in the context of the Cold War, that an independent Libya would serve their interests better. As an independent nation, Libya would be able to establish military bases and promise outside powers access to them, or to retain existing bases – something it could not have done under a United Nations trusteeship.[27] The eventual signing of military base agreements with both countries in the wake of independence added credibility to this interpretation. As Henry Villard, the first US ambassador to independent Libya, noted:

A glance at the map shows the strategic value of Libya … without which there might have been little interest in the emergence of an Arab kingdom in North Africa … if Libya had passed under any form of United Nations trusteeship, it would have been impossible for the territory to play a part in the defense arrangements of the free world.[28]

Great Britain and France (with the United States) above all proved united in their conviction that, no matter what, the Soviet Union should be kept from gaining a foothold or sphere of influence on the southern shores of the Mediterranean. If not for that fact, as Dr. Pelt later acknowledged, "Cyrenaica, Tripolitania, and the Fazzan might have remained under foreign domination for a long time."[29] In the case of France, there was a mixture of strategic and economic concerns: Fazzan was an important staging area for French Equatorial Africa, and French engineers had started to prospect for oil across the Libyan–Algerian border.

LEGACIES AT THE EVE OF INDEPENDENCE

At the eve of its creation, the United Kingdom of Libya faced innumerable obstacles. Thrown together were two provinces whose interests and outlooks substantially diverged, and a third – Fazzan – that had barely figured into the negotiations leading to eventual independence. In a sense, the United Kingdom of Libya was an accidental state: created by, and at the behest of, Great Power interests and agreed to by the local provinces who feared other alternatives.

The legacy of the first part of the twentieth century, however, had not been kind to those who now became grouped under a single flag but who, in reality, shared few common aspirations. After a particularly brutal exercise in colonial rule, the Italian fascist government had left most future Libyans with dismal memories of their first exposure to a modern state. While the destruction of human life and the humiliating treatment of Libyans had left scars that would endure far beyond independence – even as the fascist slogans "Credere, Obedire, Combattere" were slowly obliterated from farmhouses and government buildings throughout the kingdom – the Italian legacy proved enduringly destructive to the more impersonal sense of national unity and statehood that the inhabitants of Cyrenaica, Tripolitania, and Fazzan would need to face the challenges of political, social, and economic development after 1951.

The Italian creation and maintenance of the country's *Quarta Sponda* (Fourth Shore) had been based much less on economic interest than on national pride, and as an outlet for surplus population. The colonial masters had deliberately excluded native citizens from any of the administrative and bureaucratic institutions within the colony. The result was that, in contrast to neighboring Egypt, Algeria, and Tunisia, the colonial economy had not created any clear domestic financial, commercial capitalist, or agricultural classes whose fortunes had been tied to colonial interests.

As a result – one that would be extended greatly as a result of the peculiar economic development pattern under the monarchy and beyond – Libya had neither a local bourgeoisie, nor an indigenous class of patrons, clients, and brokers that Italy could have fostered to maintain or extend a centralized administration. The Italians had, furthermore, systematically excluded local people from whatever bureaucratic and administrative institutions they created. In Libya, the colonial economy did not lead to clearly defined classes or social groups that would emerge as interested parties in future state-building efforts. Beyond the coastal line of cities, the hinterland became increasingly marginalized and had, except for agricultural settlements along the coast and into Jabal al-Akhdar, been left untransformed and economically excluded. As a result, some of these reverted back to the relative isolation they had enjoyed during the Ottoman Empire. Particularly in Cyrenaica, where the Sanusiyya had held sway, traditional kinship obligations and patterns of tribal identity became once more the primary expression of local social structures and interaction, as the negotiations leading up to independence indicated. Whatever client–patron networks had started to develop during the Ottoman period among the urban elites of Tripolitania and Cyrenaica lost their relevance as they were prevented from engaging in the local economy.

Between the end of the resistance to the Italians and the colonial power's removal from Libya, barely a decade had passed. Opposition to Italy within the provinces had differed and had remained focused largely around local, provincial interests. The differential response to the Italian presence, and the persisting distrust between the Sanusi supporters in Cyrenaica and the Tripolitanians, prevented the galvanizing of a nationalist ideology that could be readily harnessed for political and economic purposes after independence.

Equally important for what was to come, however, was the fact that, except for small groups of nationalists – primarily in Tripolitania – the future Libyans continued overwhelmingly to identify themselves with family, tribe or region, or in a larger sense as part of an Islamic community of the faithful. Out of this diversity, the Great Powers had, for essentially strategic reasons and Cold War considerations, decided to create the United Kingdom of Libya. The two northern provinces had, also for strategic considerations, decided to accept this creation under the leadership of Sayyid Idris al-Sanusi. Fazzan's voice had barely been heard during the period leading up to the creation of the kingdom, except during the inquiries the United Nations had made about its preferences. But the concept of a kingdom was an untried political concept that did not resonate within the country's history or among its people. As the negotiations for independence intensified, Sayyid Idris had already proven reluctant to assume power over all three provinces, reflecting in a personalized sense the more general suspicions Libyan citizens held.

Added to these political difficulties were the shocking economic and social realities the country faced at its independence: a largely destroyed infrastructure, virtually no trade, extremely high unemployment, a per capita income estimated at $25 per year, an infant mortality rate of 40%, and a 94% illiteracy rate. It was, at best, an inauspicious start for a newborn country.[30]

CHAPTER 3

The Sanusi monarchy as accidental state, 1951–1969

On 24 December 1951, King Idris al-Sanusi announced the creation of the United Kingdom of Libya from al-Manar Palace in Benghazi – where Rodolfo Graziani had once resided. With this proclamation, a protracted process of multilevel negotiations between international, regional, and local actors came to a close. However, the country faced enormous political and economic challenges. King Idris needed to confront a number of interrelated difficulties: to create a sense of political loyalty, to develop a sense of national identity among the three provinces' citizens, and to build a state out of their multiple and contradictory interests. The title of King – an unknown political concept in Libya – had been conferred upon Idris al-Sanusi and, as heir to the Sanusiyya Order, he certainly provided a focus of identity within Cyrenaica. For Tripolitanians, however, history was seemingly repeating itself. Much like their offer in the 1920s to extend the Sanusi amirate into Tripolitania as a last resort against Italian encroachments, the kingdom represented an uneasy compromise they had accepted overwhelmingly in the negotiations leading up to independence to avoid further colonial oversight.

Libya had passed from colonialism to independence at the behest of the Great Powers, without a unifying ideology or a movement whose goals and aspirations were shared throughout the country. In neighboring countries, independence was the end result of a drawn-out ideological or physical struggle that was instrumental in creating a sense of national identity. In Libya, however, political independence was sudden and unexpected. The manner in which it came about shattered whatever low level of historical or political continuity the new Libyan citizens possessed. As with economic independence a decade later, it arrived without efforts by the country's citizens, and yet profoundly and irrevocably changed their lives forever.

The country adopted a federal system of governance that left wide powers to the different provinces. As such, it was indicative of the weakness of the central state at the time. With few institutions to regulate its economy

43

Figure 3. Proclamation of the creation of the United Kingdom of Libya at al-Manar Palace in Benghazi. King Idris al-Sanusi stands at the right side of Prime Minister Mahmoud Muntasir who reads the proclamation on 24 December 1951.

and with an emerging political system that closely revolved around the Sanusis and affiliated tribes and families, the monarchy largely restricted the state's intervention in the economy to distributing – albeit in a highly unequal fashion – the revenues flowing into the country. The discovery of oil in 1959 immeasurably increased the use of distributive largesse at the expense of real economic and political regulation and, within half a decade after the discovery of oil, Libya was on the road to becoming a major producer of eagerly sought-after, high-quality oil. This tidal flow of revenues, into what had been a subsistence economy barely a decade before, led to the emergence of a particular kind of state. Oil revenues allowed King Idris – already reluctant to govern beyond his native Cyrenaica – to bypass the procedures that in most countries over time foster political identity and promote loyalty to the administrative mechanisms of modern states.

The independence of Libya in 1951 and its subsequent economic development also politically pulled the country inexorably into the western camp. The country was created at the behest of the western powers who provided all of the country's expertise and aid during the first decade after independence. In particular, warm relations between the United States and Libya served the interests of both parties, and US companies would assume a leading role in developing the country's oil industry. The kingdom granted the United States and Britain access to Wheelus Airbase and al-Adem Base, considered strategic by the western countries for waging the Cold War against the Soviet Union or for maintaining a declining empire. The Sanusi kingdom became a valued client, and the income from aid and from renting the military bases provided the first economic boom in a country that was one of the poorest in the world at its creation. By the end of 1959, the United States would spend more than $100 million in aid in Libya, making the country the single biggest per capita recipient of US largesse in the world.[1]

Internally, the economic, social, and political challenges raised by Libya's rapid transition from an isolated and impoverished desert country to oil exporter necessitated the creation of a large number of increasingly complex state institutions and economic bureaucracies. But those that emerged were overwhelmingly geared toward employing rapidly growing numbers of urban citizens, and distributing the accumulating oil wealth. Due to a lack of regulation, and to the absence of a need to involve Libyans in managing the country's economy and its political life, Libya's earlier difficulties in developing the concept of a modern state and in creating a political community were exacerbated.

As a result, the country during the monarchy witnessed a haphazard process of internal consolidation that made Libya's political system increasingly incapable of coming to terms with its growing internal difficulties, with its reliance on the West that put it at odds with prevailing notions of Arab socialism within the region, and with the reality of an economic and political system increasingly marked by rampant corruption and favoritism. All of these shortcomings proved easy marks for Arab nationalism that, after 1952, was fueled by the fiery rhetoric of Gamal Abdul Nasser's regime in Egypt. The kingdom proved incapable of finding its political bearings between East and West, tossed around by the discontinuities of rapid economic growth and divided loyalties. As one of the country's earliest and most astute observers noted, "when nationalism became the new mode of loyalty, especially among the new generations, the Sanusi movement began to decline."[2] Despite feeble attempts to prevent the emergence of groups with distinct political or corporate interests inside the country, its most politicized and coherent group – the Libyan military – ousted the king and assumed power in September 1969.

POLITICS OF AVOIDANCE: THE RELUCTANT MONARCHY

In Cyrenaica, Tripolitania, and Fazzan, the United Kingdom of Libya seemed to most groups to be the best compromise that could be achieved, despite the fact that the West was responsible for its creation. That calculation was largely based on the fact that an extended trusteeship under one of the victorious World War II powers remained a lingering possibility during the early post-war negotiations. Also, because there was as yet no hint of the riches the country would soon benefit from, the compromise that a unified kingdom represented had not been overly bedeviled by economic concerns among the provinces' citizens. At the same time, as the United Nations commission – headed by Dr. Adrian Pelt – and other international reports pointed out, the institutional compromise that was needed in Libya required a central government that would prove capable of bringing the different parts of the country together politically and economically while leaving sufficient autonomy to the existing provincial administrations.

Separate administrations under the British and the French in the wake of the Italian retreat during the war, lingering memories of Cyrenaica's and Tripolitiania's differential reactions to Italian colonialism, as well as the protracted negotiations after World War II at the United Nations, nurtured existing suspicions between the provinces. It was, therefore, not surprising that the United Kingdom of Libya at independence adopted a constitutional framework that left the powers of the individual provinces strong and those of the central government relatively weak. Except for some nationalists – particularly in Tripolitania – who argued from the beginning for a unitary state, the provinces were willing to accept a federal formula that determined economic and political relations between the Libyan state and its constituent provinces until 1963. Hence the centrifugal political tendencies of the provinces were somewhat curtailed. But the challenge of trying to foster the idea of a unified political community in a country that essentially remained a tribal society – i.e., where political loyalties at best extended to provincial borders and most often, among the urbanized population, barely reached beyond the cities – proved a vexing one.

When UN Commissioner Pelt arrived in Libya in December 1949, he proved instrumental in creating the National Assembly. Through a series of intense negotiations with the country's different provinces, and after querying different groups and personalities about the structure of a future constitution, Pelt attempted to balance the interests of the three provinces in the National Assembly. But while each was vying for equality of status under the proposed Constitution, this equality masked great disparities in terms of population, resources, and inclinations toward unity.[3]

Cyrenaica and Fazzan forcefully insisted on a federal formula, afraid that a unitary government would be dominated by Tripolitania where

two-thirds of the country's population lived. The Tripolitanians themselves – and particularly the province's National Congress Party, headed by
Bashir al-Sa'dawi – were openly against the federal formula, arguing that its
implementation would leave the central government with little power to
implement decisions of national interest. Several National Congress members considered the federal formula an undisguised attempt by Britain and
France to maintain their influence in the kingdom.[4] During the extended
discussions leading up to the promulgation of the Constitution, the
three provinces held divergent views on virtually all fundamental issues.
Moreover, the presence of dissident groups and numerous personal rivalries further bedeviled the work of the National Assembly.

In the end, the National Assembly adopted the federal formula and
offered the role of king to Idris al-Sanusi, the Amir of Cyrenaica. From
independence until 1963, this formula formed the bedrock of the country's Constitution. King Idris, sixty-one years old and having spent almost
thirty years in political exile in Egypt, returned to a country that had
changed considerably since his departure. He accepted the constitutional
parliamentary system as the best (temporary) compromise for the country.
He also expressed the hope, however, that this new political system could
co-exist with the kind of traditional and personal practices that had marked
political relations in Cyrenaica until then. In other words, the king hoped
that the federal formula would effectively limit popular participation in
the actual running of the government. This feeling was widely shared by
the Tripolitanian representatives, who wanted the king to retain power in
light of the lack of democratic experience in the country.

King Idris was a pious, deeply religious, and self-effacing man. He
refused, for example, to have his picture on the national currency, or to
have anything in the country, except for Tripoli's civilian airport, named
after him. Despite his reluctance to rule – a fact he conveyed on several
occasions to the first US ambassador, Henry Serrano Villard – Idris nevertheless enjoyed considerable personal power under the Constitution.[5] It
was this combination of factors – a king somewhat detached from politics, with considerable power at his disposal, and with few mechanisms to
check his entourage – that would prove so problematic for the political
future of the kingdom.

Under the Constitution's 213 articles, the formal powers of the federal and provincial governments were clearly delineated under Articles
36–39. In some areas, the Federal Government obtained both legislative
and executive power, but in others – banking, organization of imports
and exports, income tax, subsoil wealth, and mines, among others – it

possessed only legislative power. The executive power to implement this legislation remained within the competence of the provinces, "acting under the supervision of the Federal Government" (Article 38). This latter category of so-called "Joint Powers" which enabled the provinces to prevent the creation of a single, national policy, would soon form a stumbling block for the economic development of the country since in some crucial areas – taxation, electoral laws, economic development – the Federal Government had to work through the provincial governments. As the country's oil industry increasingly necessitated unified legislation, the need to surmount these limitations led to a constitutional amendment in 1963. This proved difficult in practice since, under the Constitution, the federal formula could only be changed by a two-thirds majority in each of the country's two Chambers and "must be approved, in addition ... by all the Legislative Councils of the Provinces" (Article 199).

The federal system that was put into place in 1951 created an elaborate administrative structure with – in yet another compromise – two capitals, in Tripoli and Benghazi, between which the country's Parliament shuttled. It also boasted provincial Legislative Councils and Executive Councils in Tripoli, Benghazi, and Sebha (Article 188). Later in the decade, the king would move to al-Bayda in Cyrenaica, creating a de facto Summer capital as well. If the federal system was, at least temporarily, necessary from a political viewpoint, it imposed enormous costs from an economic and social viewpoint. The country – with a population of slightly over 1 million – found itself economically burdened with four separate governments, each with its own head of state, its own Parliament, its own Cabinet, and a wide range of administrative and bureaucratic departments. In 1959, for example, Libya's Federal Government had 1,200 employees at its disposal, while Tripolitania employed 6,000 civil servants and Cyrenaica 4,000. Government payrolls at the provincial and federal level amounted to 12% of total GNP.[6]

Provincial borders remained marked by border posts, requiring expatriate personnel to obtain different visas that needed to be separately entered into passports (Article 200). Socially, the separateness and wide-ranging powers of the provincial governments caused the already weak sense of national unity to deteriorate further. The country's Senate consisted of 24 members, 8 from each province, half of which were appointed by the king. One deputy was elected to the House of Representatives for every 20,000 male inhabitants. Each province was governed by a *wali*, appointed by the king, and possessed, in addition to the Legislative Assembly, an Executive Council that included a number of *nazirs* (department heads) appointed and dismissed by the king on the advice of the wali. Libya's Cabinet was responsible both to the king – who could simply dismiss it – and to Parliament which could bring down the government with a vote of no confidence. In reality, Parliament could not really control the Cabinet since the government controlled elections. This meant that the power of the king – or, as it turned out, of his unofficial Royal *diwan* (an advisory group that until 1960 consisted largely of Cyrenaican tribal elite) was greatly enhanced. Virtually all falls of government until 1963 resulted from infighting between the palace entourage and the Cabinet.

After the declaration of independence, the National Congress Party in Tripolitania and the Umar al-Mukhtar Club in Cyrenaica were abolished on the grounds that the country could not afford the instability they generated. In the wake of the first election for the House of Representatives, all remaining political parties were also forbidden to operate. Thus, after January 1952, all candidates for the lower house were government nominees, leading an observer to note caustically that, "After the dissolution of parties ... the electorate showed less eagerness to go to the polls ... due to the rigid control exercised by the government."[7] In effect, Libya's first experiment with elections was also its last – neither under the monarchy nor under its successor regime after 1969 would free, multi-party elections take place again.

During the period of the federal formula (1951–1963) a succession of governments – led by Mahmud al-Muntasir, Muhammad al-Saqizli, Mustafa Bin Halim, Abd al-Majid Ku'bar and Muhammad Bin Uthman – attempted to implement a number of economic decisions that would extend across the three provinces. But, as they were all aware, the functioning of the central government remained hampered by the extensive power that had been left to the provinces, and by the king's entourage. Under the federal formula, King Idris – advised by the members of the royal diwan and by successive Cabinets – dominated the country's political life. Although Ministers were responsible to Parliament, it rarely exerted any force to influence the direction of the country's political or economic development for the first decade of the country's existence. It was not until increasing corruption caused such an uproar in the early 1960s that the members of Parliament finally stirred into action, and forced the resignation of Prime Minister Abd al-Majid Ku'bar. Many of Cyrenaica's elites and powerful families had found their way into the Council of Ministers, the diplomatic corps, and the top of the national bureaucracies. Many had been recruited more on the basis of political expediency than on the grounds of administrative or bureaucratic competence.

King Idris remained a crucial player in the country's political life. Unfortunately, however, the Libyan leader proved a very "reluctant monarch."[8] In talks with the first US ambassador to the country and with one of the country's first academic observers, he made it clear that the burden of leadership over a unified Libya was one he had not truly desired. As recounted by Villard, "He was not very anxious to rule over Tripolitania and ... would have been satisfied with the Amirate of Cyrenaica, but accepted the throne of Libya as a patriotic duty in order to supply leadership for a divided country."[9] The king's own sense of political community then did not, initially at least, extend beyond the country's eastern province. As Ambassador Villard noted, "the unfailing subject of interest to him was the past, present and future of Cyrenaica ... he gave the impression that he would be content to reign over that territory alone."[10]

It was the oil industry and the revenues it generated that, with their unrelenting pressure for unified economic policies and clear, national legislation, would have the greatest impact on the political life of the country after 1961. After that time, the growth of the economy steadily eroded the king's ability to depend on tribal and family ties to rule. Despite its deeply traditional and essentially pre-bureaucratic society, the kingdom could not avoid the impact of rapidly growing revenues. The federal bureaucracy, by being able to attract the best-trained technocrats and experienced administrators, slowly but steadily increased its strength vis-à-vis the provincial governments. The same applied to the country's political life where the most capable politicians often moved from provincial Executive Councils into the federal Cabinet as the central government slowly assumed greater importance in directing the country's development.

THE DEVELOPMENT CHALLENGES OF THE FIRST DECADE

From an economic viewpoint, Libya's situation at independence looked decidedly dismal. Benjamin Higgins, the economist appointed by the United Nations to draw up plans for the country, reflected that "Libya combines within the borders of one country virtually all the obstacles to development that can be found anywhere: geographic, economic, political, sociological, technological. If Libya can be brought to a stage of sustained growth, there is hope for every country in the world."[11]

Higgins's prognosis for Libya echoed that of the British government – which questioned the viability and continued existence of Libya – during the Four Power Commission talks that led up to the country's creation.[12] The economic challenges were formidable indeed. The country's population was estimated at slightly over 1 million people: 300,000 in Cyrenaica and 750,000 in Tripolitania. Fazzan's population of slightly under 60,000 was smaller than it had been during the Ottoman Empire, and continued to decline. An estimated 40,000–50,000 Italian settlers remained in Tripolitania and possessed most of the available fertile land. In Cyrenaica, much of the cultivated land had reverted back to pastoral use after the Italian population left during World War II. Except for a handful of oases, small towns, and cities, most Libyans who had fled the countryside during the period of Italian rule were clustered in a narrow coastal strip along the Mediterranean. Despite this inflow of people into urban areas during the colonial period, 80% of the country's population still lived in the hinterlands. The high birth rate of the country – in 1954 the population was growing at a rate of 1.25% annually – was tempered by the fact that one infant out of every two born died within its first year.

At the time of independence, 90% of the population was illiterate.[13] Most of the population, rural and urban, lived at subsistence level. Annual per capita income was $25–35, making Libya one of the poorest countries in the world. Despite Italian agricultural schemes, the overall percentage of arable land had remained at roughly 1% of the total land area, while another 3–4% was usable for pastoralism. Despite this, the majority of Libyans still depended on agriculture for their livelihood. For the first few years of the new kingdom's existence, its formal economy relied principally on the export of castor seeds, esparto grass – used for making currency – and scrap metal scavenged from the materiel left behind by the World War II belligerents, as well as on financial and technical assistance received from the United Kingdom, the United States, the United Nations, and a handful of other friendly countries.[14] There were, at the time, no known mineral deposits that would justify exploitation.

Cyrenaica's infrastructure, including many of its agricultural areas, had been destroyed during World War II by the British, Italian, and German armies. The country's industrial sector was almost non-existent, virtually without capital formation or indigenous entrepreneurship. Its banking system was primitive. Of most worry was the fact that the system of tribal land and water ownership formed an almost insurmountable barrier to any possible reform in the agricultural sector. According to the World Bank report, the lack of security or incentives made the possibility of individual ownership highly problematic.

It was clear from the beginning that the new kingdom would be dependent for considerable time on foreign aid, both for economic reconstruction and for balancing its budgets, which were in chronic and heavy deficit. Part of the economic assistance Great Britain and the United States extended was a quid pro quo for the leasing of military bases in the country. Three United Nations technical assistance teams assessed the prospects for the country's economic development in 1950 and 1951. Benjamin Higgins noted some characteristics of the Libyan economy that, he believed, either had been acquired since the country's independence or simply reflected long-held beliefs. The first was that appointments to government jobs were frequently made on the basis of personal or family connections rather than on merit. Further, he observed that manual labor in Libya was increasingly viewed as undignified. Finally, he wrote at some length about the status of women in Libya, and how their absence from the workforce deprived the economy of a valuable and available pool of resources. Jobs traditionally reserved for women in even conservative societies – in nursing, administrative support positions, even as teachers – were simply off limits in Libya.

Higgins's team prepared a six-year social and economic development plan that was adopted by Libya after the creation of the country's Development Council on 7 June 1956. Also created were a Libyan Public Development and Stabilization Agency and the Libyan Finance Corporation which was charged with providing credit to the Italian farmers in Tripolitania who remained the backbone of the province's economic life. On a deeper level, Higgins's observations on the Libyan economy reflected the fact that the kingdom had remained a deeply conservative country where the impersonal mechanisms of a modern state had not yet taken hold. Commissioner Pelt noted the underlying problem: the persistence of "protagonists of unitarianism" in Tripolitania and "extreme federalists" in Benghazi indicated the different outlooks of the two northern provinces.

These opposing viewpoints were all the more worrisome since Libya in 1960 stood on the cusp of a vertiginous path of development. The problems Higgins, Pelt, and their successors identified were those of traditional societies that are faced with problems of rapid development, western-dominated modernization, and with internal disagreement on the best political formula for development. With little indigenous economic expertise, and without a politically seasoned group or class that could be expected to challenge him, King Idris seemingly possessed the power to strengthen the monarchy and to make it politically relevant to all Libyans. One might have assumed that the discretionary power of the state would inevitably increase as oil revenues gathered. The federal formula, however, left an inordinate amount of power in the hands of provincial authorities, and the persistence of a traditional network of family and tribal allegiances had already started to infiltrate the state's networks of patronage. Whether Idris – as always the well-meaning but reluctant ruler – would confront these challenges was uncertain. In the end, as shown below, Libya would solve its institutional problem by abandoning the federal formula in 1963. But the second challenge, of creating state structures that would prevent narrow coalitions and groups from profiting extraordinarily at the expense of the country as a whole, was never seriously addressed – even if the king would repeatedly condemn the favoritism and corruption this situation provoked.

THE LIBYAN OIL INDUSTRY

As King Idris struggled with these political issues, Libya, within a decade after independence, also faced the challenge of economic modernization and development. The presence of oil traces in water wells along the Libyan coast had led Italian geologists before World War II to speculate on the possibility of the presence of oil in Libya. In 1940, the Italian government ordered Aziendi Generale Italiana Petroliche to search for oil in the Sirt Basin. The efforts were abandoned as the war spread across North Africa. At independence in 1951, few contemporary economists viewed the development of a Libyan oil industry as a viable possibility. Current international markets already possessed an overabundance of oil, and much of the capacity available in the Middle East was deliberately left undeveloped as a result. There seemed little reason to expect that, under the circumstances, the so-called "Majors" – the eight vertically integrated multinational oil companies that dominated worldwide production – would be interested in exploring the Libyan desert for oil.

Despite this, and lacking any legal basis for their explorations, several major oil companies – including D'Arcy Exploration Co. Ltd. (British Petroleum), Royal Dutch Shell, and Standard Oil of New Jersey (Esso Standard) – decided to send teams to the area. Esso had already concluded in 1947 that Libya likely contained oil in commercial quantities.[15] The Minerals Law of 1953, published in the country's *Official Gazette* on 18 September, delineated the conditions under which companies could officially carry out the necessary surveys – but did not allow for either seismic operations or actual drilling, and made no guarantees that permit holders would be entitled to an actual production license in the future. While the country gathered a group of expatriate experts to help local officials draft the 1955 Libyan Petroleum Law, nine companies – a mixture of Majors and smaller companies – were granted one-year survey permits.[16]

Within a few years, however, Libya would become the world's fourth most prolific producer of oil. This phenomenal growth was triggered by a combination of circumstances that made the country's oil an eagerly sought-after commodity. The first of these was the fact that, despite an overabundance of oil on the world market, the post-war European demand for oil was increasing at an accelerated pace. This was prompted in part by the European countries' determination to replace their coal industry with a more efficient and more environmentally friendly fuel, and also by the Continent's rapidly expanding transportation network. Libyan oil would prove ideal for meeting this demand. As the result of geological factors, the oil deposits that were discovered in the Sirt Basin proved light in gravity and contained very little sulphur. They were particularly of interest to European refiners trying to meet increasingly stringent rules on sulphur emissions.

Libya's location also proved to be an important asset. Situated close to the European market, Libyan oil commanded an important advantage over Middle East oil: lower transportation costs, particularly to the southern European ports. In addition, there were few geo-political consequences to consider in developing the Libyan oil industry: the country's oil export pipelines – unlike those of some of the Arab Gulf states – would run solely across the country's own territory, making them unlikely to be damaged or closed down. Similarly, Libya would not have to ship its oil through the Suez Canal, a lesson that was not lost on the oil companies when the canal was closed after the 1967 Middle East War.

Libya's most important asset in attracting international oil companies, however, had relatively little to do with the advantages of geographical location or possible pricing schemes. In the end, it was the skill of the Libyans, aided by an expatriate team they recruited for the purpose, that created the right conditions for attracting companies to explore, and then to market Libyan petroleum. Libya's oil legislation, starting with the 1955 Libyan Petroleum Law, incorporated the realization that effective competition for oil concessions, if carefully managed and if offering the right mixture of incentives and penalties, would yield considerable benefits to the kingdom. The abundance of oil worldwide meant that the Libyans would need to offer attractive financial terms to interested companies. At the same time, they also needed to ensure that companies did not simply buy concessions and then allow them to remain unexplored in light of abundant reserves they might possess elsewhere in the world. Such "preemption" had been part and parcel of the global oil industry until then, and the Libyan planners were determined to avoid it at all costs. Finally, they were cautious to fashion arrangements that would prevent oil companies from limiting production to suit their own needs. They did so by building in measures that would force the companies – or give them incentives – to produce at a level that would guarantee an income the Libyan government judged adequate for its overall development needs.

The Libyan Petroleum Law of 1955 skillfully blended these tactics, and structured the country's burgeoning oil industry to provide the Libyan government with an uncommon amount of leverage over its direction. Based on earlier drafts that had been composed in consultation with some of the companies interested in exploring for oil and published in the *Official Gazette* on 19 June 1955, the final text and its two schedules laid out in great detail the mixture of incentives and penalties that would make the Libyan Petroleum Law one of the most progressive and creative in the Middle East and beyond.[17]

For purposes of the allocation of concessions, the country was divided into four zones – two to the north of the 28th degree parallel (Zones I and II), two to the south (Zones III and IV). Although the divisions were allegedly based on geological and geographical characteristics of importance to the industry, they also reflected the reality of the country's provincial boundaries under the federal formula. There was, however, a constitutional problem. Under Article 38 of the Constitution, all subsoil wealth belonged to the state, but provincial authorities retained the right to grant exploration permits for areas that were not already included in existing permits or that were part of pending concession applications. This was problematic because the Sirt Basin, which would become the major producing area of the country, straddled the territories of Tripolitania and Cyrenaica.

To resolve the issue of competing claims between the state and the provinces and among the two northern provinces themselves, the 1955 law established a Petroleum Commission that enjoyed wide latitude in administering the new directives, and was charged with implementing all the rules and regulations contained within the law. It had the authority to grant, assign, and revoke permits and concessions subject to the approval or rejection of the kingdom's Minister of the National Economy. In addition, it was entitled to collect all fees, royalties, rents, and taxes from the operating oil companies, to appoint the Director of Petroleum Affairs for the kingdom, and to propose any regulation for the "safe and efficient performance of operations" or the "conservation of the petroleum resources of Libya" (Article 24). Members of the Libyan government or Parliament were expressly excluded from the Commission's board. In order to ensure that the country could retain expatriate expertise on the board, non-Libyans could serve on the Commission. A retired Royal Dutch Shell executive was appointed as initial director, a position he retained until the Commission was dissolved in 1963 along with the country's federal formula.

The size of concessions was limited to 30,000 square kilometers in the north and 80,000 in the south. A company could hold a limited number of concessions in each zone. Significantly, the law also included requirements that forced companies to relinquish one quarter of its concessions in the fifth year after signing a contract, followed by another quarter in the eighth year. In the tenth year, all companies were obligated to reduce their concession areas to one-third of the original size in Zones I and II, and to one quarter of their original size in Zones III and IV. Applications for concessions were granted on a first-come, first-serve basis under the new law, although the Petroleum Commission could intervene and arbitrate if needed.

In language that would later prove important – for both positive and negative reasons – the law also stipulated that the Petroleum Commission could take the "public interest" into account while awarding concessions. This encouraged the use of so-called "sweeteners" – such as increased royalty payments, higher rent payments, higher minimum investments, the initiation of non-oil-related public projects, and the willingness to include the Libyan government in production operations – to influence the Commission. Finally, the law also gave companies the right to enter into joint operations, and set taxes, after annual depletion allowances, at 25% of gross income up to a maximum of 50% of net income.

The stipulations of the Petroleum Law of 1955 were crucial for the direction of the country's industry, for the incentives and conditions of exploration it offered, and, ultimately, for Libya's power vis-à-vis the oil companies. Part of the incentives was the low entry fee per concession. At a price of £500 plus annual rent of £10–20 pounds per 100 square kilometers, even small independent companies could afford to drill. Only in the eighth year did rents increase significantly and, by then, companies either had found oil or would simply relinquish the concession.

The way profits were taxed further encouraged those companies that managed to find oil. Taxation only began when the company's exports reached a certain level and was based on net profits, calculated after the companies had deducted fees, rents, expenses, losses, as well as royalty payments. Allowable expenses were broadly defined: prospecting and exploration costs could either be deducted during the year in which they occurred or amortized at a rate of 20% annually. In addition, there was an annual depletion allowance of one quarter of gross income up to a maximum of

50% of net income. Royalties, at 12.5%, were calculated not on a posted price but on a more competitive "market price, free on board" mechanism which excluded handling and transportation costs. Concessions were, with some limits, guaranteed for five or six decades.

The difficulties surrounding the different zones of exploration, the delineation of which could possibly infringe upon provincial royalties, indicated the lingering difficulties the federal formula posed for the economic development of Libya. In this regard, the appointment of the Petroleum Commission had a salutary effect, for it dramatically increased the power of a national organization – the Petroleum Commission – at the expense of the provincial walis (governors). The original draft of the Libyan Petroleum Law of 1955 had included the provisos that each wali was entitled to appoint one member of the Commission and that the three walis jointly had the power to appoint the Commission's director. Under the original draft, the walis also were entitled to make the final decisions on the granting or refusal of concessions. However, in one of the very rare instances, until 1963, where the national interest prevailed over that of the provinces the final version of the Petroleum Law allowed the Petroleum Commission to implement its decisions "in the name of each and every Province." The formula for distributing the royalties from oil sales, however, hinted at lingering uncertainties: 70% would be devoted to economic development and were to be assigned to the Development Council, while the remaining 30% was divided into two equal parts, one half being transferred to the regular budget of the federal government and the other half to that of the province where the oil was extracted.

The Commission's independence also had the positive effect of making clear to the international oil industry that issues of economic and commercial concern would be handled in a manner that attempted to relegate the politics of the kingdom to the sidelines. The fact that companies had been consulted in the original drafts of the oil legislation added another measure of confidence, and the continued presence in the country of a large number of international advisory boards and technical missions further strengthened the image of Libya as a trustworthy and stable place of investment.

The limitations on the number and size of concessions meant that no single company could lay claim to a large area, and the need to relinquish parts of each concession rapidly encouraged companies to use their acreage actively to produce oil at levels the government thought appropriate. While the Libyan government was successful in pressuring individual companies to adhere to the requirements of the 1955 Libyan Petroleum Law – by making no company crucial to the Libyan oil industry – the unforeseen and major downside of the competitive program it fostered was that the oil companies had a vested interest in producing as much oil as they could, as quickly as possible. These conditions were not conducive to the careful management of the oilfields, and the charge that the government allowed the conditions of the oilfields to deteriorate would later form one of the revolutionary regime's major charges against Libyan oil officials.

As a result of the 1955 Petroleum Law, Libya's territory by early 1962 resembled a checkerboard of 84 concessions, operated by 19 companies. Several of the companies were US independents and small companies – including Marathon, Amerada and Continental (the Oasis group), and Nelson Bunker Hunt – that were attracted by the conditions under which they could acquire acreage. By the end of 1959, companies had drilled 122 wells. Four years later, in 1963, the country possessed 437 producing wells, and petroleum made up 98.7% of the country's exports.[18] By 1968, the Libyan government had granted a total of 137 concessions to 39 Major and independent companies that were producing a total of roughly 2.6 million barrels per day.[19]

As the Libyan government became aware of the size and quality of the country's oil reserves, it gradually adjusted the terms under which companies could operate, and it applied pressure to have them hand over more of their profits to the government. Throughout the 1960s, the monarchy promulgated policies that systematically increased its control of the country's oil industry – policies the revolutionary regime after 1969 would be able to build upon for its own concessions. The large number of "sweetened" applications in 1959 and throughout the 1960s was a clear indication of how attractive the Libyan oil market was for the oil companies. For example, British Petroleum, in late 1959, agreed to restrict its depletion allowance. The Petroleum Commission, as on all occasions when sweeteners were included in contracts, promptly noted that "old concession holders will naturally stand a better chance of increasing their acreage if they follow BP's example."[20] In one of the best-known sweeteners, Occidental, a small US independent eager to obtain acreage relinquished by the Oasis group, outbid 20 other companies in 1966. As part of its contract, it agreed to spend 5% of its pre-tax profits on an agricultural scheme that included the financing of an ammonia fertilizer plant, and to drill for water around the Kufra oasis – an area for historical reasons important to the Sanusi monarchy.

Throughout the 1960s, the Libyan government incrementally adjusted the 1955 Petroleum Law, each time using carrot-and-stick measures to wrest greater control over pricing and production from the oil companies. The 1961 and 1965 amendments to the original law were meant to change the basis on which royalty was calculated and to review allowable cost deductions. The government was determined to increase its royalty income by having the final say over the posted price level, and wanted to eventually obtain a 50% share of oil company profits. Simultaneously, the Petroleum Commission kept insisting that sweeteners – now called "Elements of Preference" – would be instrumental in future concessions. In addition, in November 1965, the government abolished the system whereby the independent producers paid substantially less taxes than the Majors; this situation would come to haunt the small independents when, after the 1969 coup, the revolutionary government would further increase pressure for higher taxation.

Libya joined the Organization of Petroleum Exporting Countries (OPEC) in 1962 and, after a year of a hands-off policy designed not to antagonize producing companies in the kingdom by falling in with OPEC demands for greater taxation, endorsed the organization's plans to create greater refinery capacity in producing countries, to help create national oil companies, and to realize greater cooperation among members. When the federal formula was abolished in 1963, the Petroleum Commission was replaced by a Ministry of Petroleum Affairs and a High Council of Petroleum Affairs. Soon thereafter the government created the Libyan National Oil Company (LNOC) and, in April 1968, the Libyan Petroleum Company (LIPETCO) that would become the country's most important institution for entering into partnerships with foreign oil companies, subject to the Council of Ministers' approval of all participation agreements. After 1968, further concession agreements could only be awarded as joint ventures with LIPETCO.

By mid-1966, Libya had deliberately withheld concessions for almost five years. At the time, the Ministry of Petroleum Affairs had before it more than 100 bids from 50 different companies. By the end of 1968, when the granting of concessions was terminated, 41 new ones had been allotted – virtually all containing substantial sweeteners. The government deliberately included more independents in the mixture of companies, seeking out European state-owned oil companies to secure access to long-term markets on the Continent, with the hope of creating government-to-government agreements, a policy that continues today.

During the 1960s, the monarchy was able to achieve considerable success in dealing with the oil companies in the country. Its policies forced concession holders to base their tax liabilities on posted prices, allowing only minimal discounts. It had created a competitive framework for exploring and marketing its oil that had led to virtually undreamt of riches for the country. During its last year in power, in early 1969, the monarchy drew up legislation that would significantly increase the country's power over its oil industry, as well as its per-barrel take. Regulation 8 of 1969 required companies to provide the government with advance information on proposed drilling operations. The regulation was in part meant to control production; the Libyan government rightly realized that under existing conditions it was to the companies' advantage to produce as much as possible and as quickly as possible, a strategy which sometimes jeopardized the oilfields' recovery rates. Production was inching upward toward the maximum 3.7 million barrels per day the country's pipelines could carry – a record it would reach in April 1970. Regulation 9 transferred the authority to set posted prices from the companies to the government. The issue was temporarily left unresolved, for while the Libyan government and the oil companies were still negotiating over the issue, the September 1969 coup took place.

In retrospect, all of the concessions gradually and grudgingly made by the oil companies throughout the 1950s and 1960s flowed from the nature and structure of Libya's oil legislation, beginning with the 1955 Petroleum Law. In particular, the system of granting small concessions that needed to be relinquished after a few years made for a very competitive environment, providing as it did incentives for other companies to take over acreage where the original holders had failed to strike oil. As a result, the Libyan government – although aware that it could not exploit these favorable circumstances to the point where it would provoke a general exodus of the oil companies – was in a powerful position to negotiate with their representatives. The smaller, independent companies were particularly vulnerable since they did not possess either the integrated structure, or the global diversification, or the financial resources of the Majors that would have allowed them to stand up to the Libyan government.

By 1969, the Libyan government had proven to be a skilled and determined negotiator, making pragmatic adjustments when needed but unrelentingly pressing for greater control over the production and pricing of its oil. The revolutionary regime that took over in September that year inherited all the tools, expertise, and knowledge that had been skillfully acquired in the decade before. With very few exceptions, it would continue the policies of its predecessor in a neutral and technocratic fashion that stood in sharp contrast to its revolutionary edicts and pronouncements. The kingdom's policy of attracting independent companies would furthermore prove an invaluable asset to the Qadhafi government: it allowed the

Libyan oil industry, much to the chagrin of the United States, to continue virtually unimpeded when the American government ordered its companies to leave the country in 1986.

THE UNIFICATION OF THE KINGDOM

Long before the *Esso Canterbury* took away Libya's first crude oil from the Marsa al-Burayqa harbor in the fall of 1961, the impact of an emerging oil industry had already started to affect Libya's economy. In a dramatic fashion, the sale of increasingly large quantities of oil changed the parameters of both the challenges of, and opportunities for, economic development the monarchy faced in its second decade in power. Although the money foreign aid agencies had spent in Libya between 1952 and 1958 now seemed small in comparison to oil revenues, it had been of great value to the country and had been accompanied by a large amount of expertise provided by the international donors.

The country's leadership now faced a twofold dilemma. First, how to use the resources from this first oil boom in a manner that was efficient and equitable, and that promoted the long-term development of the country. Second, how to adjust a federal system that had assigned a great deal of political authority and independent economic power to the hands of the provinces. Under this federal formula, the central government had been hampered in its budget planning by the fact that its taxation policy was subject to provincial agreement. As such, the government could not establish either a national income or a business tax. This stipulation was aggravated by the fact that, under Article 174 of the Constitution, the federal government was obliged to make up provincial budget deficits over which it had no control. As oil revenues started to flow into government coffers, it was clear that this was a recipe for economic disaster.

If the oil industry had been a good example of how a relatively isolated group of technocrats might construct a national institution and legislation that potentially could benefit all, it was not so clear in light of Article 174 how the country's political structures would channel the profits from the oil industry to the country at large. By 1960, Higgins observed what became known as "rent-seeking behavior" by individuals and groups, particularly those close to the monarchy, providing the first indications that Libya, like most other oil exporters, would find it difficult to suppress the urge to use economic resources for political purposes.

Adding, furthermore, to King Idris's worries – as the government stood poised to take over the management of the national economy in the wake of the oil discoveries – was the fact that the initial funding and much of the expertise of the international community would substantially diminish. For the first time, Libyans had to plan for their own economic future. Few developing countries in the world could boast the number of background studies and advisory reports the international community and individual countries had provided to the Libyan monarch. In the years leading up to independence, and during its first decade as a country, it had enjoyed extensive advice that could now serve as background for Libya's own development plans. In particular, and with considerable care, the United Nations had studied the country's economy and its sociopolitical system, and had made a large number of recommendations. These included warnings about the potentially nefarious impact of oil money if considerable changes to the country's existing political and economic structures were not enacted. Indeed, Higgins's observations cited above were implicit warnings about the climate of economic permissiveness Libya was in danger of creating as oil revenues entered its economy.

The economic riches that accrued to the country were astonishing. Per capita annual income, estimated at $25–35 at independence as noted above, mushroomed to $2,000 by 1969. Libya's annual growth rate during the second decade of the monarchy had been in excess of 20% annually, stimulated exclusively by the production of oil that had climbed from 20,000 barrels per day in 1960 to almost 3 million barrels when the military coup took place in September 1969.[21]

From the beginning, it was clear to most informed Libyans and to the international agencies that the federal formula was at best a temporary compromise that would eventually outlive its usefulness as the country slowly coalesced into a single economic and political community. Its enactment had essentially been a compromise made for political purposes, before the interests of the different provinces were affected by the country's riches.

By the time the issue of federal versus provincial powers was solved in 1963, it had already preoccupied King Idris and some of his top advisors for more than a decade.[22] After the assassination of the king's close advisor Ibrahim al-Shalhi in 1954, Idris had left the Cyrenaican capital Benghazi – never to return – for Tubruq, disgusted by the Sanusi family intrigues surrounding his succession. When Prime Minister Mustafa Ben Halim suggested to him that the federal formula be abolished and the monarchy transformed into a republic – with King Idris as president of the republic for life, but with a ten-year tenure term limit for all successors – the king ordered his prime minister to write up a formal draft. Under the plan, the president, as head of state, would be responsible for provincial administration, thus eliminating any further need for their separate bureaucracies. The proposed solution would solve the problem of federal versus provincial power once and for always, and would settle the festering succession issue within the Sanusi family. Ben Halim's draft was discussed at several meetings in the king's new residence in Tubruq in January 1955, with Adrian Pelt and several Libyan officials present. Ben Halim strenuously defended his proposal on the grounds of economic efficiency, but the king in the end backed away from it when Cyrenaican tribal chiefs, through the royal diwan, exerted pressure to abandon the plan. As always during the monarchy, the country's prime minister had found himself caught between the weak powers of his own office, the extensive authority of the provincial walis, and the power of the palace entourage.[23]

The idea of unification was further stimulated by a study produced by the International Bank of Reconstruction and Development in 1960, just as oil revenues were starting to course through the country's weakly developed economic institutions. It clearly pointed out that the distinctions, different fields of jurisdiction, and different levels of decision-making powers that had marked the interaction between the federal and provincial governments during the country's first decade of existence precluded consistent planning. The IBRD obliquely noted the existing political difficulties in the country as oil was being discovered, and the potential benefits of its commercialization:

Economic development demands unity of purpose and action. No development program can succeed in Libya unless the federal and provincial governments are ready to put their full weight behind it and join together in a common endeavor to raise the standard of living of the nation as a whole. The discovery of oil presents the Libyan people with great opportunities. It can also help to weld the three provinces together and to create a new sense of national unity ... [T]hough it was apparently the intention of the Constitution (Articles 36–38) that the federal government should be responsible for making economic policy and supervising its execution, the federal authorities have been hesitant and irresolute in asserting their rights, and the provinces have been jealous of surrendering their privileges.[24]

The carefully calibrated federal system had, of course, been the price Libya had paid to make independence possible, and in order to construct the United Kingdom of Libya out of the different interests of the independent-minded provinces. The monarchy's dilemma in 1963 was to ascertain whether the existing political system of the country – centered around this federal formula – and the emerging need for economic integration for purposes of its development as an oil exporter could be reconciled. The reform of the oil sector, and the creation of the Petroleum Commission, had been crucial in setting a precedent for the economic unification of the country. Could the country's political and administrative systems, which by now had started to function as important access points for economic patronage, be similarly reformed? It was in part to avoid this debilitating political situation – and to create clearer guidelines for the country's oil industry – that the federal formula was abolished in 1963. Its abandonment was also meant to more clearly assert national control over economic development, as well as to streamline and make more transparent the operation of the government.

The abolition of the federal formula in April 1963 was a watershed for Libya: it constituted the single most critical political act during the monarchy's tenure in office and would indicate whether the country could really become a unified political and economic community. The country's unitary form of government concentrated economic, administrative, and planning power at the national level, creating, at least in principle, a unified state apparatus under which all citizens would be equal. Although some nationalist groups and technocrats applauded its adoption, it did not enjoy particular support within the provinces or the provinces' municipalities, whose powers – both from a constitutional and an institutional viewpoint – it dramatically reduced. The 1963 amendments to the Constitution that effected the unification brought in their wake the re-organization of many of the country's administrative and bureaucratic institutions. The amended Constitution centralized the power of the national government by assigning it the sole right for all transactions involving ports, customs, commercial entities, finance, transportation, economic development, and, most importantly, taxation.

The provincial legislative assemblies were disbanded, along with the provinces' juridical systems. The amended Constitution bestowed upon King Idris the right to make appointments to these local administrative councils and to choose all the country's senators. The automatic subsidies to the provinces were halted, and the country's name was officially changed from "The United Kingdom of Libya" to "The Kingdom of Libya." Oil revenues and company and individual taxation now accrued directly to the central government. The abolition of provincial bureaucracies and administrations allowed the central government to start staffing the newly created, proliferating governmental institutions. The country's banking system was re-organized, and the Central Bank, whose governor reported directly to the royal diwan, further concentrated power at the top of the country's political system. The amendments also included the expansion of the

Libyan Public Development and Stabilization Agency and of the Libyan Petroleum Commission (turned into LIPETCO in 1968), the replacement of the Development Council by an enlarged National Planning Council, and the creation of a Ministry of Planning and Development, as well as the creation of a number of development funds. Finally, outstanding border disputes – except for the Aouzou strip on the Chadian–Libyan border, which Idris considered part of Libyan territory – were settled as oil companies needed clear property rights to the areas assigned to them.[25]

The unitary system thus put an inordinate amount of power directly into the hands of the king – and indirectly into those of the royal diwan – by creating the essential machinery of a centralized state in Libya. But, as the Libyan monarch realized so well, creating state institutions and appropriate bureaucracies by itself was not enough. The unresolved question in 1963 was whether the state could provide enough incentives – or enforcement in case of transgressions – to make the system as a whole work. A crucial issue was whether or not individuals would be able to circumvent the rules and formal institutions that had been put into place. In retrospect, the role and power of the state in Libya after 1963 did not significantly increase as a mechanism to regulate and arbitrate, despite the newly created state machinery and changed constitutional powers. As the country's revenues escalated dramatically, the newly created bureaucratic and administrative institutions increasingly became mechanisms for distributing them.

The fact that unification was adopted in 1963, whereas Ben Halim's 1955 quest for a unitary state had failed, hinted at some of the changes Libya had experienced during the intervening years. The kinship links that had still marked the first decade of independence were slowly being replaced by the creation of a number of groups who all had an economic interest in the state's largesse as income from oil grew. As in the past, Cyrenaican tribal elites received their traditional share of political appointments to the top positions in the state's newly created bureaucracies. But these were now shared with a growing number of Tripolitanian businessmen who were systematically incorporated by King Idris as part of his attempt to help temper what he perceived as the sometimes nefarious power of the country's tribes.[26]

Also, by 1963, the traditional agricultural nature of the country was slowly eroding as increasing numbers of Libyans left the rural areas in search of employment in the cities. As national income rose, wages for skilled workers increased, and educational facilities started to produce a young generation of Libyans who were more articulate than their parents.

The creation of new infrastructures altered not only the country's physical landscape, but its social structures as well. Internal political realities changed slowly, due in part to the fact that the bulk of the country's oil had been found beneath Cyrenaican soil, lessening its unease about Tripolitania's perceived dominance. As a result, relationships between the provinces became less problematic, and Cyrenaica's fear of being controlled by a unitary government dominated by Tripolitiania was substantially reduced. Still, Cyrenaica – in a move that would haunt the kingdom at the time of the 1969 coup – insisted as part of the unitary formula that the position of head of the national police (the only effective security force in the country that was both larger and better equipped than the country's army) be filled by a Cyrenaican. Membership in the new national police force overlapped almost completely with that of the Cyrenaican Defense Force (CYDEF), made up in large part by Sanusi tribal elements that would assure Cyrenaica's rights under the unitary system. In effect, the national police and CYDEF were meant to act as a tripwire against potential attempts to overthrow the monarchy.

Undoubtedly, however, it was oil that once more provided the biggest impetus for changing the federal into a unitary system. Under the formula of Article 174 of the original Constitution, provincial income rose as the country's overall revenues increased. With the burgeoning income from oil, this would effectively have heightened provincial capacities for independent actions, whether or not those were consistent with national objectives and priorities. This, many Libyans and outsiders realized, was once more a recipe for disaster among the provinces. Although both northern provinces had been opposed to unification during the first decade of independence, the provincial governments – but particularly the Cyrenaican tribal elites who had forced Idris to withdraw Ben Halim's 1955 proposal – realized that only real financial, administrative, and bureaucratic integration would allow all three provinces to enjoy the benefits of oil.[27] This would require the creation of formal institutions and mechanisms necessary to allow for state control of the economy.

The post-1963 impact of the oil revenues on the kingdom was perhaps not unexpected in light of the weak existing national planning institutions, a centralized political system that left decision-making power for economic projects in the hands of a few individuals, and the informal system in which the royal diwan was the most powerful player. As the economic boom expanded beyond any Libyan planner's comprehension, the second decade of the kingdom witnessed a further weakening of state administrative capacity to regulate the Libyan economy – despite, or perhaps because of, the increased income. This erosion was so dramatic that, halfway through its projected life, the country's first development plan (1963–1968) was abandoned, replaced by unrestrained spending that continued for the remainder of the kingdom's existence.

By the end of 1965, the country had thirteen ministries. At least another dozen individuals from research institutes, the Central Bank, and some members of the royal diwan possessed ministerial rank, and thus the power to dispense revenues.[28] The five most important ministries, which allocated roughly 80% of the budget – Housing and State Property, Public Works, Planning and Development, Communications, and Industry – were initially headed by tribal supporters of the king, and by two Tripolitanian technocrats. These ministries, as well as the development funds, became the most important formal mechanisms for distributing the growing wealth. As financial discipline was lost in the mid-1960s, they also became important instruments of corruption. At the same time, their ability to regulate – particularly that of the Ministry of Planning and Development, which was in charge of sector development allocations – declined along with information-gathering capabilities. The system of sweeteners in the oil industry undermined many of the legal guidelines the drafters of the 1955 Petroleum Law had been so careful to construct and allowed for a high level of corruption to proceed.[29]

As a result of the unified taxation regime, the power of the state to collect taxes increased in principle. In reality, however, direct and indirect taxes on individuals, entrepreneurs, and businesses declined after 1963. Import duty levels were dramatically reduced, and the enforcement mechanisms of both the Department of Taxation and of the Customs Department atrophied.[30] In the midst of the boom, the state failed to enforce investment codes and ignored whatever import regulations still existed. In addition to the ministries, the country's proliferating development commissions and agencies became channels for food program subsidies, for interest-free loans, and for government-sponsored contracts. Particularly after 1965, when public criticism over high inflation rates became more vocal, welfare, social security, interest-free loans for housing, and educational allowances were used in primarily urban settings to protect average citizens.

The king and the royal diwan also controlled two more informal but powerful and highly lucrative mechanisms to distribute the country's wealth. The first was inside information about future contracts that could then informally be used to negotiate commissions with potential foreign contractors. Second was the ability of the king to personally dispense grants to urban and rural properties that had been evacuated by the Italians and had become state lands. For those who became landowners, there were further riches down the road: they became eligible for subsidies through the newly created industrial, farming, and construction funds. Foreign companies also relied on access to those individuals who could approach high-level civil servants or the royal diwan. Hence, being an influential tribal leader – particularly in Cyrenaica – or belonging to one of the influential families, to the royal diwan, or to the Sanusi family became literally a paying proposition since these individuals effectively controlled the economic bureaucracy. For example, throughout the decade, the skyrocketing prices of urban real estate made those who had access to this informal mechanism wealthy overnight.

Certainly, as one of the kingdom's most astute observers has argued, "tribalism [in the country] had been waning" as a result of the profound changes that took place particularly after the discovery of oil.[31] Particularly, as young university graduates entered the different levels of the country's burgeoning bureaucracies, they brought with them an individual professionalism that often transcended tribal interests or affiliation. To state that tribal representation became "purely symbolic" after the abrogation of the federal system, however, was only true if one concentrated solely on the country's bureaucracies where the more impersonal processes of bureaucratization and of professional recruitment were to some extent proceeding.[32] But this ignores the larger context – the royal diwan, CYDEF and the Tripolitanian Defense Force (TRIDEF), the top echelons of the bureaucracies, the informal mechanisms for patronage – within which those bureaucracies functioned, and where tribal affiliation still provided a persisting and balancing mechanism.

THE SOCIAL IMPACT OF OIL AND THE EARLY
SEEDS OF REVOLUTION

The impact of the oil revenues within the kingdom – and the opportunities created by the country's institutions to use oil income for personal advancement and riches – immeasurably added to its difficulties. This impact would prove so disastrous to its survival in part because it reverberated within a country whose citizens had effectively been reduced to bystanders in its political system. The suspension of the country's inexperienced political parties in 1952 had perhaps been comprehensible within the chaos surrounding independence, but the lack of participation became increasingly unacceptable – not only as the chance for a representative system was being frittered away, but also because it could have acted as a counterweight or a channeling device for the messages of Arab socialism that Radio Cairo was broadcasting across the region. In a sense, it was clear that the lingering suspicion between the provinces continued to play a role. Cyrenacian tribal affiliation remained centered around loyalty to Idris and the Sanusis. Individuals within the eastern province were less inclined to find resonance in Gamal Abdul Nasser's admonitions. In Tripolitania, however, the Arab nationalist calls reverberated among a much more receptive audience.

King Idris was not unaware of the country's dilemma. Although he tried to cast his own pronouncements within an Arab and Muslim tradition, the reality was that Libya had been created by the West – his successor would call what happened on 24 December 1951 a "false independence" – and western advisors played a highly visible role as the kingdom became an oil economy that needed extensive foreign inputs and investment. The kingdom had few, if any, options or inclinations to distance itself from those who had helped to create and develop it. While it tried to be more responsive to Arab concerns that resonated among many younger Libyans, the Arab socialist harangues against regional monarchies that were anachronistic and corrupt could hardly be countered. The anti-British and anti-US riots in Tripoli and Benghazi in June 1967 during the Six Day War were widely interpreted as essentially an expression of frustration at the pro-western policies of the regime. Despite government appeals, oil workers refused to reopen the oil terminals that had been closed during the conflict in sympathy with the Arab countries fighting against Israel. Even the government's subsequent request for the eventual evacuation of all British and US military bases was seen as a palliative to public opinion that had arrived too late.

Despite his reluctance to immerse himself, King Idris was not unaware of the growing unrest. He was particularly conscious of the corroding effect of the growing corruption and political intrigue. He realized that even – or particularly – at the highest levels of government, the distinction between what was private and what was public had often become indistinguishable. Prime Minister Bin Halim's close connections to the Shalhi brothers, who had intimate links to the royal diwan and were widely considered as utterly corrupt, raised considerable concerns. So did a number of scandals that reached into the office of Abd al-Majid Ku'bar, Ben Halim's successor. The machinations of al-Busiri al-Shalhi, the son of Ibrahim al-Shalhi, and nazir of the royal diwan after his assassination, managed to edge Bin Halim out of office in 1957, a move indicating the undiminished power of informal connections. The fact that a number of unknown independent oil companies managed to obtain concessions under undisclosed conditions prior to 1963 proved that the "sweetener" system had also led to further corruption. Indeed, so rampant had charges of mismanagement and corruption become that the king himself felt obliged in July 1960 to issue a public letter denouncing developments inside the country:

Matters have come to climax, as have deafening reports of the misconduct of responsible state personnel in taking bribes – in secret and in public – and in practicing nepotism – the two [evils] which will destroy the very existence of the state and its good reputation both at home and abroad, as well as the squandering of the [country's] wealth in secret and in public.[33]

The king's message had been prompted in part by one of the country's most notorious scandals: the assignment by the Ku'bar government of a construction contract for a road from Fazzan to the Mediterranean coast to Sayyid Abdallah Abid, a close associate of Abdallah al-Shalhi and of Ben Halim (together known in Libyan business circles as "the triumvirate"). The cost of the project, originally projected at £1 million, skyrocketed by several million more pounds, but was approved by the Ku'bar government anyway. The ensuing crisis led Ku'bar to ask the king to dissolve Parliament as only he was entitled to do under the Constitution. Beyond his concern about setting a regrettable precedent, Idris also realized that the growing corruption scandals would inevitably involve the monarchy. Hence his public letter of July 1960.

In the letter, he had ended his admonition with several references to the Qur'an and vowed to remedy the situation "by God's blessing and His might." But despite the king's intentions, Libya's political system after the abandonment of the federal formula in 1963 remained characterized by intrigue, by personal, family, and royal diwan politics, and by a growing inability to control the extensive corruption that existed – leading to what one sympathetic observer euphemistically called a "deterioration in ad-ministration."[34] The years surrounding the abandonment of the federal formula coincided with an influx of income the likes of which Libya had never seen. The persistence of personal connections providing access to those revenues, despite slowly increasing state regulation, made personal enrichment at the expense of the country's overall development inevitably attractive. Libya's political system was slowly running out of time to make itself meaningful to its citizens, unable to halt the onslaught on state revenues by well-connected individuals.

By the mid-1960s, the extensive use of the country's revenues for reasons of patronage, in addition to the political exclusion that marked the monarchy, created a state where citizens were de-politicized but all enjoyed the economic benefits and hand-outs of an oil exporter. King Idris – old, enfeebled, caught up in extensive power struggles and the palace intrigue he so despised – increasingly retreated from active involvement in the country's life. Having left Benghazi and then al-Bayda behind, the king's own literal journeys in search of solitude, away from the corrupting influence of the kingdom's main cities, reflected the country s sense of uncertainty writ large.[35]

Ultimately, however, some of the blame for the lingering inability to create a state that could appeal to all Libyans must be laid at the feet of the king himself. In his astute memoirs, former Prime Minister Mustafa Ben Halim encapsulated in a single passage the paralysis that marked the king's dealings with the country's need for political and economic reform throughout the 1960s, and the stultifying patrimonial regime that had come to dominate the Libyan political landscape: "I was sure also that he sincerely wanted reform, but I knew from experience that he became hesitant when he felt that such reform would affect the interests of his entourage. He would gradually pull back until he abandoned the reform plans, moved by the whisperings of his entourage.[36]

Unfortunately, that entourage included too many individuals for whom personal self-enrichment had become an all-consuming passion. They operated within the larger reality of a country where regulations and checks and balances, even if existing in principle, had been eroded by the persisting informality that marked the politics and economic development of the kingdom.

Perhaps emblematic of the inability to conceive of a truly unitary nation was an article in the *Libyan Review* – a local magazine aimed primarily at the country's expatriate population – published in August 1969, on the eve of the coup, containing on its front page a picture of a military parade in honor of the country's Army Day. Inside, the magazine's main article reminded its audience that Army Day marked the "anniversary of the establishment of the Sanussi army." The failure to mention the country's regular army, or to ignore that the Sanusi-commanded forces during World War II had overwhelmingly consisted of Cyrenaican tribal forces, provided one final and stark indication of how King Idris at the end of his reign, after spending eighteen years in power, still failed to envision Libya as a single political community. In the end, however, even the king's praetorian guard – the Cyrenaican Defense Force and the Tripolitanian Defense Force – remained in their barracks when the coup took place. It revealed how the country's traditional system of tribal loyalty, based on family and regional interests, had seemingly run its course in the country.

THE MONARCHY IN PERSPECTIVE

When the Sanusi monarchy was overthrown on 1 September 1969, the Kingdom of Libya had experienced eighteen tumultuous years, marked by dramatic social, political, and economic changes. Its government had confronted a number of multilayered and virtually simultaneous challenges few leaders of any country could hope to face and emerge unscathed. Libya was a unitary state for only six of those years. A destitute, illiterate, traditional society with few interests beyond those of family, tribe, or province had been catapulted into becoming an increasingly affluent society, buffeted by strong ideological regional currents, and by persisting uncertainties in choosing between the certainties of the past and the exigencies and discontinuities of an oil state.

At independence in 1951, very few of Libya's new citizens could realistically think of their kingdom as a distinct political community. Whatever had been created at the behest of the Great Powers seemed a state in a minimalist and territorial sense. The new country had been conferred juridical statehood, but the federal system – so carefully enshrined with its multiple jurisdictions, capitals, and legislatures – demonstrated the compromise, the uncertainties, and the unwillingness of the country's different regions and elites to hand over power to a stronger, centralized state. While the 1963 new Constitution attempted to create the latter, what actually resulted was a more centralized government whose ability to retain power within a narrow circle of elites and intimates left state institutions and bureaucracies devoid of real purpose. In the process, it helped to maintain a political system where primordial ties could be used to circumvent the country's more formal state institutions and rules.

King Idris's repeated calls to be left alone in his native Cyrenaica and his numerous threats and offers to resign were but one indication of the lack of political identity and interest that remained in the country – even among its top elites. Not surprisingly, therefore, a national political identity centered around effective state institutions failed to emerge – even as the state bureaucracies grew tremendously. That these essentially anti-state feelings expressed by Idris were allowed to linger owed much to the fact that the monarchy had never been politically or financially beholden to its citizens – but only to a group of favored individuals, families, and tribes it judged necessary for its own survival.

This independence from society was striking. It would ultimately prove a major factor in the monarchy's demise, for, when the young officers waiting in the wings staged their coup in September 1969, the kingdom's

Figure 4. Vice-President Richard Nixon meets with representatives from Libya's
Parliament during his visit in March 1957.

historical allies proved too inept or unwilling to stand up and unite. This, of course, was no coincidence. During the monarchy, as a result of the process of de-politicization and selective patronage described in this chapter, individuals had not managed to form themselves into groups with distinct and common economic interests that possessed either a corporate or a class identity. The burgeoning provincial bureaucracies created within the kingdom after 1951, and those of the unitary government after 1963, had left plenty of room for personal, family, and even tribal advancement. Neither the country's traditional grand families nor the tribal elites developed truly national interests that would have allowed them to transcend their personal or, at best, regional interests. Without this historical record of a collective or class memory that could be turned into political energy, they were, not surprisingly, unable to confront the one group – the Libyan military – that had developed and was willing to act upon its corporate interests.

The sales of oil after 1960 had an economic impact on Libyan society arguably far beyond those the oil booms of the 1970s would have. Inexorably, as the state started on its path of development and bureaucrat-ization during that decade, the kingdom's personalized system of political management and economic patronage was questioned by those who had been excluded from real participation, by those who believed in the messages of Radio Cairo, and by those who believed in a more equitable and professionally managed country. Oil revenues initially allowed the monarchy to create a large number of institutions and bureaucracies that, beneath their veneer of modernity, in effect extended the monarchy's ability to use them for patronage and for the distribution of growing oil money. The process of political exclusion and rent-seeking thus created a highly corrosive system of governance that starkly revealed a weak state. The Sanusi monarchy had willy-nilly created this minimalist state. It created a receptive environment for the military regime after 1969 to pursue and extend what one observer so eloquently called the "tradition of the rejection of states" that had, inadvertently perhaps, so clearly marked the kingdom.[37]

In most of the accounts that appeared after its overthrow, the monarchy has often been portrayed as weak, inept, utterly corrupt, ideologically bankrupt, lacking nationalist credentials, and as an anachronistic political system that had outlived its usefulness. Many of these charges reflected those leveled against it in 1969 by the young revolutionaries when they assumed power. Although often exaggerated, often based on incomplete knowledge of the historical record, or simply ignorant of the enormous difficulties the monarchy faced, there is no sense denying that the kingdom was not able to respond adequately to the challenges it faced. In its defense, this was perhaps not surprising in light of the dismal political and economic legacies left to the country in 1951, and when taking into account the kind of challenges it faced within a territory where tribal, family, and provincial structures and interests often acted at cross-purposes to those of the state. The explosive influx of revenues, and the unchecked manner in which they could be spent by those at the pinnacle of power in the country, added to the monarchy's difficulties. Libya's close affiliation with the West, politically suspect at a time when anti-westernism provided a convenient theme for a wide range of grievances in the Arab world, exacerbated matters further.

But when the young revolutionaries took over the reins of power in September 1969, Libyan citizens had known a unitary state for barely six years. During that short period, the combination of historical memory and the actions of the Sanusi monarchy had not significantly strengthened their sense of identity as Libyan citizens, or made modern statehood particularly attractive to them. The political apathy the young military coup leaders found, the lack of support for the king when the coup came, and, above all, the skeptical pronouncements of the coup's leader regarding the usefulness of a modern state, were a publicly voiced reflection of the calculations many Libyans had privately already made. In a spectacular form, after a period of assessment and tentative political initiatives described in the next chapter, the new Libyan government would adopt a strategy to turn those calculations into an actual policy of reducing the power of the state even further. Such a strategy required a revolution in the classical sense in which the new regime would use the word: a complete upheaval of the country's economic, social, and political structures.

CHAPTER 4

A Libyan sandstorm: from monarchy to republic, 1969–1973

The overthrow of the Libyan monarchy came not unexpectedly. Throughout the 1960s, a number of political incidents had revealed the low level of legitimacy the kingdom enjoyed outside Cyrenaica. They had also revealed the inability of King Idris to institute reform that could break up the highly corrupt patrimonial system that had grown up around him and the royal diwan. For months preceding the actual coup, there had been consistent rumors of plans for a military take-over, forcing the king to shift army units around the country's territory repeatedly in an ultimately vain attempt to prevent a coordinated effort against his rule.

The king's hesitancy to rule effectively, the wrenching social dislocations caused by the rapid inflows of oil money, the halting and incomplete transition from a traditional to a more modern society, the rampant corruption and cronyism that followed the rapid inflow of oil revenues, and the kingdom's conservative positions in inter-Arab politics within a region seething with Arab nationalism in the aftermath of the 1967 Arab-Israeli war: all these had hollowed out the monarchy to such a degree that few careful observers in the region, or beyond, were surprised when the actual coup took place. While the general expectation in the West and much of the Middle East had been that a number of senior military leaders would take over, the coup leaders turned out to be overwhelmingly young officers and captains with no links to the monarchy or to senior military figures. Although the first few days brought the unavoidable confusion over who constituted its leadership, from the first official communiques onward it was clear that Libya's military rulers were inspired by Arab nationalism and by a resentment of the West's role in regional politics. They also seemed determined to chart a new political course for Libya within the Arab world and within the world at large.

After the lackluster performance of the monarchy in dealing with the challenges posed by a traditional society exposed to modernization and to the demands of an outward-oriented oil economy, the arrival of

Figure 5. Qadhafi, Arafat, Hussein, and Nasser, 1970. The young revolutionary
Mu'ammar al-Qadhafi meets with his hero Gamal Abdul Nasser in the wake of the 1969
coup. It marked the beginning of Qadhafi's pursuit of Arab nationalism, a dream he
would abandon two decades later.

Libya's new leaders raised a number of tantalizing questions about how
they would deal with the dilemmas the monarchy had left unresolved.
Would the young military officers use their power to counter the process
of political and bureaucratic benign neglect that had marked the country
since independence? Would they be able and willing to construct the new
political community they envisioned while simultaneously, and for the
first time, bringing a greater sense of participation by incorporating the
country's citizens, who had been sidelined during the monarchy? Finally,
what would the impact of these efforts be on the structures of the country's traditional society, and on the elaborate patterns of patronage that
dominated Libya's public life?

The first four years of the new regime provided only some tentative
answers to these questions. After dislodging some of the monarchy's key
elites, Libya's young revolutionaries turned their attention to creating and
invigorating new political structures for the country. With Mu'ammar
al-Qadhafi – who was only 27 years old at the time of the coup – emerging
as the charismatic *primus inter pares* within the Revolutionary Command
Council (RCC) that guided the revolution, the country embarked upon
a period of political mobilization that was soon judged unsatisfactory.
On the economic front, the RCC had to proceed cautiously. The new
Libyan rulers had neither the expertise nor the educational background

to run an oil economy that relied on continued access to world markets for its materiel, its supplies, and its expertise. Despite their antipathy for the West, oil was the lifeblood of the country's economy, and much of the needed capital and supplies for the industry's infrastructure could only be acquired there.

LIBYA'S YOUNG REVOLUTIONARIES

The 1 September 1969 coup in Libya put an end to a political system that was considered anachronistic by most of its observers. The coup had been a bloodless event as, in the end, the king's praetorian guard units (CYDEF and TRIDEF) decided not to intervene. For several days, there remained uncertainty as to the identities of the country's new rulers. A week after the actual coup took place, the name of the regime's commander-in-chief, Mu'ammar al-Qadhafi, was revealed. He was identified as the chairman of a Revolutionary Command Council that was put in charge of the revolution. It would take another four months – until January 1970 – before the names of the RCC members were made public. They included Major Abd as-Salam Jallud, Major Bashir Hawadi, Captain Mukhtar Abdallah Gerwy, Captain Abd al-Munim Tahir al-Huni, Captain Mustafa al-Kharubi, Captain al-Khuwaylidi al-Hamidi, Captain Muhammad Nejm, Captain Ali Awad Hamza, Captain Abu Bakr Yunis Jabr, and Captain Omar Abdallah al-Muhayshi.[1]

The new Libyan leaders clearly represented a break with the country's past. Their populist and revolutionary rhetoric was no coincidence. Their socio-economic and political backgrounds stood in sharp contrast to those who had provided leadership during the monarchy. Virtually all of them came from the country's middle class, and from less prestigious tribes and families than those who had been affiliated with the Sanusi government. Most came from rural backgrounds and they were all young: all except two had graduated from the Military Academy in 1963, barely six years before the actual coup. Some of them were still captains at the time, including Mu'ammar al-Qadhafi. These Free Officers, as they were collectively known, had all attended the Military Academy, largely because under the restrictive policies of the monarchy they had not been able to qualify for a university education, which required a special certificate.

If their backgrounds set the Free Officers apart from those who had managed the monarchy, their ideological program differentiated them even more. Plainly guided by Qadhafi, who possessed an unlimited admiration for the Egyptian President Nasser, Libya's new leaders clearly articulated their own vision for Libya in words and images that resonated strongly within the ongoing Arab nationalist language swirling around the region at the time. Qadhafi, like other young Arab nationalists who had followed the ideological debates and struggles within Arab nationalism, viewed Egypt's Nasser as a dedicated Arab revolutionary who could return to the Arab world much of the grandeur and the power it had once possessed. That Nasser cloaked much of his vision in language taking the West to task only added to his appeal for the new Libyan leaders who viewed the presence of British and American military bases as an unacceptable compromise made by a corrupt monarchy – ignoring that negotiations regarding the US withdrawal from Wheelus Airbase had already started during the last years of the monarchy. As Qadhafi commented in a remark that acutely captured the frustration of many of his fellow RCC members: "How can a soldier remain passive and salute a king who has filled the country with foreign forces? How can you accept being stopped on the street by an American? That happened to me personally. When I wanted to enter Wheelus base, I was turned away."[2]

The emergence of Nasser as a prime nationalist figure within the Arab world after the 1955 Bandung Conference in Indonesia, as well as his success in nationalizing the Suez Canal the following year, had made him an enduring symbol of Arab unity. To Qadhafi and the Free Officers, the possibility for renewed respect and power for the region had not yet been exhausted, and Libya's oil revenues could serve as part of this strategy of renewal. Reflecting this enthusiasm for pan-Arab courage and unity, Qadhafi was willing to commit his country's resources to the pursuit of unity with other Arab countries, thus establishing a precedent that would remain a *Leitmotiv* for the next two decades: "Tell President Nasser we made this revolution for him. He can take everything of ours and add it to the rest of the Arab world's resources to be used for the battle [against Israel, and for Arab unity]."[3]

When his hero died within a year after the coup, Qadhafi became the self-appointed guardian of Nasser's legacy, nurturing the notion of Arab nationalism and unity as part and parcel of the Libyan revolution. Within Libya, however, the regime found it more difficult to design and implement a coherent ideological program. It was not until 16 December 1970 that the regime's first clear political agenda emerged.[4] It included a call for the removal of foreign bases and troops from Libyan territory, for neutrality, for national unity, and – mirroring the monarchy's actions in 1952 – for the suppression of all political parties. Much of the program was carefully interspersed with references to Islam, an attempt by the new regime to establish its own religious credentials in opposition to the old *ulama* once associated with the Sanusi leadership.

It is important to measure the context of the Libyan revolution in the ideological and international political climate of its time. In a part of the world where the failures of non-alignment and of Third World initiatives were keenly felt, Qadhafi represented, despite his blustering and often absurdly simple solutions, a voice for what many Arab rulers could no longer say. He spoke the unpalatable truths that others did not dare to articulate. He attacked both friends and foes alike with a sense of righteousness that antagonized his closest partners in the region and beyond as much as his enemies. But, to many in Libya and within the region, there was something riveting and audacious about his analyses and his proposed solutions. No doubt in other capitals of the Arab world where revolutions and popular upheavals had already taken place decades earlier, his often naive speeches were received by an older generation with a mixture of disbelief and a shaking of heads. To many of them, who had dealt with the West since the independence of their countries in the interwar period, his speeches and exhortations often seemed out-of-date. But this was a new era – or at least so Libya's new rulers believed. Qadhafi and his young revolutionaries represented a dramatic change from the conservative and timid generations before them, and a concrete embodiment of what the Egyptian journalist and Nasser confidant Mohammed Heikal called the "post-setback [i.e. 1967] generation."

It is also important to keep in mind that the young captains and officers came to power in Libya with few credentials of any kind. They lacked political and economic skills, and they simply did not have enough legitimacy during the initial three or four years of the revolution to ride roughshod over whatever resistance the coup had provoked. As a result, while the regime consolidated itself, the impact of their actions was considerably less harsh than what their revolutionary rhetoric prescribed.[5] The coup had been essentially bloodless, and the subsequent removal of anti-revolutionary elements and the monarchy's old bourgeoisie figures led to modest jail terms and exhortations rather than repression and executions. It was a sign of the de-politicization during the monarchy that the coup provoked little reaction beyond some rhetorical opposition.

What the young revolutionaries may have possessed in charismatic appeal and ideological rhetoric, however, they lacked in programmatic clarity. There was no clear outline of how the new regime's ambitious internal and international goals were to be accomplished at first. This oversight, and Qadhafi's penchant for projecting political energy (and eventually much of the country's riches) at the regional rather than the national level, would open up fissures within the regime. Meanwhile, the RCC proceeded in 1970 with an attempt to destroy the lingering power of the monarchy's economic and political elites. Throughout the year, it targeted high-level bureaucrats and businessmen in Cyrenaica, Tripolitania, and Fazzan. It removed Sanusi army officers from the regular army, incorporated CYDEF and TRIDEF into the regular army, and dislodged Cyrenaican tribal and rural elites as well as prominent *ulama* who had served under the monarchy. The new regime did not encounter significant opposition in doing so.

In purging the old regime elites, the RCC was forced in practice to act much more gingerly than its rhetoric suggested, simply because the new regime did not possess the requisite skilled manpower to staff, overnight, all the bureaucratic, diplomatic, and oil-related positions. An anti-corruption campaign that started in early 1970 was meant to replace the old regime's top bureaucrats, but the effort largely faltered for lack of adequate replacements. By that time, however, many of the country's top civilian administrators were already resigning. Sulayman al-Maghribi, the country's last civilian Prime Minister, left office in early 1970.

The country's new Constitution of December 1969 designated the RCC as the highest political authority in the country, empowering it to appoint the Council of Ministers. By October 1970, all the country's ministries – except for the Ministry of Oil where the regime simply did not have the expertise to replace existing personnel – were directly run by RCC members. At the same time, the Libyan army started to emerge as a major employment outlet for a young generation of Libyans. All former officers above the rank of major were removed, and the army's size almost doubled overnight. Clearly the country's military academies were now privileged institutions that were meant to be channels for social advancement, and for creating a new cadre that could carry the revolution's message forward.

With its position solidified, the regime turned toward mobilization of the population in earnest. On 14 January 1971, Qadhafi announced at Zawiya that the country would move toward popular rule: Popular Congresses would appoint representatives to the country's parliament, and would directly elect the country's president. RCC members fanned out across the country's territory to encourage people to participate. Despite their efforts, however, the country's first version of popular rule was quickly abandoned. Aware of the existing political apathy, the leadership then turned toward a more controlled system of mobilization. It announced the creation of the Arab Socialist Union (ASU) on 12 June 1971, following Nasser's earlier example in Egypt. Much like Egypt's ASU, the Libyan version was seen as a vanguard party that would not only mobilize the masses for political participation, but also help to consolidate the revolution.

In order to reduce further the power of traditional identities and institutions, a structure of local, provincial, and national assemblies for the ASU was put into place. Elections for the local and provincial congresses took place in December 1971 and January 1972, respectively, followed by the ASU's first national congress over which Colonel Qadhafi personally presided. On 30 May 1972, Law Number 71 made any political activity outside the ASU a crime that could be punished by death under certain circumstances. Using the word *hizbiya* in the original text – a word that could be interpreted to mean virtually any action that could sow dissent among the country's citizens – the law in effect dampened all hope for independent political initiatives.[6]

In retrospect, the ASU never enjoyed the confidence of the RCC or of Qadhafi himself. Although it lingered on a while longer, it never assumed any real power. Much like the earlier attempt at establishing Popular Congresses, the ASU had not been able to mobilize Libyans sufficiently. Instead of producing a new revolutionary leadership, as Qadhafi had hoped, it recruited many of the country's middle-class citizens and modernizing young bureaucrats, all of whom remained politically neutral. Tribal, personal, and regional solidarities still marked Libya to some extent, particularly in the rural areas. By 1973, as the regime took stock of its two experiments in popular mobilization, a sense of failure prevailed. Qadhafi then opted for a more radical strategy: removing all political barriers or intermediaries that stood between the country's leadership and the people. The first glimmerings of Libya's experiment with self-representation and self-rule were about to reveal themselves more fully in the country's political system.

POPULAR REVOLUTION, PARTICIPATION, AND LEGITIMACY

In November 1972, the first meeting of the Higher Council on National Orientation – a committee created to facilitate, the exchange of ideas among the regime's top leadership – spurred discussion of the country's political and economic options. Despite the ASU's attempt to create loyalties across regional and provincial boundaries, the experiment had been deemed a failure. Reducing the remaining power of the country's tribal chiefs had been more arduous than expected. Where the regime had been able to replace the monarchy's bureaucrats with its own younger and modernizing recruits – primarily from less prestigious tribes – they proved overwhelmingly apolitical. Many were better educated than the RCC members themselves, and Qadhafi's attempt to include these non-military technocrats in the RCC increasingly caused friction. Qadhafi clearly preferred civilians within the Cabinet at the time, and ordered Abd as-Salam Jallud – the regime's most powerful figure after Qadhafi – to redesign it. The division between the RCC and the Cabinet hardened when fifteen of its seventeen available ministries – including the important Ministry of Planning – were assigned to civilians.[7]

The infighting over the composition of the Cabinet and the emerging struggle between its more technologically inclined – civilian – members and those who were revolutionary figures was cut short, however, by Qadhafi. On 16 April 1973, the anniversary of the prophet Muhammad's death, he launched at Zuwara what he described as a Popular Revolution. Rather than mobilizing Libya's citizens from above – as the ASU had attempted – the new strategy would rely on bottom-up mobilization. The five-point program announced at Zuwara obliterated the country's existing political structures and intensified the popular direction of the revolution. It included measures to accelerate the removal of regime opponents, to encourage an administrative and cultural revolution, to arm Libyan citizens, and to suspend the country's existing laws.

Qadhafi's announced Popular Revolution was clearly meant to remove whatever administrative and legal obstacles still stood in the way of revolutionary change. It initially targeted local and regional bureaucrats who were considered hostile to the revolution: mayors and managers, including those in charge of the country's national radio and television station, Libyan Arab Airlines, and the country's Petroleum Institute. The governors of Benghazi, Darna, and Gharyan were replaced. In Tripoli, the entire municipal council was forced to resign, as was the president of the country's main university. The second wave of reforms – *zahf* in Arabic – consisted of actually establishing Popular Committees within the country's enterprises and public and community organizations. By the end of August 1973, an estimated 2,400 committees had been approved by the RCC and had taken up their tasks.[8]

In reality, and despite the veneer of what was known as Popular Rule or People's Power, the RCC remained firmly in control. Indeed, the Popular Revolution marked the beginning of what would become an enduring

feature of Libyan political life that lasts until today: a growing bifurcation between the formal and informal instruments of political control
and power in the country. When the Popular Committee Law was finally
promulgated on 12 October 1973, it carefully excluded vital sectors of the
economy from popular management. Qadhafi strenuously objected to this
restriction and refused to sign the law into effect. The incident indicated
the persisting disagreement between the country's top technocrats, and
those who, like Qadhafi, favored revolutionary measures to pursue popular mobilization and management. It also indicated that, at least until the
end of 1973, the Libyan political system was not yet totally consolidated
around Qadhafi, but left some (rapidly diminishing) opportunities for
disagreement.

The Zuwara announcement was an indication of Qadhafi's frustration at
the political apathy within the country. The real revolution, he argued, was
obscured and frustrated by elements within Libyan society that wanted to
obstruct the country's progress. The only solution, he proposed, was to let
"people govern themselves by themselves." The speech thus also marked an
intensification of Qadhafi's populist rhetoric, and foreshadowed the three
elements that would come to dominate the more spectacular revolutionary
directives after 1973: the dismantling of a host of political and economic
institutions that could provide coherence to the country, the destruction
of representative political institutions, and the emergence of what would
eventually become known as the Third Universal Theory as the country's
ideological guideline.

The 1973 Popular Revolution was meant to create a locally based, youth-
ful leadership, drawn from the lower-middle and lower classes, that would
have a substantially different socialization and education from that of the
country's traditional elites. The revolution's success in achieving this aim
also meant that many of the country's new bureaucratic cadres were highly
inexperienced. The regime's inclination, furthermore, to create a growing
number of government agencies whose activities were not coordinated created even greater confusion. This was exacerbated further by the fact that
offices were often physically shifted around at short notice – a precur-
sor of Qadhafi's later attempts to shift ministries and institutions away
from Tripoli. The combination of these factors produced a large amount
of administrative and bureaucratic chaos in the country. By mid-1973, the
country's bureaucratic structures, which the regime along with the army
saw as an outlet for indoctrination, had nearly doubled in size. The country's bureaucracies – much like the army – were targeted as a means for
social advancement and control by the new regime.

CHARISMA AND RHETORIC AS MOBILIZATIONAL TOOLS

From the beginning of his take-over on 1 September 1969, Qadhafi was eager to portray what had taken place that day as not simply an *inqilab* (military coup) but a genuine *thawra* (revolution) within Libya:

> It is impossible to give the specific date for the beginning of the Libyan revolution ... no one can determine the beginning of any revolution. This differs from a coup which is a casual event occurring at the pleasure of senior officers ... A revolution is the opposite, even if the practical application of the idea partakes of the same appearance as a military coup.[9]

Ignoring the fact that it had in reality been a *putsch* that owed its success more to the relative incompetence of the old regime than to an expression of popular sentiment, or to widespread support within the army, the new regime understood the value of ideologically situating the coup within ongoing events in Libya and in the region. From the opening speeches of the revolutionary regime in September 1969, it was clear that a strong ideological agenda, deeply infused with a number of traditional historical, cultural and symbolic references that resonated within Libya's history, would become part and parcel of the leaders' quest for legitimacy.

The early references to the disastrous legacy of Italian colonialism, and to the "neo-colonial arrangements" imposed on Libya after World War II – Qadhafi would forever refer to 1951 as a "false independence" and to 1 September 1969 as the true independence day of Libya – provided a backdrop to a much larger historical tapestry into which the Libyan leader skillfully wove his vision for a new Libyan society. The confrontation with the West – still exclusively verbal during this initial phase – formed a theme in his search for personal legitimacy, and for the legitimacy of his revolution, from which Qadhafi would not waver for more than three decades. There was, as yet, no hint of the open confrontation with the West that would emerge full-blown within a decade. Relations between Libya and the United States, in particular, remained initially cordial. Though cautious, Washington hoped that Libya could be kept outside the Soviet orbit, and that Libya's close business ties to the United States, and the earlier special relationship between the two countries, could be maintained. As the single most important contributor to Libya's development since its independence, and as the country that had played the single largest role in constructing the country's oil industry, the United States clearly did not favor a confrontation with the new regime.[10]

The presence of American and British bases on Libyan soil, however, provided an easy target for the Qadhafi regime that resonated strongly within the wider ideological pursuits of its revolution. Although the removal of the bases had already been discussed and decided upon during the monarchy, Qadhafi quickly seized upon their lingering presence as yet one more sign of the monarchy's collusion with western interests. Their abandonment soon after the September 1969 coup was portrayed as a victory for Libya's revolutionaries. At the same time, the regime skillfully extended its leverage over its oil industry, relying on mechanisms for confronting the international companies that had been developed during the monarchy. Throughout 1970 and 1971, the RCC increased royalties and taxes with seeming impunity. The rapidly growing revenues in the wake of higher posted prices of Libyan crude oil added to the conviction within the RCC that Qadhafi's emphatic call for greater economic sovereignty could be fulfilled.

All of these pursuits were cloaked within the language of Arab nationalism that brightly fueled the regime's political energy. Qadhafi's identification with Nasser, and with his dream of a unified Arab world able to stand up to the West, marked the cornerstones of his early speeches. In Qadhafi's estimation, Libya's oil revenues could seemingly make up for the fact that Libya's small size and relative unimportance would forever make it a junior partner in any relationship with Egypt or any other Arab country. Egypt's – and then Syria's – willingness to consider a union with Libya provided a sharp contrast to the days when the monarchy had been ostracized in the region. Within less than two decades Libya would pursue seven different unity plans to help bring about greater integration in the Arab world: in 1969 with Egypt and Sudan (the Tripoli Charter), in 1971 with Egypt and Syria (Benghazi Treaty), between Egypt and Libya in 1972, with Algeria in 1973 (Hassi Messaoud Accords), with Tunisia in 1974 (Djerba Treaty), with Chad in 1981 (Tripoli Communique), and, finally, with Morocco in 1984 (Oujda Treaty). Although all eventually foundered, they indicated the degree to which Tripoli cherished Arab unity – a dream to be abandoned, with rancor, within the next two decades, in favor of pan-African unity.

A third element in Qadhafi's search for legitimacy focused on the social background of those who had led the revolution. Portraying the revolution as a reaction of the country's hinterland – where Qadhafi and most RCC members came from – against its exclusion during the monarchy, the systematic recruitment and emergence of members of the country's secondary tribes provided a powerful focus for the regime.[11] This would no longer be a defining characteristic of the regime in later years as it started to create its own coalitions of support, as economic differentiation proceeded, and as rapid urbanization continued. However, the initial appeal to the hinterlands reflected once more an aspect of Qadhafi's populism: the fact that a new political community could be created that relied on the consultative mechanisms of a tribal system that had characterized the country before the Italian invasion.

The Libyan leader was initially cautious in appropriating Islam as part of the revolution, determined to stress that Islam should constitute a direct relationship between an individual and God, and should not be used for political purposes.[12] Although the country's *ulama* had been largely discredited by their affiliation with the Sanusi government, the regime put them on notice that organized opposition would not be tolerated. Through a number of largely symbolic acts that were meant to show their dedication to Islam and the values it embodies, the young revolutionaries banned alcohol, closed a number of churches and nightclubs, and, at least in principle, re-introduced Islamic criminal penalties. It was not until the revolution was more fully consolidated that the regime would more openly confront the *ulama* and that Qadhafi would publicly debate them.

The final aspect of legitimacy was derived from the economic patronage provided by increasing oil revenues. National expenditures on literacy, health care, and education expanded rapidly under the new regime. Minimum wages were raised and interest-free loans provided – with the regime waiving repayment for the poorest of its citizens on the first anniversary of the revolution. Starting in 1970, confiscated land, that had once belonged to the Italians or the Sanusi monarchy, was distributed to farmers who became eligible for purchases of livestock and for farming implements at greatly reduced prices. Farmers furthermore enjoyed government salaries until their farms could make a profit. After taking over the banking system in 1970, the government freely provided subsidies for the construction of houses, particularly in the countryside where abandoned Italian farmhouses and newly constructed Libyan dwellings stood side by side.

A "Libya first" policy assigned all government contracts to Libyan citizens, while local entrepreneurs could freely vie for government tenders on a large number of contracts. Commercial business ventures and industrial projects enjoyed protection under laws that provided the overwhelming share of funding. Local entrepreneurs were then free to sublease such ventures to foreigners. Thousands of new small businesses were established in this manner throughout the country, benefiting average Libyans who had once been excluded from such activities.[13] Although many of these ventures proved uneconomical and were later singled out repeatedly by Qadhafi for their wastefulness and inefficiency, they indicated how, until the publication of *The Green Book*, the regime curried favor among the Libyan population through a careful combination of populism and distributive largesse. This group of consumers and entrepreneurs, on one hand, and the RCC and Free Officers, on the other, were the two main constituencies that now enjoyed the government's favors.

OIL AND ECONOMIC MANAGEMENT

During the first few months after the revolution, the country's new leadership – preoccupied with consolidating the revolution and aware of its inexperience in economic management – had proceeded cautiously with its economic programs. Their concerns initially focused on two readily visible economic and social problems within Libya: the fact that the country had become a dualistic economy where, beyond the oil sector, a number of other inefficient sectors still employed the majority of the Libyan population. Furthermore, oil production in 1970 had reached a record 3.7 million barrels per day – a figure which represented the entire capacity of the country's pipeline systems. It was a development the RCC considered detrimental to the long-term health of the oilfields. One year after the revolution, oil provided almost 99% of Libya's revenues and constituted all of its exports. In addition, the young officers were worried that the oil sector employed only 1% of the country's active population, and that oil development had produced a number of undesirable social and economic ripple effects that could not easily be reconciled with the egalitarian tenets of the revolution.

At the same time, the technocratic nature of the oil industry meant that Libya's new rulers had little choice but to continue relying on whatever expertise was present in the country, much of it consisting of expatriate personnel. Libya by 1970 had one of the world's most sophisticated oil infrastructures that constantly needed fine-tuning and upgrading. Under those circumstances, Qadhafi and his entourage realized that the nationalization of the Libyan oil industry was not an option at the time. By default, they turned to the country's oil pricing mechanism as the one aspect of the oil extracting and marketing process over which they had some control.

As described above, in Chapter 3, Libya's oil sector exhibited some unique traits that could now be exploited effectively to the regime's bargaining advantage. The assignment of large tracts of oil exploration areas to small independent producers, in addition to the Majors, during the monarchy now gave the military regime the opportunity to press consistently for higher profits from Libyan oil through a divide-and-rule strategy. The weak bargaining position of the independents at the time – many relied on Libyan oil for a substantial portion of their revenues – facilitated the regime's strategy. For example, one of the country's two major independents, Occidental Petroleum, received 97% of its total production from Libya. Under those circumstances, the independents were clearly more vulnerable to threats of cutbacks in production, or of expropriation, even if only implied, than the Majors for whom Libyan production constituted a small part of their global output.

The independents furthermore had few incentives to join the Majors to cut production in 1970, a move undertaken globally to restore prices as an oil glut developed. As a result of the 1961 amendments to the country's Petroleum Law, the independents in Libya had paid substantially less tax per barrel of oil than the Majors did.[14] This favored position now hurt the independents as the Majors refused to help them when the revolutionary regime demanded higher taxes. By systematically targeting the smaller companies – their situation made worse by an acute shortage in Europe at the time – the Qadhafi government cut back their production, forcing them to acquiesce to the regime's demand for higher prices.

The government aggressively continued to pursue a policy of higher prices, greater ownership, and greater control over production. The frustration over the level of posted prices, determined by the oil companies and left unaddressed during the monarchy's last few months in office, led the government to establish a committee in December 1969 to discuss the increase of posted prices with the oil companies. The same month, it reduced production allowances for individual companies, following and closely cooperating with Algerian authorities, who had started to take a series of increasingly aggressive measures aimed at the French oil interests in their country. When the small independents in Libya – who produced more than half of the country's crude oil at the time – capitulated to the government's demands for higher posted prices, the rest of the industry had no choice but to fall into line. In January 1971, the government further ratcheted up both tax rates and posted prices.

When the companies attempted to develop a common strategy vis-à-vis the Libyan government – the so-called Libyan Producers' Agreements of 1971 – the regime's divide-and-rule tactic enabled it to withstand the companies' collective actions. Bypassing the arrangements made between oil companies and certain OPEC countries during the December 1970 Tehran Agreement, Libya lambasted OPEC for what it considered insufficient price increases and inadequate premiums for its short-haul advantage. Since the LNOC had managed to sell oil on its own – at prices substantially higher than the posted prices then available for Libyan crude – it pressed for even higher posted prices. The result of the negotiations – the Tripoli Agreement of 20 March 1971 – raised the posted price for Libyan crude to $3.32 per barrel, a figure that included a Suez Canal Allowance, as well as a freight and low sulphur premium, and provisions for annual adjustments. By 1974, the price differential between Libyan and Persian Gulf crude was $4.12 per barrel – causing Libya to lose its cost advantage, creating temporary difficulties for the country later that year. But the Libyan revolutionaries, in a series of audacious measures that added to their revolutionary elan, had proven themselves capable of inexorably ratcheting up their demands for greater revenues. In doing so, they laid the groundwork for the more intrusive demands they would make before, during, and after the oil crisis of 1973, which eventually led to a wave of nationalizations.

Although the increases between September 1969 and October 1973 were small compared to what the quadrupling of oil prices would bring by the end of 1973, the actions of the Libyan government propelled the Qadhafi regime to a stature within the region that only its most ardent supporters had thought achievable. They also provided the Libyan leader with an unprecedented level of internal legitimacy. By the beginning of the 1973 October War, Libya had amassed reserves that would allow it to outlast a four-year economic embargo if necessary. In the wake of its victories against the oil companies, the government then turned toward strengthening the position of the LNOC, aiming to play a larger role in the actual management of the country's oil industry. The LNOC took under its management twenty-three concessions that had been abandoned by the oil companies during and after the oil price negotiations.

Outside the oil sector, however, economic realities looked distinctly less attractive. During the last decade of the monarchy, the share of oil in the country's GDP had jumped from 27 to 65%. By 1973, oil was the only commodity the country exported. Libya's population in 1969 was estimated at roughly 2 million people – almost a doubling since independence. Of those, a few hundred, at best, were employed within the oil sector. The country's other sectors were those of a more traditional economy, largely underdeveloped and marked by low investment, inefficiencies, and with a labor force that lacked the requisite skills for the kind of economic plans upon which the new revolutionary government would soon embark. As an example of the wrenching changes oil economies can engender, in

1969 agriculture and manufacturing contributed only 2.4% and 2% of the country's GDP, respectively.

In many ways, Libya had already become the dualistic economy characteristic of many oil states. Although per capita income at $2,168 in 1969 had improved dramatically from the subsistence level at the beginning of the monarchy, the increase was almost solely due to aid and, later, to hydrocarbon revenues.[15] The agricultural sector in particular was a cause for concerns for the new government. Despite the cultivation of additional acreage during the colonial period, only marginal additions had been made. Only 260,000 acres were irrigated (an estimated 220,000 acres belonged to the Sanusi family) while the remainder was left for unproductive dry farming. The Italian settlers had occupied most of the fertile land, leaving behind modernized farms that the Qadhafi government began expropriating in 1970. A telling fact was that, by 1969, Libya only managed to produce enough food on an annual basis to feed its own population "for one third of a single day."[16] Even more troubling, 34% of the country's active population worked in a sector that contributed only 4% of GDP. Faced with these realities, and without the requisite expertise, the revolutionary government took essentially stopgap measures during its first four years in power. They were populist measures that focused on the distribution of Sanusi and Italian-controlled land, starting in February 1970, and the expropriation of the latter in July 1970. The rapid exodus of the remaining Italian settlers in the wake of the government's measures further lowered the already dismally low level of available skilled labor in the country.

When the first tentative and cautious directives for the country's economy emerged in March 1970, it was not surprising that they were marked by a suspicion of the role of the private sector, and aimed to bring substantial parts of the non-oil sectors under state control. The country's history of crony capitalism during the monarchy had sparked much anger among those who had led the coup, and they clearly considered private entrepreneurship suspect. The private sector was, at least temporarily, retained, but the new decrees clearly stated that it could not impinge upon or contradict the economic policies of the government. It was also clear that retaining the private sector was a policy the regime intended to correct when they were in a position to do so.

Besides its directives for the private sector, the regime gingerly embarked upon a number of industrial projects: a petrochemical plant in Marsa al-Burayqa, two steel plants that were meant to use the considerable reserves of iron ore in Fazzan, and the construction of three new oil refineries. A number of turnkey contracts were signed for the production of construction materials, and the Libyan Industrial Bank financed a number of investments for the production of consumer goods. By 1973, the regime had started to spend considerable amounts on the extension of electricity grids throughout the country's coastal areas, and had started to enlarge the harbors of Misrata and Tripoli.

The country's first multi-year plan after the revolution was made public in April 1973. The *Three Year Economic and Social Development Plan 1973– 75* provided an initial comprehensive and systematic look at how the Qadhafi government – now in power for almost four years – would address the country's economic problems. It was an ambitious plan that projected annual growth at 11% – perhaps not unreasonable in light of the low economic level that served as its baseline, and in light of the fact that oil revenues were steadily increasing. That the plan clearly targeted the non-oil sectors of the economy – which were expected to grow at 16.5% annually versus 5% in the oil sector – indicated the emphasis the government put on diversification of the economy. The total contribution of the non-oil sectors to the national economy was expected to rise to almost 50% by the end of the plan. It therefore allocated substantial amounts of long-term investment to the agricultural and manufacturing sectors.

Rhetorically perhaps, the plan envisioned that the agricultural sector would be able to meet the country's internal food needs. By doing so, the government hoped to slow down the country's unabated rural flight. Clearly, the agricultural sector enjoyed priority, and several large contracts for land reclamation, for agricultural and geological research, and for the construction of new farms were signed. During the first year of the plan alone, the contracts included agreements with East European and Arab companies to bring into production a total of 356,000 new acres. This constituted only part of a much larger agricultural project that was meant to exploit more than a million acres in four distinct geographical areas: the Gafara Plain in Tripolitania; an area around Kufra and Sarir where ample water resources were known to exist; in the Barce-Tukra plain in Cyrenaica; and several wadis in Fazzan. Many, if not most, of these planned investments remained little more than indicators of the revolutionary regime's intentions. Taking into account that the Italians had managed to bring less than 300,000 acres of agricultural land into production over almost three decades, these projections seemed unrealistic, despite the availability of considerably greater economic resources. As one long-time observer noted, the RCC since 1969 had been "long in enthusiasm for managing a national economy but ... very short on experience."[17] Following the dramatic increases in oil revenues after October 1973, the plan's allocations increased dramatically. But – in a fashion that closely mirrored the predicament of the monarchy during the country's first oil boom – unlimited spending, rather than a coherent, integrated strategy, became the norm.

THE REVOLUTION ON THE EVE OF THE 1973 OIL CRISIS

The four years between the start of Libya's self-styled revolution in 1969 and the 1973 oil crisis can most logically be considered as an interlude for Libya and for the new regime. The transition from a politically conservative monarchy to an increasingly activist military regime – seemingly ready to use the country's resources in pursuit of its ideological agenda – had taken place without generating much support among ordinary Libyans. Nevertheless, by the time the first oil boom took place in 1973, the RCC – increasingly yielding its power to Qadhafi – had managed to achieve a number of the aims it formulated after coming to power. Libya's new rulers had consolidated their political power. They had also managed to replace a sizeable portion of the bureaucracies that had been part of royal patronage and that had proven resistant to their political agenda. In the process, they had reduced the power of traditional rural notables and tribal figures, and had managed to dismantle much of the monarchy's patterns of patronage by targeting its social, political, and economic structures of support.

To the country's new institutions, the young military leaders had been able to attract a younger population whose outlook differed substantially from that of the educated officials and tribal and family elites that had held similar positions during the monarchy. The creation of new administrative boundaries across tribal lines helped to obscure traditional loyalties, but the nationalization of the country's oil industry had left economic power once more at the pinnacle of the country's political system – with no real institutional constraints on how these revenues were to be used by the country's rulers. At the same time, Qadhafi managed to stand up to the multinational companies involved in the exploitation and sale of the country's hydrocarbons, and had been able to remove most of the entrenched economic, commercial, and landed elites of the monarchy. Heavy industry, insurance companies, and hospitals had either been nationalized or were on the cusp of being brought under state control.

Many of the achievements during these first four years – in light of the existing circumstances and lack of political and social cohesion during the monarchy – had been relatively easy. The monarchy had enjoyed oil revenues for less than a decade, and the patterns of economic competition and differentiation that invariably lead to organized and entrenched groups in oil exporters had not yet become visible in Libya when the coup took place. Hence the relative ease with which the old elites could be replaced – heightened by the fact that the monarchy had retained few supporters that were willing to oppose the revolutionary regime. Much of this was nevertheless a remarkable achievement by the RCC in light of the difficult tasks they faced, not only in developing plans for the country's future, but also in persuading Libyans to participate in economic and political enterprises from which they had been systematically excluded during the eighteen years of the monarchy.

But much harder tasks lay ahead. The transition toward the ASU, and then its abandonment, had been the first indication that political mobilization and indoctrination had not been as successful as the RCC had hoped. Libyans remained largely politically apathetic and showed little interest in the affairs of their country. To Qadhafi, who wanted to mobilize his citizens in support of his revolution so that the country could then become the vanguard of a larger regional movement, this was clearly unacceptable. His emergence as the charismatic leader of the revolution – which relied for its success on a skillful blend of traditional and modern ways to legitimate his rule – and the concentration of power at his disposal had started to turn the Libyan revolution into a personal crusade.

With a growing lack of checks and balances on the power of its leader, or on his ability to use the country's resources in pursuit of his ideological zeal, it was highly problematic that the revolutionary regime showed little interest in systematically extending the power of the state. Beyond its nationalist and Arab nationalist language, the RCC had barely articulated a clear vision or program that could consolidate the country. The demise of the ASU as a political party, the repeated references to state institutions as antithetical to the implementation of the revolution, and the sustained use of populist rhetoric, all indicated Qadhafi's frustration with the slow pace of reform. The adoption of People's Power in 1973 had been the culmination of efforts to bypass the frictions that slowed down these reforms. As yet, however, the ideas behind its adoption did not contain the kind of programmatic unity and revolutionary fervor *The Green Book* would soon provide.

On the eve of the influx of massive oil revenues that would forever alter the direction and intensity of the country's revolution, Libya stood at an important crossroads. Qadhafi and the RCC seemed truly interested in mobilizing the population for the country's political and economic development, and in pursuing a viable, long-term economic strategy for the country. But they had also, virtually overnight, come into possession of the physical and economic resources that would allow them to shape both pro-cesses in an extraordinary fashion, devoid of checks and balances. Until the beginning of the country's second oil boom in 1973, Libya's military leader-ship had in many ways already started to repeat the essentially distributive policies of its predecessor in order to correct what it rightly considered as a pattern of inequitable development during the monarchy. Whether they could, or would, go beyond this seemed much less certain. The Libyan revolutionaries had started to embark upon a course of increasingly dra-matic and contradictory policies that simultaneously aimed at putting the state in charge of all economic activity, and tried to make it irrelevant as a focus for political identity. The contradiction between the two pursuits was seemingly lost on the Libyan leadership.

All options still appeared available to the revolutionary regime in mid-1973. The growing resort to populism and to concentrating ever-growing amounts of power at the pinnacle of the country's political system, how-ever, hinted at the fact that it stood poised to forgo once more the difficult process of trying to regulate its economy and seemed reluctant to incorp-orate the country's population into a true political community and state. The revolutionary regime's populism, much like the monarchy's benign neglect, also seemed destined to limit the economic and regulatory power of the state to the low common denominator often visible in oil exporters: distributing the riches of a hydrocarbon state. In principle at least, and according to official regime language that continually stressed popular par-ticipation, Qadhafi seemed determined not to demand what many other rulers of hydrocarbon states traditionally and implicitly request in return for economic largesse: political quiescence. Whether they could manage to dovetail the contradictory demands of economic and political devel-opment under the onslaught of oil revenues after October 1973 forms the subject of the next chapter.

CHAPTER 5

The Green Book's *stateless society, 1973–1986*

After four years of stocktaking and its first tentative attempts at mobilizing Libya's population, the Qadhafi government in 1973 stood poised to embark upon a number of breathtaking economic and political initiatives. These would form the foundation of its long revolutionary decade from 1973 until 1986. These experiments were fueled by an estimated $95 billion of oil revenues, propelling Libyan per capita income from $2,216 in 1969 to almost $10,000 a decade later. Some of the characteristics that had already emerged during the new regime's first four years – the impatience with bureaucratic and political mechanisms that in Qadhafi's mind prevented the Libyan population from participating directly in the country's revolution, and the distrust of the lingering impact of traditional forces in the country – now became central features of what the Libyan leader referred to as his Third Universal Theory. Codified in Qadhafi's *Green Book*, the Third Universal Theory was, according to its author, an alternative to capitalism and Marxism. Its directives, reflecting a profound distrust of political parties and bureaucratic institutions as obstacles to popular participation, provided the theme for a number of increasingly dramatic economic, social, and political initiatives. These culminated in the creation of a Jamahiriyya – a country directly governed by its citizens, without the intervention of intermediaries.

The massive inflows of revenues after 1973, and during the second oil crisis of 1979, presented Qadhafi with an economic windfall it would systematically use to pursue his vision of a just, egalitarian, and participatory society – and to adopt an increasingly activist confrontation with the West. For purposes of the former, the government simply expended the revenues at its disposal in an attempt to bring about Qadhafi's populist agenda. That much of the population had been indifferent to his mobi-lizational rhetoric during the first four years of the revolution, however, had not been lost on the Libyan leader. His solution to political apathy consisted in part of the creation of Revolutionary Committees that were expected to implement *The Green Book* directives.

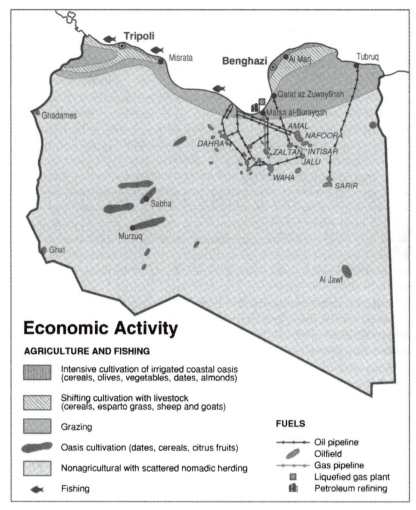

Economic Activity

AGRICULTURE AND FISHING

Intensive cultivation of irrigated coastal oasis (cereals, olives, vegetables, dates, almonds)

Shifting cultivation with livestock (cereals, esparto grass, sheep and goats)

Grazing

Oasis cultivation (dates, cereals, citrus fruits)

Nonagricultural with scattered nomadic herding

Fishing

FUELS

— Oil pipeline
Oilfield
— Gas pipeline
Liquefied gas plant
Petroleum refining

Map 3. Economic activity

The publication of *The Green Book* codified many of the regime's earlier inclinations toward top-down management, and unleashed upon Libya a further wave of contradictory policies that put the state in charge of all economic and social activity, while simultaneously trying to make it irrelevant as a focus for political identity. Whatever formal attempts at economic planning the government undertook were matched and then overtaken by virtually unrestrained spending. In an effort to maintain the allegiance of those groups the regime considered its main supporters, it made major economic outlays through an unbridled program of welfare measures, military purchases, and government contracts.

As economic decision-making became even more concentrated, tension between distributive proclivities and regulatory intervention became an acute political challenge for the regime, pitting factions within the Revolutionary Command Council against each other. The disagreement led to the country's first attempted coup in August 1975. It proved to be a watershed for the regime. In its wake, the revolution turned increasingly populist at the expense of careful management. The prospects for a viable public sector in the country were eviscerated, and Qadhafi consolidated his position as undisputed leader of the revolution. When the massive capital inflows started to slow down perceptibly in the early 1980s, the regime found itself forced to evaluate its economic plans. Libya, however, showed no inclination to seriously reform its economy and became the region's last great spender of petrodollars. It was not until March 1987 that the regime would gingerly adopt some economic reform measures.

By that time, the economic difficulties inside the country had become seriously exacerbated by an increasingly activist foreign policy that brought the regime ineluctably into an open confrontation with the West. Within its ideological framework, the confrontation with the West became a self-fulfilling prophecy it eagerly embraced as a vindication of its own ideological stance. It became as well as a rallying point around which the revolution could be deepened internally. At the end of 1981, the United States halted all crude oil imports from Libya. This was of relatively little importance to Libya since it could easily divert those exports to the European market. The United States then gradually extended its economic boycott, however, until it included products crucial to Libya's oil industry. The rupture of diplomatic relations with the United States and Great Britain was the temporary culmination of a period of escalating confrontation between Libya and the West that left the country diplomatically and economically isolated after 1986.[1] As Libya headed into headlong confrontation with the US administration, Washington assiduously pursued its attempts to limit Libya's behavior in several distinct areas, seeking to oppose its support of extremist and terrorist groups, to curtail its foreign policy adventurism, to halt its unwavering opposition to US-sponsored attempts to settle the Arab–Israeli conflict, and to prevent its attempts to acquire or produce non-conventional weapons and weapons of mass destruction. The April 1986 bombing of Tripoli and Benghazi by the United States marked a turning point in Libya's revolutionary period. As a long decade of revolution came to an end that year, the regime faced numerous internal economic problems and a slowly growing international isolation.

REVOLUTIONARIES, TECHNOCRATS, AND "*THE GREEN BOOK*" AS POLITICAL PRIMER

Ever since the creation of the ASU, Libya's revolutionary leaders had remained concerned about its mobilizational potential. Qadhafi's Zuwara speech, inaugurating the Popular Revolution, had been an attempt to bring some programmatic unity to the different initiatives meant to overcome political apathy. The two years following the Zuwara announcement were marked by chaos and confusion inside the country, in part because the division of labor between the still existing but almost moribund ASU and the popular committees created at Zuwara had not been clearly articulated. The creation of the popular committee system was an attempt by Qadhafi to bypass the more regularized procedures of the ASU. The attempt, however, led to conflict within the RCC. At the November 1974 meeting of the ASU, a split between two factions emerged publicly for the first time. It pitted those who wanted a more orderly, planned course of action that included a carefully designed economic plan – a technocratic solution to the country's problems – against those who wanted to pursue a more activist policy that sacrificed some of the country's riches for the sake of Arab unity and other ideological pursuits. As the struggle continued throughout 1974 and into 1975, the fortunes of both sides waxed and waned.[2] Student unrest erupted in early 1975 and added to the tension, resulting in the RCC's announcement of compulsory military service. Despite the measure, the unrest continued and spread further, leading to the first large-scale arrests of students in April 1975.

Rumors of attempted coups surfaced in the Arab press throughout the summer and, at one point in July 1975, army units loyal to Qadhafi surrounded Tripoli. When the government was restructured in the wake of the ASU Congress, the technocrats seemed to have gained the upper hand: only four RCC members remained, while a number of newly created ministries were assigned to young intellectuals with no broad, nationalist credentials. But the ongoing debate within the RCC indicated the lingering disagreements over what some considered Qadhafi's growing personal power and over the rising costs of his pan-Arab pursuits, foreign adventures, and his aborted unity attempt with Egypt. There was also growing unease about the political interference of Qadhafi and his supporters in economic and development projects that some argued should be evaluated on purely technical merits.

The conflict between the two sides was highly ideological, focusing almost exclusively on the purposes to which Libya's oil wealth should be put and, in a related matter, on the role the state should play in the country's economic development. As the conflict intensified, both sides attempted to attract allies within the Libyan army to their side, leading to fears of another coup.[3] In August 1975, RCC members Bashir Hawadi and Umar al-Muhayshi launched a coup attempt against the regime. Muhayshi, who was Minister of Planning at the time, refused to give up funds that had been earmarked for local development projects, and fled with a number of his supporters to Tunis in the aftermath of the failed coup.

The event marked a political, economic, and ideological breaking point in the politics of revolutionary Libya, lurching the country forward in an activist direction that would not be deviated from for more than a decade. The RCC, still the most powerful organization in Libya, was now reduced to five members: Mu'ammar al-Qadhafi, Abu-Bakr Yunis Jabr, al-Khuwaylidi al-Hamidi, Mustafa al-Kharubi, and Abd as-Salam Jallud. The way had been cleared for increasingly draconian measures to implement Qadhafi's vision of a stateless society. With no institutionalized opposition left, Qadhafi quickly moved to consolidate his own position, and the revolution inexorably became identified with his own personal vision. Throughout the remainder of 1975, civilian, military, professional, and technical personnel suspected of potential disloyalty were removed from the country's planning institutes and ministries. Those who argued for a greater prudence in the country's financial and economic affairs were systematically sidelined. Muhammad Mugharyif, the country's comptroller and – later, after his own defection – one of the regime's most virulent and eloquent critics, was replaced. The coup attempt also marked the end of professional and technical criteria for military recruitment, and the beginning of a steady but noticeable influx of individual members of Qadhafi's tribe – and later of his family – into a number of sensitive security and army positions.

In the wake of the attempted coup, Qadhafi seized the opportunity to push forward his revolutionary agenda. What was still missing was a coherent ideological treatise that could serve as the guideline for the revolution. That treatise was to be a collection of three slim volumes, containing Qadhafi's ideas about economics, political systems, and social relationships. Known collectively as *The Green Book*, these volumes became the ideological focal point of the regime's activist internal and international policies. Its publication therefore came at a particularly crucial point in Libya's young life as a revolutionary state.[4] The disagreement within the RCC had indicated that, even at the country's highest level, opposition to the revolution remained strong. The ASU, the 1973 Congress of which had been postponed in the wake of intra-RCC disagreements, had proven to be an unreliable mechanism for mobilizing the population. There remained a high level of apathy toward the new regime.

Piecemeal efforts at reform had been judged unsuccessful. *The Green Book* was meant to replace these incremental efforts of the past with a thorough reform of the country's political and economic structures. These, in turn, would transform Libya and its citizens into active mechanisms for creating a stateless society. The modern oil state, with all its trappings of specialized institutions, of course, could no longer be eliminated or ignored. But, what the Libyan leader viewed as the necessarily deleterious social impact of such a state could, he argued, be circumscribed and reduced. The impact of its institutions could be curtailed, handed over to the masses, and managed by popular committees. To those goals the Qadhafi government committed itself – and virtually unlimited resources – after 1975.

The Green Book, the first volume of which appeared within weeks of the August 1975 coup attempt, constituted an elaboration of Qadhafi's earlier Zuwara speech and of the short, abortive effort at popular rule in 1971. The publication of its first volume in *Al-Fajr al-Jadid*, the country's main newspaper, confirmed Qadhafi's position as the undisputed leader within the RCC. His earlier pronouncements on how Libyan society should be reshaped to make citizens fully participate in the country's political life formed the basis for what emerged as the ideological primer of the revolutionary government. It became the guide that systematically legitimated and extended the directives of the regime.

The Green Book contains a compilation of Qadhafi's utopian ideas on what Libya's social, political, and economic organization should look like. He refers to this new state as a Jamahiriyya – a political community marked by consultation, rather than representation. In it, ordinary citizens own the country's resources, they exercise authority, and directly manage the country's administration and its bureaucracy through a system of popular congresses and committees. Each volume of *The Green Book* contains common themes: a distrust of the hierarchical bureaucratic structures inherent in modern states, and Qadhafi's abhorrence for the presence of intermediaries who – via the impersonal structures of bureaucracies and administrative institutions – prevent individuals from directly managing their own lives. Qadhafi himself clearly viewed *The Green Book* as, above

all, a manifesto for action. It was meant to intensify his earlier mobilizational efforts that had been frustrated so far, he argued, because the country's political system could not express the true voice of the Libyan people
(Volume 1), because Libyans were not directly in charge of the economic
resources of the country (Volume 2), and because of the country's archaic
social structures (Volume 3).

The ideas are simple and, with their insistence on egalitarianism and
lack of hierarchy, reflect a tribal ethos. *The Green Book*'s central tenet is that
ordinary citizens can directly manage the bureaucratic and administrative
institutions that shape their lives, and devise their own solutions to their
economic and social problems. Hence, *The Green Book* contains the essential idea of statelessness, and of people managing their own affairs without
state institutions. There is, as well, an emphasis on consultation and equality, and an explicitly voiced aversion to hierarchy and to the handing over
of authority to state functionaries. There is, finally, a repeated insistence on
"direct democracy" through which citizens will take control of the state.
None of this, the Libyan leader argued, could be accomplished without
removing a number of "archaic elements" that in the past had prevented
citizens from becoming true revolutionaries.[5]

The most basic problems faced by human societies, according to *The
Green Book*, are political systems and states that rely on representation.
These are inherently repressive because representation involves the surrender by individuals of their natural, personal sovereignty to the advantage of
others. Political parties invariably involve winners and losers. This inherently conflictual process, even in electoral systems, inevitably means "the
defeat of the people ... of true democracy" since "even if 51% of the vote
is obtained by the victorious party," 49% of the electorate is ruled by those
for whom they did not vote. Representation, therefore, is a deception, and
parliamentary systems only create false democracies. By extension, political parties are simply the means by which a narrow majority can usurp the
right to speak in the name of all. Votes can be bought, leaving the poor
without a voice. The struggle for power between political parties, much
like between classes and tribes, is destructive. Such a system cannot serve
as the basis for a truly democratic society.

Above all, *The Green Book* stresses, the authority of the individual and
group spirit needs to be preserved in modern societies, something modern
states cannot guarantee since they are a form of either political or bureaucratic
representation.[6] Constitutional guarantees to preserve individual authority
are suspect since they represent the interests of the most powerful in society.
The only possible solution is "direct democracy" through the establishment

of local popular congresses to which every Libyan citizen belongs. These congresses in turn delegate power to higher congresses and to popular committees that can represent their interest at the national level.

First, the people are divided into basic popular congresses. Each congress chooses its working committee. The working committees together form popular congresses for each district. Then the masses of those basic popular congresses choose administrative people's committees to replace government administration. Thus all the public utilities are run by people's committees which will be responsible to the basic popular congresses, and these dictate the policy to be followed by the people's committees and supervise its execution. Thus, both the administration and [its] supervision become popular, and the outdated definition of democracy – "democracy is the supervision of the government by the people" – comes to an end. It will be replaced by the correct definition: "Democracy is the supervision of the people by the people."[7]

The popular congresses and committees represent the legislative and executive branches, respectively. At the top are the General People's Congress (GPC) and the General People's Committee – the equivalent of a Cabinet. The latter, in principle, has no independent authority. Members of both branches are appointed through consultation or through choice. Basic People's Congresses (BPCs) appoint Basic People's Committees that are in charge of the local administration. Their representatives report to counterparts at the national level, therefore ensuring that each of the country's districts remains autonomous and possesses the ability to channel local demands up to the national level. Thus, the political system is constructed from the bottom up, rather than from the top down.

By the end of 1975, *The Green Book*'s populist slogans – such as "lijan fi kulli makan" (Committees Everywhere) – started to appear throughout the country. The ASU was renamed the General People's Congress (GPC) in January 1976. At the same time, however, it became clear that the system of popular rule was also meant to further reduce opposition to the regime: political activities were restricted to Basic People's Congresses, and foreign policy decisions were excluded from their competence. This new and cumbersome system of political governance – which included a total of almost 1,000 representatives from throughout the country – was finally implemented on 2 March 1977. On that day, Qadhafi at Sabha announced that the "Era of the Masses" had arrived, and he renamed Libya "Al-Jamahiriyya al-arabiyya al-Libiyya al-sha'abiyya al-ishtirakiyya" (The Socialist People's Libyan Arab Jamahiriyya).[8]

Some minor changes would follow – most notably the addition of municipal committees (*sha'biyat*) in the mid-1990s, as well as the creation of "technocrat advisory groups" within the General People's Congress to help decide on technical issues regarding economic development and oil-related issues – but, in principle, the country's new political structures were in place by 1980. All political control in Libya was now vested in the people through the congress and committee system. The RCC was formally abolished. Qadhafi and the four other original remaining RCC members nevertheless retained crucial positions – Qadhafi and Abu-Bakr Yunis Jabr as heads of the Libyan army; Khuwaylidi al-Hamidi as commander of the police; Mustafa al-Kharubi as chief of staff; and Abd as-Salam Jallud as roving economic ambassador for the regime. In principle, Libyans were ruling themselves directly, and replaced or directly appointed those staffing the country's bureaucratic and administrative institutions. At the annual GPC meetings, they were able to discuss a large number of national issues that had been channeled up from the local and municipal levels.

There were also clearly limits to the level of competence and authority of the General People's Congress. In principle, the GPC appointed its own Secretariat – equivalent to a Cabinet in western parliamentary systems. In practice, the Secretariat determined the agenda of GPC proceedings and, together with the technical committees, determined much of the day-to-day business of the country. Although Secretaries (ministers) were in principle elected by the GPC, they were actually appointed by the regime – and remain so until today. Furthermore, several areas were clearly off-limits to the competence of the GPC, including foreign policy, the army, the police, the country's budget, and the petroleum sector. The functioning and competence of the GPC thus provided a clear indication of the selectivity of Qadhafi's acclaimed *sult ash-sha'ab* (People's Power). Finally (see below), the creation of Revolutionary Committees in 1977 would further curtail the GPC's authority, and would be a clear indication of the fact that the country's leadership was eager to supplement the country's formal structure of authority with a rivaling system of revolutionary rule. These "revolutionary means of governing" would prove more agile and more responsive to Qadhafi's rhetoric, and would serve as safeguards for the regime. This bifurcation would be officially confirmed by the separation of formal and revolutionary authority – *fasl as-sulta wa ath-thawra* – at the second session of the GPC in March 1979.

"*THE GREEN BOOK*'s" ECONOMIC AND SOCIAL DIRECTIVES

The publication of *The Green Book*'s second and third volumes, *The Solution of the Economic Problem: Socialism* and *The Social Basis of the*

Third Universal Theory, marked the extension of populist measures to the country's economy in a fashion that dramatically interfered with economic management after November 1977. The two volumes provided the most explicit statement of Qadhafi's vision of a stateless society: "To an individual, the family is more important than the state ... Mankind ... is the individual and the family. The state is an artificial economic and political system, sometimes a military system, with which mankind has no relationship and has nothing to do."[9] The economic role of the individual within this stateless society forms the subject of the second volume. Qadhafi argues that everyone should be allowed to share and profit equally from the country's wealth and productive activities. Citizens must no longer be simply salaried employees, who are nothing but "wage-workers" who can be exploited within the enterprises where they work. Rather, they must become "partners in production." State ownership of enterprises, as under Marxism, is also inadequate, since the wage-worker remains nothing but "a slave to the master [the state] who hires him." As encapsulated by what became one of the revolution's most famous slogans – *shuraka' la ujara'* (Partners, not wage earners) – *The Green Book* declared that neither private nor public enterprises could use "wage-labor," which is nothing but the "exploitation of man by man." Workers must "abolish the bureaucracy of the public sector and the dictatorship of the private sector" by directly taking control of economic enterprises.

Qadhafi furthermore aimed at an even more radical re-division of wealth by eliminating ownership of certain economic goods altogether. Not only should all citizens profit from the country's wealth, but, by becoming partners, they should profit equally. Individuals and families should not possess economic assets that can be used to exploit other Libyans. Qadhafi singled out housing in particular, no doubt in light of the real-estate frenzy the country had experienced as it urbanized during the oil booms. To own several houses "will [prevent] another from obtaining his ... Renting ... is the beginning of a process of controlling another person's needs." This introduced into the country another omnipresent slogan: *Al-bayt li sakinihi* (The house belongs to [those] who live in it). The implication of these simple ideas was clear: the wealth of the nation should be shared equally, and this equality could only be established if no individual was dependent economically upon another. As a result, services – such as hiring taxis or employing maids – were no longer allowed either, since they did not constitute a productive economic activity.

Outside those institutions and sectors that were off-limits to its commands, the impact of the second volume's directives within Libya after

1977 was enormous. With the help of the Revolutionary Committees the regime systematically implemented the ideas of the Libyan leader. The nationalization of all non-occupied dwellings began in 1976. The government reduced apartment purchase prices by 30% in late 1977. In May 1978, the GPC formally adopted a new real-estate law that effectively implemented the *al-bayt li sakinihi* policy, distributing confiscated real estate to mostly low-income earners.[10] Renters of apartments and houses suddenly found themselves owners of their dwellings, paying off small monthly mortgages to the government.

The impact of the directives regarding the abolishing of "wage-labor" had an equally profound impact. Starting in earnest following his 1978 speech on the anniversary of the revolution, the first wave of business takeovers took place. Overnight, the country's merchants and small businessmen were reduced to passive onlookers in the country's economic life. These groups of small-scale business entrepreneurs, retailers, and private farmers had initially formed the backbone of support for the revolutionary government following 1 September 1969. Clearly, the regime now felt emboldened enough to move against their interests. Indeed, when the GPC had debated and adopted the 1976–80 development plan two years earlier, attempts to nationalize all internal commercial transactions had been rebuked by the coalitions of entrepreneurs and businessmen that still existed at the congress in large numbers. By the end of 1980, the more important large industries were put in the hands of Basic Production Committees – selected groups of workers within each business or enterprise. Popular Committees replaced their administrators. Only the banking system and oil-related industries were, once more, saved from these popular takeovers.

The role of traders was abolished. Those that managed to survive until 1980 had already been subject to the Secretariat of Finance's selective and increasingly restrictive use of awarding or denying permits for business arrangements. In principle, the agricultural sector remained outside popular management. In practice, all available land in the countryside already belonged to the public sector from 1977 on, and survived only through heavy government subsidies. Individual farmers were only allowed to lease as much as they needed for their own requirements. By that time, the only land remaining in private hands was located along the coastal strip, owned by remnants of old land-owning families or tribes. They would hold onto their land until 1980.

In his speech of 1 September 1980, Qadhafi emphasized that the country's entrepreneurs (an estimated 40,000 individuals) were nothing but parasites because their economic activities did not contribute to productive activity within the Jamahiriyya. Private businesses closed throughout the country, often with the help of the Revolutionary Committees. Their function was taken over by a number of state supermarkets that soon dotted the country's landscape. Their construction effectively spelled the end of private commercial and retail transactions in Libya. Ten government agencies were responsible for the provision of all the country's import needs ranging from oil technology to consumer goods.[11]

The disappearance of the private sector was soon followed by similar constraints on the country's legal community and other professionals. Professional organizations were now represented as a group at the GPC, subject to the same restrictions and limited competence as the GPC as a whole. Private practices were abolished. In a move that culminated all its previous directives, the GPC's General Secretariat in early 1981 announced the state takeover of all export, import, and distribution networks. All *waqf* (religious endowment property) was also abolished, thus undermining whatever economic power the *ulama* still possessed.

In a decision that was aimed primarily at controlling private wealth and extending *The Green Book*'s directives regarding equality, the regime in March 1980 decided to change the country's currency. All Libyans were thereby forced to declare their assets and to exchange their old currency, within one week, for limited amounts of new dinars. In a country without a functioning banking system, where currency was widely hoarded and where cash transactions were omnipresent, this undoubtedly represented the regime's most intrusive populist measure. The uncertainty led to enormous spending sprees in the country – primarily on gold – much as the *al-bayt li sakinihi* policy had led to a spate of marriages to keep real estate within families. It also further undermined the confidence of the population to participate in the country's economic life, a legacy that would come to haunt the regime when it attempted its privatization efforts in the 1980s and 1990s. Although highly effective, the demonetization was, as one seasoned observer noted, "a rather blunt instrument" that indicated the inability or unwillingness of the Qadhafi regime to manage a national economy that had grown tremendously complex.[12]

Not surprisingly, the country's banking system no longer functioned as a financial intermediary, but had largely become a repository of surplus funds. In light of the evisceration of the private sector, the country's five commercial banks lost whatever role they had once played. The functions of the industrial and agricultural banks declined similarly, while the Real Estate Bank was reformed to dispense interest-free loans to poor families.

Although the country's Central Bank remained a privileged institution, outside Popular Committee management, the lack of information and the overall style of management of the economy highly reduced its effectiveness and importance.

By the end of 1981, the Libyan regime had implemented – in some cases through coercive means at the hands of the Revolutionary Committees – measures to distribute and redistribute much of the country's assets. Through a number of legislative actions, simple administrative controls, and the construction of supermarkets, the state controlled the distribution of all basic necessities, including food. Small factories, commercial firms, agricultural land, urban real estate, and private residences had been confiscated and were either redistributed or simply kept by the state which, paradoxically, showed little inclination for active regulation beyond the oil sector.

OIL AND DEVELOPMENT

Ultimately, Qadhafi's entire *Green Book* experiment crucially depended for its implementation on the income from oil sales. Perhaps not surprisingly, therefore, the country's oil industry remained carefully shielded from the revolutionary fervor swirling around it. The October 1973 Arab– Israeli War and the oil boom in its aftermath found Libya halfway through the revolutionary regime's first development plan. A few months earlier, in July 1973, the regime had followed up its earlier suspension of awarding acreage to oil companies by introducing so-called Exploration and Production-Sharing Arrangements (EPSAs). Under these new arrangements – which had been pioneered in Indonesia and gradually adopted by other OPEC members – Libya's National Oil Company retained title to whatever acreage was exploited by international oil companies, and the latter in effect simply became contractors. By the time the first contracts under the new arrangement (known as EPSA I) were signed, the price of the country's oil had risen from $4.605 at the beginning of the month to $9.061 by 16 October, and then to $15.768 on 1 January 1974. By 1978, LNOC authorized EPSA I agreements with Occidental, Exxon, Mobil, Total, Elf Aquitaine, Braspetro, and AGIP, and proceeded to sign contracts with a consortium involving Elf Aquitaine, Wintershall, and LNOC itself. In general, and reflecting once more the desirability of Libyan oil, the conditions under which the companies signed EPSAs were highly favorable to the Jamahiriyya.

As a result of the 1973 oil crisis and the regime's hard bargaining, the country was awash with petrodollars by the end of 1974. However, despite its growing power over oil companies' operations within the country, it remained highly vulnerable to the fickle conditions of the international oil market: by the end of 1974, the price of Libyan oil had dropped to slightly above $11. Some of the damage had been self-inflicted: in support of the Arab oil embargo, Libya voluntarily cut its production to the United States and the Caribbean refineries supplying the US market to roughly 1.5 million barrels per day. It abandoned this boycott only in early 1975, almost a year after most producers had done so. The country's oil output dropped 26.4% in 1974, and its exports fell to 912,000 barrels per day by mid-February 1975, the lowest level in more than a decade. This forced the Libyan government to rely on a substantial part of its financial reserves for the daily running of its economy. The result was a short-term financial crisis in the summer of 1975, fueled in part by the continuing heavy outlays for military purchases and for foreign adventures that had provoked the August coup. In 1975, Libya's balance-of-trade dropped from a surplus of $1.8 billion to a deficit of $.5 billion. The government requested financial aid from Saudi Arabia, which was promptly denied. The rapid inflows of oil money, however, resolved the country's crisis soon thereafter, and Libya's planners faced once more the dilemma familiar to many oil exporters during the 1970s: how to distribute revenues they could not expect their economies to use efficiently.

In the wake of the 1973 oil boom, but before the August 1975 attempted coup, Libya's technocrats had started to draw up preliminary plans for the country's future development. The blueprints of what eventually emerged as the *1976–1980 Five-Year Social and Economic Development Plan* represented a solution to what Libyan planners viewed as the economic problems the country faced in the immediate wake of the oil boom. In their estimation, Libya faced multiple challenges. There was a need for greater regulatory control over an economy and a population that was already showing signs of becoming used to the riches of an oil state, and when saddled with a ruler who viewed the country's riches as a means to implement his revolutionary directives. Within a year of the plan's publication, Libya's technocrats faced an additional challenge that would profoundly alter whatever prescriptions they offered: under the directives of *The Green Book*, the country's administration and bureaucracy were, at least in theory, in the hands of the people.

While the first five-year plan represented an ambitious, systematic blueprint for Libya's economy, the real question was whether and to what extent the political goals pursued by the country's leader were compatible with the imperatives of economic development. The country's planners clearly indicated that the country would have no choice but to rely on technical expertise for economic development, and on integrated and centralized policymaking at the national level. They also asked for the establishment and implementation of more rational criteria for the creation and maintenance of the country's burgeoning bureaucracy and they pointed out that Libya increasingly demonstrated the characteristics typical of an oil economy: expatriates still provided 55% of Libya's unskilled labor in 1975, 27% of its semi-skilled and skilled personnel, 35% of its technicians, and 58% of its managers. The country's food production had continued to drop since 1969, with food from abroad consuming 15% of the total import budget. By 1975, Tripoli had swollen to over half a million people, for whom the government had been moderately successful in providing housing and education.[13] The plan further noted that the country's main challenges would be to channel the population's energy into productive economic activities, to revitalize the agricultural sector, to create a manufacturing sector, and to ensure that the government's investments were conducive to further efficient development.[14]

Of its $26.3 billion budget, $23 billion of the plan would be provided by the government, the remainder by the private sector. The plan advocated a greater and more efficient use of economic decision-making and stressed the importance of technocratic advice and input. Its main recommendation was to use the revenues from oil for the development of the economy's non-oil sectors, creating a more diversified economic structure that would put more of the country's population to work, as well as spurring long-term growth. Agriculture was projected to grow 30%, manufacturing 16%, and provisions of electricity and water 23%. Except for the oil and housing sectors, where private investment was deemed indispensable, funding in the other sectors was overwhelmingly provided by the state. Food self-sufficiency was projected in eight to ten years, and all needs for meat, grain, fruit, vegetables, and dairy products were to be met by local production by 1980. Expatriate manual labor was expected by that time to constitute not more than 40% of the total working population, while expatriates with technocratic expertise would be reduced dramatically.

To make this possible, the government was to make heavy investments in education, hoping to reduce its dependence on skilled expatriates. By the end of the 1970s, university enrollment had increased six-fold to 20,000 students annually. The takeover of the universities by Revolutionary Committees and *The Green Book*'s ideological intrusion into the country's educational system and curriculum, however, had a profound impact. Also deeply disturbing was the fact that, by the end of 1979, an estimated 100,000 Libyans, many of them well-educated and possessing advanced degrees from western universities, had left the country. As a result, the need for expatriate labor remained undiminished, particularly in areas requiring managerial, professional, and technical personnel. By 1980, this need included non-technical areas as well – agriculture and construction in particular – as Libyans increasingly demanded employment they viewed as desirable, often in service occupations within one of the country's bureaucracies.

The modernized part of the agricultural sector was staffed almost exclusively by foreign labor. Furthermore, its capacity to absorb increased capital remained limited. During the monarchy, allocations of roughly 12% of annual budgets had already proven problematic. The Qadhafi government now planned to invest 17% of a much larger budget in the sector. With no financial restrictions, several research projects that under normal circumstances would have been unfeasible enjoyed massive support. Two of the best-known were the agricultural project at Kufra, and the Gefara Wheat Project. The Kufra project dated back to the monarchy and involved sophisticated irrigation systems for thousands of acres of soil with low organic content. Labor was 80% expatriate. Efforts to raise cattle at the project had already been abandoned in 1977, and the land was used once more for grain production. Transport costs to the coast alone, per ton of grain produced at Kufra, exceeded world prices in 1979. Total cost per ton was estimated to be between ten and twenty times the world price for grain in the late 1970s. The Gefara Wheat Project was similarly problematic, once more involving sophisticated irrigation technology. It was telling but ironic that, for both projects, the revolutionary regime had not taken into account the kind of long-term crop predictions that both the Ottoman Empire and the monarchy had incorporated in their earlier planning.

Regarding the country's oil industry, the government seemingly paid little attention to the instability of the market throughout the 1970s, even though the country's dependence on oil revenues now amounted to 99.9% of total income. Despite new contracts for offshore production in 1979, the "spontaneous take-overs" of the economic sectors by the regime's militants – although still restricted to the non-oil and non-banking sectors – had a chilling effect on company–government relations, particularly with regard to European companies. The growing animosity toward Libya forced several American companies – despite highly profitable contract terms – to start reconsidering their investments in the Jamahiriyya. The government judged that, in the wake of the Iranian revolution, which more than doubled the price of Libyan crude between December of 1978 and December of 1979, actual divestment was unlikely. The 1978–79 price hikes pushed Libyan revenues to unprecedented levels, allowing the government to keep production levels untouched.

Technocrats at the LNOC, however, did not fail to notice that the real price of oil, even after discounting for indexation and inflation, had started to lag behind posted prices, indicating that a buyer's market was on the horizon. By 1979, government officials were sufficiently worried about possible depletion of its oil reserves to move aggressively toward new exploration contracts known as EPSA IIs. Despite growing unease about the country's international reputation and the fact that the terms of EPSA IIs were even less favorable to oil companies than those of its predecessor, interest proved high. As part of an attempt to make itself less vulnerable to outside pressure, the government also attracted East European companies to its upstream activities – a move that would consistently be resisted by the LNOC who viewed these corporations as unreliable.

The involvement of the East European companies was an indication that, despite Libya's continuing ability to attract participants to its oil industry, its fortunes were slowly starting to wane. Already in 1978 the United States had started to place restrictions on trade with Libya because of its suspected involvement in terrorist activities. The withdrawal of some US oil companies from the country in 1981 and the US embargo against Libyan oil that started in 1982 were further indications of Libya's changing fortunes. In 1981, oil production tumbled from 1,700,000 barrels per day (bpd) in the first quarter to 600,000 bpd by the end of the year. Total production for 1981 was 40% below that of 1980. Of this reduction, roughly 500,000 bpd had routinely been delivered to the United States; the remainder of the cutback was due to phase-outs in production and the annulment of existing contracts by multinational companies. Furthermore, as a result of Libya's need to offer incentives to the remaining companies, the price of its oil had dropped by $4–5 per barrel. Libya's balance-of-payments for 1981 showed a deficit of $4.8 billion, and the country's international reserves tumbled from $15.5 to $2.4 billion.

Throughout the 1970s, inflation, rising prices of industrial imports, a fluctuating oil market, and heavy reliance on a few countries for oil exports added to Libya's difficulties. Inflation was estimated at 20% annually throughout the decade, forcing the government to adjust its development budget repeatedly. The rising prices of all needed imports – from food to high-technology items and machinery imports – added to the problem. In addition, the Jamahiriyya failed to develop a systematic strategy to deal with its technology purchases. It took no advantage of access to international capital markets, nor did it develop a financial system that could have dampened the wild oscillations of its revenue income. Actual income and reserves were consistently used to ride out the turmoil created by the fluctuations – a strategy Libya would also use in the next decade when US and multilateral economic sanctions were imposed. The country had no outstanding debt, but its unsophisticated method of financing a burgeoning economy produced occasional cash flow shortages.

When the *Five-Year Social and Economic Development Plan* was launched in 1976, its authors had been optimistic about the chances of successfully implementing their ideas. Trade and financial surpluses had recovered rapidly in the wake of the 1974–75 financial crisis, and the country's income had boomed to $8.8 billion. A consortium of foreign oil companies – including Aquitaine, Elf-Erap, OMV, and Wintershall – had discovered new offshore oil approximately 60 miles north of Zuwara. Halfway through the plan, however, the populist edicts of the regime and the dramatically increased revenues at its disposal started to interfere with its recommendations and, as a result, few of the problems it had identified were systematically addressed. By 1977, Libya's development budget was four times greater, on a per capita basis, than that of the rest of the Arab world combined.[15] The ratio of development spending to total expenditure was 72.3%, the highest in the region. How much of that spending was adding actual productive capacity to the country's economy seemed of little concern at the time to the regime, and its planners had little choice but to observe Libya's resources being used for purposes that added little to the development of the country.

The combination of rapidly fluctuating income and popular management of the country's economy took a heavy toll. The state's ability to function as an effective regulator suffered tremendously. By the early 1980s, Libya exhibited all the characteristics of a resource-rich but badly managed economy where efficiency and real concerns for development had yielded to the political imperatives of the regime. Small handouts were used to keep the population quiescent, and more substantial outlays were given to the regime's coalition of supporters, necessary to ensure the survival of the regime. The decline in the country's oil revenues, and the obvious need for serious economic reform after the country's oil boom, provoked no serious corrective measures. In retrospect, whatever the 1976–81 Five-Year Plan achieved differed substantially from the original intentions of its technocratic planning team. It demonstrated the corrosive impact both of the popular management style the country had adopted, and of planning that became increasingly politicized as the popular base of the regime narrowed.

In 1980, the government simultaneously announced a twenty-year, long-term economic plan and an intermediary Five-Year Plan.[16] Both contained the by-now familiar ingredients of previous plans: self-sufficiency in basic foodstuffs, provision of adequate housing and social services, growth of the manufacturing sector and the development of heavy industry, as well as the creation of a local workforce able to assume positions within an economy that relied heavily on technological inputs.

Total expenditures for the Five-Year Plan were almost two-and-a-half times those of the previous plan, despite clear indications that the previous plan had already produced absorptive capacity problems. Oil production would be reduced to a level sufficient to meet the country's economic needs, and non-oil contribution to GDP was to increase from 35.7% to 53% by 1985. Projections for the plan relied on the assumption that oil sales would match those of the late 1970s, when both the United States and Europe absorbed virtually all of the country's output. Despite the relative success of EPSA II, this looked increasingly unlikely, and the contracts with East European companies indicated that the regime in the early 1980s had fewer options than before.

Heavy industry, particularly steel and petrochemicals, was once more singled out for large investments. The government hoped to turn the Misrata steel complex into a hub for other industrial enterprises, creating in turn regional centers for future industrial development. The agricultural sector, plagued by enduring shortages of water, was targeted for increased land reclamation. Preliminary plans were drawn up to bring massive amounts of fossil water from aquifers near Tazerbu and Sarir to the coast. These outlays, for what became known as the Great Man-made River Project (MMRP), would eventually rise to an estimated $27 billion by the end of the 1990s. The MMRP was meant, in various stages, to provide water not only for agricultural purposes but also for cities along the coastal strip. Its completion would arguably mark one of the few successful ventures undertaken by the regime.

At the end of the country's second Five-Year Plan, the regime's goal of creating a more diversified and integrated economy seemed as far-fetched as ever. Oil still provided the overwhelming share of the country's income, economic activities in all other sectors were heavily subsidized, and Libya remained highly dependent on expatriates and their technical expertise to complete economic activities its own citizens no longer wanted to perform. The agricultural sector remained unproductive and highly inefficient: whatever successful projects existed could only be maintained at a staggering cost. Attempts to create a heavy industry and a downstream hydrocarbon sector remained highly problematic, in part because the country had neither the ability to integrate them into the remainder of the country's economy nor, if it were to develop the capacity, a strategy for doing so. The presence of an inordinate amount of expatriate technocrats, with little stake in efficient procurement decisions, became more pronounced in 1982 when the Reagan administration embargoed technology items. At the end of the plan, Libya still relied on expatriate labor for 35% of its technicians and 60% of its managers, the largest share of which originated in the United States and Europe.

Between 1982 and 1986, the country's revenues tumbled from $21 billion to $5.4 billion annually. Despite this, and despite the growing need for economic reform, the half-decade after the 1979 oil boom witnessed an unabated spending of the country's resources and a continued resistance to economic reform. That the regime managed to both spend and hold reforms in abeyance while its local and international political and economic fortunes declined is testimony once more to the extraordinary, but highly specific, power that oil revenues bestow upon the leaders of oil exporters like Libya: the ability to outspend emerging crises, without accountability, even if such expenditures fundamentally jeopardize the country's economic future.

By 1982, the revolutionary regime had managed to transform Libya thoroughly. Except for a few enterprises like the LNOC, the state's bureaucratic and administrative institutions had been put directly into the hands of the people through a system of political congresses and committees, and all private economic activity had been outlawed. Revolutionary Committees were in charge of supervising and implementing the economic directives. But that same year also marked the beginning of another period of uncertainty for the regime. In light of the declining revenues noted above, the regime had a number of options it could pursue. All involved more rational and efficient use of the country's revenues: reducing consumption at home, cutting back on its development plans, and curtailing its foreign adventures and military expenditures. None of these was particularly attractive since every measure meant cutting back on programs that, for political or ideological reasons, were linked to important constituencies of the regime and, as a result, had become part and parcel of the revolution.

Furthermore, diplomatic issues made the regime cautious about borrowing on the international market, and Libya had little medium-or long-term debt. Initially, the government used some temporary measures to overcome its emerging difficulties – most notably shifting the economic hardships toward the expatriate labor in the country, increasing its reliance on East European and Soviet Union expertise, and limiting consumer imports. But the growing difficulties and increasing restrictions as a result of the country's confrontation with the West slowly but steadily decreased the number of economic options available to Libya.

Those options had also become more limited by the emerging realities within the Libyan economy since 1973: the massive, almost unregulated capital inflows; the removal of the country's technocrats from virtually all institutions except the LNOC; the populist directives that stressed distribution at the expense of regulation; and the lackluster attention paid to efficiency and consistent planning. The turn toward popular rule – without built-in measures for transparency or accountability – and the ability to circumvent popular rule further when it suited the regime, meant that regulation and planning, much like the country's judicial and administrative institutions, fell victim to the ideological pursuits of the revolution during this long decade. What the kingdom had managed to accomplish through benign neglect, the revolutionary regime had achieved with a more deliberate, but equally disastrous, approach. Under both rulers, whatever formal mechanisms, rules, and checks existed to manage the country's economy for the benefit of all Libyan citizens were easily avoided by relatively narrow cliques of supporters of each regime.

The quadrupling of oil prices in 1973–74 had created a greater need for financial and monetary management if serious inflation was to be avoided and sustained development pursued. The country's leadership needed to decide whether oil production should be limited and how to recycle oil revenues. This would have required the creation of much more elaborate and integrated information-gathering institutions for the country, as well as the implementation of a number of legal, disclosure, and accounting requirements that would have limited the political, revolutionary energy of the regime. Additionally, the rapid inflows of oil revenues vitiated any need for local, domestic savings, taxation, or other policies capable of curbing consumption throughout Libyan society.

Controlling the country's inflation would have necessitated a deliberate and sustained management of its revenue flows – which the regime was seemingly uninterested in doing. Much like the king before him, Libya's revolutionary leader primarily used economic resources to solve strategic political puzzles. The government abandoned serious attempts at planning rather than carefully managing the country's economy as a hedge against the difficulties of operating a volatile oil economy that needed access to external resources for its expansion, management, and survival. Its actions inevitably provoked a massive brain drain and left local and international investors weary of operating in an environment devoid of some essential legal guarantees. At the same time, and little noticed because of the country's non-transparent budgeting procedures, the regime invested heavily in military hardware throughout the decade.

At the end of the 1980–85 plan, economic management had suffered to such an extent that several of the country's ministries no longer produced annual reports that could accurately be relied upon for future use. In 1986, Libya's Central Bank temporarily suspended its yearly assessment of the country's economic performance. A dispute with neighboring countries in August and September 1985 that led to the expulsion of approximately 100,000 expatriate laborers – many involved in providing the day-to-day goods that average Libyans needed – added to hardships inside the country.

By that time, the country's research institutions collected little primary information that would have allowed for more consistent and efficient planning. Many of the ministries' and research institutions' reports and planning papers became simple regurgitations of data provided by outside experts – data that often reflected the scenarios preferred by the regime without incorporating any real critical insights or suggestions. Except for the LNOC – which remained a privileged institution whose employees could collect data in an atmosphere untainted by revolutionary pursuits – most institutions in charge of gathering data, needed for an efficient planning and management of the country's economy, produced idealistic projections divorced from reality.

THE REVOLUTIONARY SOCIETY

The creation of Revolutionary Authority in March 1979 marked the end of one aspect of the Libyan revolution and the beginning of another. On one hand, it constituted an admission that Libyan society was not reforming itself as quickly or as thoroughly as Qadhafi wanted. But it also marked the beginning of what has remained a dominant feature of Libyan politics until today: the persistence of a formal structure of government – centered around the Popular Congresses and Committees – and an informal structure of power and authority. The latter includes a narrow circle of intimates around the Libyan leader (later formalized as the Forum of Companions of Qadhafi), supported and kept in place by a number of security sector institutions (most notably the country's layers of intelligence organizations) and the Revolutionary Committees.

In principle, the GPC and the General People's Committee constituted the legislative and executive institutions of the Jamahiriyya and were empowered to make and act upon a wide range of decisions. Perhaps inadvertently, however, Qadhafi at the end of the first volume of *The Green Book* noted the reality that came to dominate the Jamahiriyya's political life after 1980: "theoretically, this [the Popular Congress and Committee system] is genuine democracy. But realistically the stronger part in society is the one that rules."

The concluding sentence of *The Green Book*'s first volume encapsulated the reality that Libya's formal mechanisms of power paled in comparison to its informal ones. The fact that there were clear limitations on the competence and authority of the Popular Committees, and the fact that all of the country's security sector institutions – army, police, and intelligence – were outside the Jamahiriyya system indicated that, much like in the economic sphere (where the LNOC was excluded from popular rule), the ultimate control functions in the Jamahiriyya remained tightly guarded at the top. Furthermore, the regime administered the country's budget without any real oversight by the GPC – budgets were normally approved pro forma, without discussion. Even now, Qadhafi continues to argue that he cannot be held responsible for economic or political setbacks since he no longer holds an official position. Every decision, once *The Green Book*'s directives had been adopted, was now the people's responsibility. Qadhafi was, according to his own pronouncements, no longer a part of the country's formal structure of authority:

You should understand that since 1977 we no longer have any constitutional prerogative on your economic, political, and administrative matters. Please, let us be clear about this point. You may seek our advice; we are ready to play the role of revolutionary instigators as our presence warrants this. However, we are restricted by people's authority ... People's authority has become restrictive even on revolutionaries ... it restricts even Mu'ammar al-Qadhdhafi; I cannot act.[17]

In reality, however, the people's authority had been challenged by the emergence of an institution whose existence had not been part of the ideological blueprint detailed in *The Green Book*: the country's Revolutionary Committees, created after November 1977.[18] Consisting of young, carefully selected individuals who were responsible directly to Qadhafi, they were seen as instruments for further mobilization and indoctrination. In particular, they were charged with encouraging greater popular participation in the Basic People's Congresses, where high levels of absenteeism persist until today. Clearly meant as an independent institution outside the control of the GPC – who, in principle, possessed all formal authority – their initial role, beyond indoctrination, remained undefined.

At the 1 September celebrations in 1979, however, Qadhafi clearly indicated that they would function as a security mechanism for the revolution: "The members of the popular committees ... are not less patriotic or revolutionary than the revolutionary committees, but the latter have announced that they are, as of now, ready to die to defend and consolidate the revolution."[19]

Qadhafi's pronouncement created, for the first time, a clear separation between those in power (in principle the BPCs and GPC) and those guiding the revolution. The distinction further consolidated Qadhafi's position since the Revolutionary Committees were entitled to replace BPC members judged unacceptable, thus allowing Qadhafi to have appointed the people he preferred. The Revolutionary Committees were, furthermore, directly responsible to Qadhafi, who coordinated their activities through a special Central Coordinating Committee for the Revolutionary Committees, housed at Bab al-Aziziyya and headed by Ali al-Kilani, Qadhafi's personal secretary and a member of the Qadhadhfa tribe. For the indoctrination of committee members, the regime organized *mu'askarat*, a special series of seminars, that had already started in 1976.

To make the distinction between formal and revolutionary authority more clear, Qadhafi resigned from the GPC – of which he had remained Secretary-General – to commit himself fully to revolutionary activities.[20] The formal separation came at the GPC's second session on 2 March 1979. The remaining RCC members – Jallud, Yunus Jabr, al-Kharubi, and al-Hamidi – were also appointed to head the revolutionary authority structure, while all top positions within the formal authority structure became civilian. By the end of 1979, the Revolutionary Committees had fully insinuated themselves into the formal authority structure of the Jamahiriyya and its public institutions: within the Popular Committees, the Popular Congresses, the Municipal People's General Committees (MPGC; these had been created as an additional layer of administration in 1979), as well as within the universities and the professional organizations. They quickly became – except for the remaining RCC members and an informal entourage around Qadhafi – the most powerful group in the country. At the January 1980 GPC meeting, the country's new civilian prime minister, Abd al-Ati al-Ubaydi, announced that "all People's Congresses, no matter what their level, as well as the Secretariat of the General People's Congress, and the secretaries of the Basic People's Congresses are under the permanent control of the revolution and the Revolutionary Committees."[21] Some members of the Committees' coordinating office at Bab al-Aziziyya became secretaries (ministers) within the formal authority structure.

The Revolutionary Committees produced their own publications – *Al-Zahf al-Akhdar* (The Green March) and *Al-Jamahiriyya* – that quickly turned into unofficial mouthpieces of the regime, Qadhafi himself anonymously contributing to the former on numerous occasions. They also infiltrated the country's police system and were put in charge of a number of special security assignments that further strengthened the Libyan leader's control. In effect, the Committees had become the regime's vanguard in charge of protecting the revolution. From 1979 onward, they were also put in charge of coordinating the BPC elections, capable of vetoing candidates judged as not possessing enough revolutionary zeal. By doing so, they partly controlled the agenda of the GPC, contrary to the directives that had been adopted at the creation of the Jamahiriyya in 1977.

When *The Green Book*'s second volume, on economic relations, was published, the Committees were put in charge of supervising the implementation of its directives. They were further charged with rooting out corruption and the misappropriation of funds, charges that were often leveled against individuals – including remnants of the monarchy's elites – the regime considered undesirable. In October 1980, they took over the country's press, thereby concluding their first activist phase. Throughout the early 1980s, their functions expanded once more to include officially the right to propagate, guide, and control the revolution. Their final task was to defend the revolution at all costs, which included the power to pursue, hunt down, and physically liquidate (*al-tasfiya al-jasadiya*) "enemies of the revolution" abroad and at home. This led to a number of reprisals and assassinations abroad that would later contribute to the country's worsening relations with the West.

Perhaps the most worrisome development in the struggle between formal and revolutionary authority, however, centered on the infiltration of the country's legal system by the Revolutionary Committees, a process in which legitimacy was bestowed upon the use of violence.[22] In 1980, the Committees were formally assigned the right to create revolutionary courts (*mahkama thawriya*) based on the "law of the revolution" (*qanun al-thawra*). Since 1969, the revolutionary regime had attempted to devise a legal system that would underpin and enforce its social, political, and economic directives. Initially, the country's leadership had put forward the *sharia* as the only source of law applicable in Libya. With its clearly prescribed legal remedies and an emphasis on codification, however, it was hardly suited to the continual and changing nature of a regime that deliberately attempted to bypass formal and structured institutions. Several of the well-established principles of Islamic law regarding contracts and commerce, as well as the *sharia* protections of private property rights, for example, were inimical to the intentions of the government.

Already at Zuwara, Qadhafi had announced the suspension of all the country's laws then in force. The creation of the Jamahiriyya in Sabha made the directives of *The Green Book* the guiding legal norms of Libyan society, norms that superseded the regime's first Constitution of December 1969. In a number of major speeches throughout the 1970s, and then more formally during a prolonged and major debate with the country's *ulama* at the Moulay Muhammad Mosque on 3 July 1978, Qadhafi argued that Islamic legal rules could no longer be used as a guideline for economic and political relations in modern societies. He furthermore insisted that those who argued for their application were not entitled to do so.[23] At the same time, he also reiterated that the traditional guidelines for commerce and property rights in Muslim societies, based on the prophet Muhammad's actions and sayings, had no legal standing in modern societies. The elimination of the private practice of law in May 1980 – a measure that included all other professional occupations as well – removed the last obstacle to the implementation of a virtually unsupervised revolutionary court system that could be used by the Qadhafi government to pursue its own policies.[24] Rather than relying on regular judges, the revolutionary courts were staffed by Revolutionary Committee members who were not bound by the country's penal code. Not surprisingly in light of the absence of legal safeguards, the revolutionary court system was left open to a large number of well-documented abuses, including several executions, throughout the 1980s and 1990s.

By 1980, the bifurcation between formal and revolutionary authority, as well as the manipulation of the Jamahiriyya's legal system, provided a clear indication of the narrowing power base within Libya. Although officially outside the formal framework of authority, Qadhafi made virtually all important policy decisions, channeling them, if necessary for purposes of legitimacy, through the GPC. In this, he was aided by his small group of loyalists in a fashion that much resembled the workings of the former royal diwan. As in all oil states where decision-making is concentrated in a small circle of elites and a praetorian guard, this kind of rule depended on careful management of coalitions crucial to the Libyan leader's survival.

In Libya, this creation and re-creation of coalitions was inevitably accompanied throughout the 1980s by yet another *zahf* (wave, or march) of revolutionary activities and edicts that, hopefully, translated into support for the regime. The Revolutionary Committees were the most visible – but certainly not the last – of such attempts at (selective) mobilization and the retention of power at the top of the country's political system. By their unpredictability, Revolutionary Committees and revolutionary justice also ensured that groups and individuals were left politically unbalanced. The Revolutionary Committees – once meant to invigorate the revolution – quickly turned into one more instrument of control, meant to ensure the physical survival of the regime. For almost a decade, the regime would pay little attention to formal legal rules. The increasingly repressive revolutionary justice system that enforced the regime's directives would eventually be a major factor contributing to the growing tension within the Jamahiriyya – and would lead to a number of restrictions on the Revolutionary Committees' powers.

Qadhafi, however, quickly developed reservations about the effectiveness of the Revolutionary Committees. In his 1 September speech following the downing of two Libyan planes by the United States in August 1981 over the Gulf of Sirt, he reiterated the need for further mobilization and called for the creation of a new type of vanguard, the so-called "Guards of the Revolution."[25] In the same speech, he announced further popular takeovers, including those of overseas embassies, which were turned into People's Bureaus. The Guards of the Revolution, however, never became a viable organization. The rapid rise and partial curtailment of the Revolutionary Committees, in the span of a single decade, was symptomatic of the balancing act the Qadhafi government skillfully performed to remain in power. Their resurgence during the early 1990s to aid in combating Islamist opposition to the regime, particularly in Cyrenaica, shows how closely their fate was directly tied to Qadhafi.

SYMBOLS, MYTHS, ISLAM, AND OPPOSITION

Although Libya with its small population could never claim equal status with other revolutionary nations, Qadhafi considered what had happened in Libya after 1969 as one of the great twentieth-century revolutions for social liberation. In *The Green Book*, the Libyan leader portrays the Libyan revolution as an inevitable, historical process of social, economic, and political development – hence the grandiloquent claim of the Jamahiriyya being the alternative to capitalism and communism. In his speeches and exhortations since 1969, the Libyan leader has constantly invoked a sense of uniqueness, grounded in Arab history and tradition, in ways that resonated within Libyan culture and experience. But, eventually, the use of a combination of symbols, myths, and careful attempts to exploit the charismatic qualities of the Libyan leader assumed an instrumental purpose as well: bridging the gap between *The Green Book*'s precise delineation of the country's formal political structures and the reality of an increasingly exclusionary political system.

When reading Qadhafi's speeches – painstakingly assembled in yearly volumes, accompanied by extensive commentaries, and published by *the Green Book* Center in Tripoli – one is struck immediately by the repeated and powerful references to shared traditions within the country and within the region, to notions of a common history that has pitted Libyans against the West, and to symbols that are uniquely Libyan and deeply embedded within local culture. The Libyan leader's speeches contain innumerable reiterations of words that reflect conditions in Arab society before state-building began in earnest: words like *turath* (heritage), *furusiyya* (chivalry), and *diafa* (hospitality). Dignity and the indignities suffered at the hands of the West have continually been mentioned by Qadhafi to invoke a powerful sense of unity. History – and historical wrongs inflicted by the West on Libya – have been used from the beginning to create a sense of shared suffering and exploitation. The realities and memories of the Fascists' brutality, the capture and hanging of Umar al-Mukhtar, and the removal of the local population from their own land in favor of Italian settlers have all provided constant focal points of Qadhafi's rhetoric.

The suspicion of outsiders was also richly nurtured as the Libyan government confronted first the oil companies and then the West more generally. Libyans were instructed to be vigilant against the West and to destroy those who would sell out the revolution for their own interests. In a speech exhorting citizens to be wary of those who would betray the Jamahiriyya to outsiders, Qadhafi deftly made the link between the past and the present:

So I must tell you that the traitors are a bigger threat to our future, freedom, and independence than colonialism. It was the traitors who enabled Italy to go deep inside Libya. The Italians on their own could not have advanced into this desert or these mountains. They would not have managed to catch Umar al-Mukhtar had it not been for a traitor who gave his whereabouts ... Now we should seek traitors, those who pave the way for the Americans, and kill them. The Americans today are like the Italians yesterday. The traitors of today are like [those] of yesterday. The traitors of October 1911 are like those of October 1993.[26]

There is little doubt that Qadhafi's statements and actions tapped deeply into a rich source of resentment among Libyans against the West. Through the oil negotiations of 1970 and 1971 and the evacuation of the military bases, the regime provided many ordinary Libyans with their own sense of dignity, even though the monarchy had started negotiations for the latter. It was similarly important therefore that what had happened on 1 September 1969 be portrayed as a collective action: the Libyan people had rejected the kingdom and its corrupt pro-western clique, and the military planners of the takeover had simply implemented their wishes. In order to convey this image, the regime needed to deflect attention from the fact that the events of 1 September had only involved a very small number of military personnel. Moreover, it needed to downplay the reality that the new leadership had very few clearly developed ideas beyond some rudimentary principles that could be condensed into anti-westernism, Arab nationalism, and populism, when it assumed power.

It was important, finally, not only in light of the existing *ulama* but because of a wider popular appeal, to portray the revolution as consistent with the general precepts of Islam. The Qadhafi regime had inherited a legal system in which codified western law enjoyed primacy over religious and customary law. Despite the fact that *The Green Book* elevated religion and custom to the status of the law of society, in practice, both were displaced as sources of law by secular policies. This break with Islamic law and Libyan custom, however, was never officially acknowledged. *The Green Book* continued to stress reliance on "a sacred law based on stable rules which are not subject to change," identified this sacred law with Islam and with the Qur'an, and Qadhafi claimed consistently that the revolution had reinstated true Islam.

The revolution of 1 September 1969, according to the regime, was meant to initiate a wholesale cleansing of perceived stains of western culture, colonialism, and the monarchy (with its links to global capital) from the country's social fabric. A number of public and highly symbolic acts in the early years of the revolution were necessary to achieve this end, including the burning of western books and musical instruments, the closing of nightclubs, the promotion of traditional Libyan dress, the conversion of churches into mosques, the adoption in principle of Islamic punishment, and the renaming of the Gregorian calendar. Oil was instrumental in achieving the regime's goals, confronting the West, and restoring to Libya and to the Arab world the cultural and political power they had once possessed. The confrontation with the West – and Libya's repeated efforts at creating alliances with other Arab countries – must thus be understood not only as a means of creating support at home but also as fulfillment of the deeply felt conviction that Qadhafi could indeed be the heir to Gamal Abdul Nasser within the region.

During the first years after 1969 in particular – but lasting until today – one of the most powerful mechanisms for creating a following for the revolution was Qadhafi's own charisma. Informal, non-institutionalized, charismatic leadership fitted perfectly within the kind of personalized politics that developed within the Jamahiriyya. In contrast to a monarchy that had been dominated by an older bourgeoisie and an aging king and lacked a desire to define Libya's position clearly within Arab politics, Qadhafi conveyed a sense of personal integrity and self-esteem. The overthrow of the Sanusi monarchy, a political system that had sidelined citizens since its creation and grew increasingly corrupt during the 1960s, initially added to the new leader's standing among the population. His hard bargaining tactics with the oil companies, and the eventual vindication of Libya's insistence on a greater share of oil profits, provided him with a stature far greater than that of those around him. His sense of righteousness and fearlessness, his willingness to take a clear position within intra-Arab politics, his sense of duty and of honor, his personal honesty: all these qualities put him in sharp contrast to what the country had experienced before. In a sense, Qadhafi was the revolution, *al-qaʾid alʾmuʾallim* (the leader and teacher) as he became known in the Jamahiriyya. His ability to insinuate himself – and the Libyan people simultaneously – into the troubled history of his country by claiming that he followed in the footsteps of Umar al-Mukhtar and all those who had resisted the West forged a sense of solidarity among Libyans.

Viewed against the backdrop of the monarchy, he seemingly possessed all the qualities Arab nationalism touted: militancy in opposing the West, youthfulness, and a high level of political energy. Above all, he possessed the will to pursue his own vision of what a political community should look like, despite numerous setbacks and (often self-inflicted) crises. Charisma is by its nature a fleeting political resource that needs constant rejuvenation and renewal to remain valid. Thus, successive waves of mobilization and consistently unbalanced politics were powerful mechanisms Qadhafi used to prevent the routinization of his charisma, no matter how seemingly incoherent or irrational these policies appeared to observers. As a charismatic leader, Qadhafi also insisted on direct contact with ordinary Libyans that allowed him to claim a link and legitimacy no other RCC member could match. From 1969 onward, he put great emphasis on personalized exchanges with the population, continuously meeting groups of Libyans within highly formalized settings, delivering speeches throughout the country, reinforcing the message of the revolution, and exhorting citizens in a way few recent rulers in the Middle East have attempted.

Charisma, however, is an inherently unstable source of authority. Not only must the charismatic leader have extraordinary qualities, but his people must share his belief – or at least suspend their disbelief – in his vision. The revolutionary measures of the 1970s and early 1980s had, through their disarticulation and chaos, slowed down this process. As the revolutionary decade ended there were growing signs that charisma as a political force within Libyan politics had become circumscribed. Despite Qadhafi's exhortations and a clear sense that he himself had been targeted for elimination during the April 1986 US bombing, the apathy among the population clearly showed the extent to which his personal power to persuade had declined.

It was also clear that, despite this careful manipulation of symbols, myths, and charisma, the revolution had created a number of enemies: monarchical elites who had been dispossessed or forced to flee the country; fellow revolutionaries, who – like Muhayshi and Mugharyif, Qadhafi's former state comptroller and ambassador to India, respectively – took issue with the wasting of the country's resources; the *ulama* whose role had been severely restricted; and ordinary citizens who resented the unpredictability of *The Green Book*'s directives and the deep impact of the revolutionary measures on their lives. As the revolution unfolded and intensified, a multitude of Libyan opposition groups formed in the West and throughout the Middle East. Some of these regularly produced publications containing their own viewpoint. The best-known opposition group was the National Front for the Salvation of Libya (NFSL), founded in 1981 by Muhammad Mugharyif. The NFSL also had a military wing, the Salvation Forces, which, with French and US support, conducted a number of military actions against Qadhafi in the 1980s.[27] Eventually, the different groups started to organize themselves more effectively, led in part by the leadership of the NFSL. However, their cooperation remained precarious and showed the deep divisions that, in turn, reflected the different aspirations and interests of each group.[28]

The fact that opposition failed to crystallize inside Libya can only be partially explained by the presence of the security sector institutions, the effectiveness of the use of symbols, the injunction against political groupings, and by Qadhafi's appeal to the population. The constant new waves of mobilization against any group that potentially threatened the regime also provided an important clue. The regime's policies had, in addition to a level of apathy, also introduced a more insidious phenomenon: a depoliticization of the population and an atomization that took place as any type of organized activity was forbidden. This atomization was fostered by the fact that the state became virtually the sole economic provider under the directives of *The Green Book*. Under such circumstances, Libyans no

longer possessed the kind of common economic interests that in more productive economies lead to common actions – and such common interests
are, at any rate, unlikely to be expressed during economic booms. As a
result, conditions that might have facilitated the emergence of broad-based
organizations to defend particular interests lost their salience – economic
handouts and political silence became an ingrained part of politics.

In addition, when it became clear to Libyan citizens that the gap
between formal and informal mechanisms of governing had become an
insurmountable reality of politics in the Jamahiriyya, most learned to cope
with a political system they had no chance of reforming. Perhaps fitting,
in light of the regime's attempts to minimize the impact of the state on
citizens' daily lives, the state had indeed, beyond its economic largesse,
become much less relevant for most citizens. But this decreased relevance
also led to the de-politicization described above, something the regime,
at least rhetorically, had tried to avoid. This de-politicization was thus
due to the fact that Libyans stopped making claims on a state they could
not hope to reform. Indeed, in Libya, this process became so pronounced
that even opposition groups operating outside the country were unable
to develop a common plan for what the country's future should look like,
while Qadhafi remained in power.

The regime nevertheless did provide a number of symbolic outlets for
citizens to vent their frustration. Qadhafi's oft-repeated remark that every
Popular Congress to which individuals belong constitutes an opposition
may seem trivial but is nevertheless important. The congresses have allowed
individuals, without challenging the structure of the political system overall, to voice their complaints. Being officially outside the formal structure
of authority, Qadhafi has often encouraged those criticisms, even in public
settings, to extend his own plans and directives.

At the same time, his directives were meant specifically to prevent the
emergence of any group that could potentially create an independent political base of support – whether as members of a tribe, a socio-economic
class, the Libyan military, a Popular or Revolutionary Committee, one
of the country's multiple security organizations, or a class of intellectuals and students. The system of Popular Congresses and Committees was
closely supervised in Tripoli, allowing the regime to create a security sector capable of preventing the emergence of any systematic articulation of
political interests. Even the once most powerful members of that security
system – the Revolutionary Committees – were never allowed to assume
any autonomous power. Much as the king created CYDEF and TRIDEF
based on tribal affiliation as an alternative to the Libyan army, Qadhafi

repeatedly reshaped the army and prevented the emergence of a professional military by creating a popular army and popular militias as the revolution unfolded.

Effective opposition to the regime would have required the existence
of both organized networks and weakness in the regime. Although the
United States seemingly anticipated that the April 1986 bombing would
constitute a catalyst for provoking such opposition to the regime, whatever reaction took place was local, ineffective, and quickly dissipated.
But while popular reaction to the US bombing had provided a tangible
expression of Libyans' apathy and their diminishing enthusiasm for the
leader's revolution, there were other signs of slowly emerging resistance.
A number of audacious public acts of defiance in the mid-1980s hinted
at problems of control inside the country. Anti-revolutionary graffiti
increasingly appeared in public places, despite the vigilance of the country's security agencies. A number of arson cases involving public buildings
and Revolutionary Committee headquarters occurred in several cities. In
August 1986, opponents of the regime managed to assassinate Ahmad
al-Warfalli, a prominent Revolutionary Committee member. The regime
blamed the murder on radical Islamists inside the country and used it as
an opportunity to begin a new wave of repression and confrontation that
Fall and Winter.

The absence of sustained and organized opposition until the country's
fiscal crisis became acute in the late 1980s, however, testified once more to
the resilience rulers in oil states like Libya possess in shaping, and holding
in abeyance, demands for greater political input during boom periods –
and, initially at least, during bust periods when reserves can be used to offset growing or persisting economic dislocations. By providing for Libyans'
material and everyday needs, Qadhafi was able to prevent a coalescing of
political interests based on purely economic criteria. It is this power, in
addition to a preemption of the Islamic activism described above and the
skillful manipulation of charisma, myth, and revolutionary rhetoric, that
were keys in maintaining his regime during the 1980s, even as its political
and ideological fortunes diminished dramatically.

TERRORISM, ADVENTURISM, AND CONFRONTATION
WITH THE WEST

Since 1969, Qadhafi's revolution contained a strong element of anti-
western rhetoric that resonated strongly within the Middle East and
North Africa, a region then in the throes of Arab nationalism. In Libya,

the reaction against the West among the young revolutionaries was in part based on Libyans' historical memory of the Italian colonial period. But it also encompassed a much broader resentment against the role of the West, and particularly of the United States, within the region – a role Qadhafi would describe as imperialist and linked to an unwavering support for Israel. Following from this, the Libyan leader decried the exploitation of the country's resources by multinational companies that paid scant attention, he argued, to the needs of the country.

For most of the first decade after the coup, however, Libyan–US relations remained characterized by caution and pragmatism on both sides. The United States, beyond its interests in the country's oil industry, was concerned about keeping the country outside the Soviet Union's orbit.

The Libyan government, despite the nationalization of some American and British oil interests in 1973, showed no inclination during its early years toward an open confrontation with the West. Its opposition remained a rhetorical tool used primarily for mobilization purposes inside Libya. Gradually, however, opposition to the West came to assume a larger role within the revolution during the 1970s and 1980s. When Gamal Abdul Nasser died in 1970, Qadhafi, much to the consternation and often derision of other Arab countries, thrust himself forward as the heir to the late Egyptian president's mission of creating a pan-Arab community that could blunt western policies in the region. Qadhafi's politics within North Africa, however, systematically alienated most of his neighbors, leading to a protracted skirmish with Egypt in 1977 – Qadhafi clearly viewing the Sadat regime as antithetical to the ideals of Nasser. In 1980, Saudi Arabia broke off diplomatic relations with the Libyan regime after a number of acrimonious exchanges over oil policies.[29]

That year, Libya's total development spending reached $10 billion per year. In 1981 alone, however, this still left $11 billion at the discretion of the government. Much of the money was spent in part on military purchases and international adventures. In 1981, Libya renewed its involvement in a dispute with Chad (dating from the monarchy) over the Aouzou strip. During the early 1980s, defense and military spending grew rapidly, even as development and regular administrative budgets were curtailed: defense as part of the country's declared regular budget climbed from $709 million to $1,149 million (16.7% and 23.6%, respectively) between 1982 and 1984.[30] Qadhafi's attempt to destabilize neighboring Tunisia led to a more open confrontation with France and the United States. In January 1981, the French government refused to implement a contract that had been signed between the oil parastatal Elf Aquitaine and LIPETCO, Libya's official investment company, and became more openly aligned against Libya following the latter's renewed invasion of Chad.

Libya's major confrontation, however, increasingly focused on the United States. The United States accused Libya of supporting terrorism, of engaging in subversion in sub-Saharan Africa and beyond, of boycotting the Middle East peace process, and, eventually, of attempting to produce weapons of mass destruction. The assassination of Israeli athletes at the Munich 1972 Olympics and the 1973 killing of the US ambassador to Sudan raised the first, albeit still unsubstantiated, questions about Libya's involvement with terrorist groups. These concerns were heightened further by the fact that the regime increasingly and openly expressed its support for radical Palestinian groups and attempted to ship weapons to the Irish Republican Army. Several radical Palestinian movements – including the Abu Nidal group, the Popular Front for the Liberation of Palestine – General Command, and Palestinian Islamic Jihad – had found a home in the Jamahiriyya.[31] In 1989, Washington accused Libya of supporting roughly thirty international terrorist and revolutionary movements worldwide.

Libya's rhetoric against Israel remained intransigent as Qadhafi started to oppose US efforts to resolve the Arab–Israeli conflict, culminating in the Libyan leader's public condemnation of the Camp David accords. Worried about these developments and about the growing role of a Soviet presence in Libya, the Carter administration in 1978 prohibited the sale of all military equipment to the Jamahiriyya. By the end of the following year, Libya was put on the list of state sponsors of terrorism, which extended the ban to include most economic assistance to the country. On 15 February 1980, the United States closed its embassy in Tripoli.

In several ways, Libya's confrontation with the United States became a self-fulfilling prophecy as Qadhafi and successive US presidents portrayed each other as outcasts in the international community. President Reagan's denunciation of Qadhafi as the "mad dog of the world" allowed the latter to deflect much of whatever internal criticism was gingerly voiced through the GPC, creating as it did the image of a highly unequal and hypocritical antagonism the Libyan leader gladly exploited. President Bush's later statement that "the politics and actions of the Government of Libya continue to pose an unusual and extraordinary threat to the national security and foreign policy of the United States" only added to the David-versus-Goliath image Qadhafi was able to use for his own internal purposes.

Clearly, however, the transfer of power in Washington from the Carter to the Reagan administration in January 1981 had marked a significant threshold for US – Libyan relations. President Reagan, in part eager to demonstrate American strength in the region in the wake of the Soviet invasion of Afghanistan in 1979, viewed Libya as a highly visible and worthy target of his new policy of opposing regional adversaries. The United States moved with determination to contain Libya further. Arguing that the Jamahiriyya was actively engaged in the destabilization of local regimes and in the promotion of international terrorism, the administration in May 1981 closed the Libyan People's Bureau (embassy) in Washington. The relations between the two countries continued to worsen when Washington accused Libya of attempting to assassinate US officials. In August 1981, the confrontation took on a more ominous aspect when the US's Sixth Fleet shot down two Libyan jet fighters over the Gulf of Sirt – which Libya claimed as its territorial waters but which Washington viewed as an international waterway.

The dogfight and the way the dispute was addressed by both sides indicated the rapid deterioration of relations and the unwillingness of both sides to engage in constructive talks. In December 1981, US citizens were prohibited from traveling to Libya and President Reagan urged all Americans to leave the Jamahiriyya. Soon afterwards, in March 1982, all crude oil exports from Libya were embargoed and US exports of sophisticated oil and gas equipment prohibited. Meanwhile, on 17 April 1984, personnel at the Libyan People's Bureau in St. James Square in London shot and killed Yvonne Fletcher, a local policewoman who was on duty during an anti-Qadhafi demonstration taking place in the square. Reaction to the murder marked the beginning of more concerted efforts by the Europeans to isolate the country diplomatically – although, much to Washington's consternation, the European countries proved unwilling to move toward imposing economic sanctions. On the other hand, the US boycott was further extended in November 1985 when President Reagan banned the import of refined petroleum products from Libya. A month later, terrorist attacks at the Rome and Vienna airports were linked to the Abu Nidal organization, which in turn had close ties to Libya. As a result, President Reagan in January 1986 invoked the International Emergency Economic Powers Act that put a halt to all loans and credits to the Jamahiriyya, prohibited all financial transactions of US citizens with Libya, and froze Libyan foreign assets in the United States. In a message that showed how personalized the conflict between the two leaders had become, President Reagan clearly warned that the United States was willing to take further and more decisive steps if Qadhafi did not modify his behavior.[32] That next step – the bombing of Tripoli and Benghazi in April 1986 – would prove a decisive turning point in the US– Libyan confrontation and would mark the beginning of a slow change and internal reappraisal of Libya's policies as well.

From the beginning of his tenure in office, Reagan attempted to destabilize the Qadhafi regime through covert actions, in addition to pinprick military confrontations over the Gulf of Sirt. Libyan opposition groups in the West and in Chad, where the US administration supported the Chadian government of Hissen Habre in the war over the Aouzou strip, enjoyed US support in an effort to destabilize the regime further. The covert efforts intensified after a June 1984 CIA assessment that asserted the overthrow of Qadhafi would be necessary to put a halt to Libyan aggression.[33]

The Libyan government skillfully exploited the confrontation with the West for its own purposes. In the wake of the Gulf of Sirt incident, Qadhafi in August 1981 attended a GPC meeting for the first time since 1978, contravening his own declaration that he no longer held power in the country's formal political system. At the meeting, he attempted once more to mobilize Libyans in defense of the country, deftly using anti-American rhetoric for the purpose.[34] This time the Libyan leader proposed a general militarization of the Jamahiriyya – the creation of a popular militia that would gradually take over the functions of the regular army. Although Qadhafi had mentioned the idea on several occasions previously – and some arming of villages and indoctrination had started earlier under the guidance of ex-RCC member al-Hamidi – the 1981 attack provided the catalyst for this latest *zahf*.[35]

The skirmish also acted once more as a self-fulfilling prophecy for the regime. In addition to the surrounding countries that constituted Libya's "traditional enemies" – Egypt in the east, Tunisia in the west, Chad aided by France in the south – the country's leadership could now point to the United States as having crossed its self-proclaimed "line of death" in the Gulf of Sirt. The internal effects of the growing confrontation with the West were, at the time, seemingly of little importance. In many ways, the regime skillfully managed to exploit Libya's traditional distrust of outsiders. But the combination of diplomatic isolation – which made traveling outside Libya virtually impossible for its citizens – as well as the growing economic dislocations at home had seemingly started to diminish Libyans' acceptance of their revolutionary leader's directives. In April 1986, when the United States bombed Benghazi and Tripoli, the attack was met by almost total apathy among the population: "One saw more demonstrators in Khartoum and Tunis than in Tripoli where the number of foreign journalists outnumbered Tripolitanians."[36] Several attempts by the regime to organize demonstrations in its wake were abandoned for lack of participants, and Qadhafi disappeared from the Libyan media for several weeks.

The worsening relationship with the United States, highly politicized by both sides for the sake of each country's political purposes, put increasing pressure on US oil companies to review their investments in the Jamahiriyya after the Reagan administration came to power. Exxon – which was represented in Libya by Esso Standard Libya, Inc., and Esso Sirte, Inc. – on 4 November 1981 announced that it would withdraw from operations in the country. Within a few months, on 10 March 1982, the US government adopted a measure that prohibited the import of all Libyan oil into the country, and started to restrict the flow of US goods to the Jamahiriyya. In January 1983, Mobil followed suit and withdrew from operations after months of unsuccessful negotiations with LNOC officials.[37] By that time, several other companies had reviewed their own exposure in the country and, as in the case of the French parastatal Elf Aquitaine, decided, at least temporarily, to halt the implementation of earlier signed contracts.

The Libyan government recognized the danger of a possible snowball effect and throughout the 1981–84 years consistently offered incentives to the remaining companies to maintain production. Occidental, one of the largest independent producers was offered a $4 price cut in October 1981 in order to stimulate its production. The result was that prices for Libyan oil throughout 1983 remained substantially below the already low 1982 prices. The Jamahiriyya was in the midst of an ambitious new development plan, and its planners had little choice but to offer incentives when the country's revenues were cut by one-third overnight as the United States implemented its boycott. Much of this financial crunch would be alleviated by the fact that European importers proved eager to take larger shares of Libyan production. But it meant that Libya, from July 1982 until the end of 1984, saw itself forced consistently to produce oil far in excess of the OPEC quota it had been assigned; during the first quarter of 1983, for example, it marketed 1.8 million bpd, an excess of 800,000 bpd.

THE REVOLUTIONARY DECADE REVISITED

Within a decade after the oil boom of 1973, the Qadhafi government reluctantly came to the conclusion that the political and economic transformations necessary to turn its revolutionary directives into reality were much more elusive than originally anticipated. Rapid inflows of oil revenues had not translated into real development. Libya's wealth had produced a developmental crisis the revolutionary government found difficult to address, as had scarcity of capital during the early years of independence. By 1986, the country's long decade of revolutionary upheaval had run its course, with disastrous effects. The altercations with the United States, with Britain, and with France were early indications that the Jamahiriyya was heading into a full-blown confrontation with the West. The more spectacular terrorist incidents, and ever more drastic responses to it by the western countries and by the international community, still lay in the future. It was clear, however, that the US administration in particular was determined to put a halt to Libya's adventurism and its use of terrorism. The Rome and Vienna airport attacks of December 1985 made it all but inevitable that Washington would escalate the confrontation, determined as it was to make Libya a pariah in the international community.

Internally, the regime had managed to destroy, reshape, or reorganize many of the institutions of the state in the name of popular rule. Simultaneously, it had created a carefully controlled system of patronage managed by the remaining RCC members, the top military elite, and the cluster of Qadhafi loyalists at Bab al-Aziziyya who, in contradiction to the official policies of popular rule and popular management, controlled access to the country's main spending institutions – its ministries. As one observer noted, "Libya's historical problem with central authority ... was resolved by eliminating it altogether, at least in principle."[38] But reality was starting to hem in the revolutionary rhetoric: the pursuit and implementation of statelessness could not disguise that the Popular Congress and Committee system, as well as the General People's Congress, possessed no real power. Throughout the revolutionary decade, they remained consultative mechanisms at best.

By centralizing all political expression in the Popular Committee system, by clearly stating that no political activity could take place outside it, and by awarding the revolutionary means of governing precedence over the formal political institutions in 1979, the regime ensured that it contained and controlled all political expression or dissent. Indeed, the GPC was never used to seriously debate the country's foreign adventures, the war in Chad, or to discuss the direction and goals of development and growth in the country. Furthermore, Qadhafi's central position within the country's political and economic structures, despite the lack of a formal link to the country's executive structure and his own assertion that he no longer had a formal role to play, created a system of personal politics that continued to dominate the country during the 1980s and beyond.

By the end of the 1970s, the regime had already become the only hand on the country's economic tiller. The economic directives of *The Green*

Book further strengthened this centralizing grip. The private sector and all private initiatives and entrepreneurship had been eliminated – in effect consigning the country's citizens to unproductive, rent-seeking activities. The unpredictability of the country's revolutionary legal system and the evisceration of property rights in the 1970s, furthermore, reduced all personal initiative. The regime managed to break the financial power of potential groups through a series of measures ranging from its "partners, not wage-earners" policy to outright confiscation and destruction of property. The nationalization of oil and land, and the monopoly over imports and exports, gave the state control over all sectors of the economy but kept economic regulation at a low level.

The impact of the regime's directives and the large inflows of revenues during the 1970s and the first half of the 1980s, however, had a devastating effect. Libya in fact became a centrally unplanned economy as the maintenance of patronage and a distinct social contract that relied heavily on economic distribution led to the skyrocketing of spending which took precedence over efficiency and regulation. In the absence of any need to adjudicate between different groups engaged in economic relations, the Libyan state simply became a crude monitoring agency, a development that would come to haunt its leader when the country attempted economic liberalization strategies after 1986.

Qadhafi's unceasing complaints about lack of accountability in public life, about the lack of personal initiative, and about the irresponsibility of public employees mirrored many of the complaints King Idris had made decades earlier. They indicated how little had changed – and how little Qadhafi understood that the broader economic and social structures of an oil state, in conjunction with the de-politicization of *The Green Book*'s populism and lack of systematic economic regulation, were instrumental in producing the symptoms he decried.

During the boom period that coincided with its revolutionary decade, the regime's domestic upheavals and embroilment in foreign adventures produced relatively little internal dissent. Much of this was due to the way in which the regime exercised control throughout the country – making individuals prefer exit to the uncertainty of any concerted opposition. It was also due to the fact that most Libyans, as direct or indirect beneficiaries of economic largesse, had become largely de-politicized despite the revolutionary fervor for mobilization. And despite all the excesses and uncertainties he had introduced, the Libyan leader remained someone with whom many Libyans could identify and with whose basic ideological precepts – if not his tactics – they agreed.

However, the "permanent revolution" – with its successive waves of new directives, new structures, and a high level of unpredictability – had hardly been more successful than the ASU in mobilizing the country's citizens.[39] As the revolutionary decade ended, a new constituency emerged in Libyan politics, one that would slowly come to play an important role from the late-1980s onward and assume a major role during the next decade: an educated younger generation of Libyans for whom the ideological battles and the rationale for the September revolution seemed less clear, and for whom the country's isolation and its lack of opportunities were deplorable. Their voice would come at a time when the regime's options became severely diminished and, in conjunction with a number of other factors, would lead to a dramatic reassessment of the Jamahiriyya experiment.

CHAPTER 6

The limits of the revolution, 1986–2000

In the wake of the US bombing of Tripoli and Benghazi in April 1986, the Libyan regime faced a number of internal and international challenges that gradually reduced Qadhafi's ability to pursue his activist policies abroad and at home. They limited his ability to use continuous waves of political mobilization within Libya, and, by the end of the century, brought a halt to the waves of unpredictable political and economic directives at home. His revolutionary harangues throughout the period continued unabated – at a pitch temporarily heightened by the US military operation that killed Hanna al-Qadhafi, one of his adopted children – but there was an increasingly desperate tone and hackneyed quality to his rhetoric. Caged in by a combination of economic sanctions and diplomatic isolation, the Libyan regime responded with one of the few tools still at its disposal: a deepening involvement with international terrorism that would reach its most notorious climax in 1988 and 1989. But these, in more ways than one, were measures of last resort.

The international sanctions in 1992, and particularly the Arab countries' initially neutral response to them, also prompted an important realignment of the county's foreign relations. After years of pursuing unity schemes with various Arab regimes, Qadhafi announced that he could no longer tolerate their leaders' lackluster responses to the Arab–Israeli conflict, or their passivity and their acquiescence in a political status quo throughout the region dominated by the US presence and its policies. As a result, the Libyan leader deepened his involvement with sub-Saharan Africa which he viewed as an area for projecting Libya's power, and for implementing new regional, economic, and political unity projects (see Chapter 7).

The decade and a half between 1986 and the end of the century represented the most difficult years the regime ever faced. The old certainties of Arab nationalism, of opposition to the West at all costs, and of regional integration schemes, had all disintegrated. The ideological aspirations that had once been cornerstones of the revolutionary regime's rhetoric had been countered, neutralized, and often reversed, by regional and international actors. Libya's reputation, at an all-time low, preempted any further chances at joint regional initiatives. The international community slowly but effectively isolated the regime politically, diplomatically, and economically. Libya's involvement in a number of terrorist acts – most notably the explosions of Pan Am flight 103 over Lockerbie in December 1988 and of the French UTA 772 airliner over the Niger desert in September 1989 – subjected the country to an extension of US unilateral sanctions, and to the imposition of United Nations multilateral sanctions starting in April 1992. The combination of the two, in addition to the multiple other hardships the regime faced, proved, in the end, insurmountable.

As international opposition to Libya's behavior grew, the half-hearted response at home to Qadhafi's hectoring in the wake of the US bombing provided the first tangible sign that internal dissatisfaction was also at a breaking point. For a number of reasons, and by a number of methods, however, the regime was able to contain opposition inside and outside the Jamahiriyya, but the suppression of dissent further degraded the ideological pretensions of the Leader's rhetoric. In response to these mounting difficulties, Qadhafi allowed a number of internal adjustments. The first was prompted by the realization that the mobilizational potential of the Popular Committee and Congress system had proven of limited value. But, because of its centrality to the Leader's ideology, it could not be abandoned. The control functions of the revolution – embodied in the country's Revolutionary Committees and in the multiple security apparatuses – had expanded dramatically by 1986, and provided a particular focus of popular resentment. While unwilling to change the structures of the security sector entirely, the regime focused instead on a (selective) curtailment of the Revolutionary Committee movement which had come to symbolize the most hated aspect of the revolutionary measures.

The second set of adjustments was announced in March 1987. The Libyan government announced that it would reform the country's economy, removing some of the restrictions that had been imposed after the publication of *The Green Book*'s directives on economic management. But, in the Jamahiriyya, where economic patronage and political quiescence were different sides of the same coin, economic reform would inevitably affect the overall power of the regime. It was not a surprise, therefore, that the economic liberalization, except for some measures that brought relief to Libya's citizens, proved unsuccessful.

Hemmed in by the sanctions, and opposed by powerful external adversaries who were not averse to possible regime change in the Jamahiriyya,

Qadhafi with these two sets of adjustments skillfully did away with some of the more pernicious elements of his revolution without, however, changing the fundamental structures that kept it in power. While these structures of power and authority in the Jamahiriyya remained unaffected, Qadhafi's exhortations for further resistance against western aggression sounded increasingly hollow. The unpredictability of the earlier revolutionary measures had created a mistrust and apathy that proved impossible to remedy. The revolution as a focus of political and ideological energy had yielded inexorably to the daily concerns among the country's citizens – and increasingly its leadership – over the more pressing matter of how to face the political, psychological, and economic hardships imposed by the country's isolation.

For Qadhafi, the adaptations necessary after 1986 presented enormous political and ideological challenges. At the very core of his internal political experiments, as well as his regional and international political pursuits since 1969, had been an ideology of revolution and activism, of confrontation with the West and of anti-westernism, and of revolutionary tactics, often subversion, as a legitimate means of confronting what it considered reactionary regimes. How Qadhafi dealt with those challenges under the differing circumstances after 1986, and how he tinkered with the interwoven links of economic patronage and political control – while leaving the essential control structures of his regime in place – provided the context for much of the deft maneuvering and incremental adjustments he initiated or allowed after April 1986. That the regime survived these multiple challenges proved once more the resilience and powerful tools rulers of oil states possess to contain and circumvent political dissent, international actions, and economic hardships for a considerable amount of time. One of the unintended consequences of the regime's maneuvering, however, was that by the end of the century the energy of Qadhafi's revolution had effectively been dissipated and contained.

CURTAILING REVOLUTIONARY ENERGY

It is quite clear in retrospect that the 15–16 April 1986 bombing of Tripoli and Benghazi by the United States created considerable consternation among the Libyan leadership. It also, in some ways, represented a watershed for the country's international politics. The country's defenses in the face of the attacks had proven feeble. Some Revolutionary Committee members had quietly abandoned their positions, and there were rumors of organized resistance in the eastern part of the country immediately after the attack. The response of the population to calls for massive anti-United-States rallies by the Libyan leader were at best lackluster. The psychological shock that the United States would actually target Libyan cities – and, it was hinted at, the Libyan leader himself – left a deep despondency and an initially confused attempt to evaluate what the country's options were.

For weeks after the bombing the Libyan leader did not appear on television. When he finally did so, he defiantly called for *tawsi' ath-thawra* – an extension of the revolution. But beneath the veneer of traditional rhetoric this new *zahf* (wave of reforms) represented nothing but a careful recalibration of the country's structures of control. Aware that the previous decade had witnessed the introduction of a number of nefarious measures – particularly the expansion of the unpredictable revolutionary authority system that had raised considerable concern and uncertainty among Libyan citizens – the "extension of the revolution" in reality meant its opposite: a curtailing of its more disliked political and economic measures. Qadhafi – now routinely referred to as The Leader – in his speeches castigated Libyans in his usual populist fashion about their waste and lack of initiative. He decried the impact of some of the "revolutionary means of governing" and of the isolation the country found itself in. These concerns were taken up publicly at the February 1987 GPC meeting in Sabha.[1] The delegates at the meeting as well voiced a number of public concerns about economic management of the country, their specificity and sophistication indicating that the criticisms had been approved in advance by the regime.

Throughout 1987 and in 1988, Qadhafi publicly deplored the excesses of the country's security organizations and of the Revolutionary Committees. In particular, the latter were singled out for their behavior. In May 1988, during a speech on national television that inadvertently revealed the true locus of power inside the Jamahiriyya, Qadhafi castigated the committees for their past actions: "They deviated, harmed, tortured ... [N]o one has immunity ... at all if he has deviated. The revolutionary does not practice repression. On the contrary, I want to prove that the committees ... are lovers of the masses, that they are for freedom and that they support my resolutions." Within weeks, a special committee was appointed under the leadership of the country's Minister of Justice. It was meant to investigate charges of corruption and of abuse of power by Revolutionary Committee members, and to audit the assets of several of those who belonged to the committees. By December 1988, the Revolutionary Committees started to lose power as their presence in the intelligence, police, and security sector was curtailed. A Ministry of Mass Mobilization and Revolutionary Leadership was created under Ali Al-Sha'iri, one of the regime's most trusted members. His task was to control the Revolutionary Committee movement, and to bring its task back from an overall guard dog of the regime to its original more narrow role as an ideological vanguard.[2]

Simultaneously, the regime attempted to expand its political liberalization to a wider audience. In 1987 and throughout 1988, scores of political prisoners were released. On 3 March 1988, Qadhafi personally participated in the destruction of Tripoli's central prison, making a coruscating verbal attack from the prison's tower against those who abused the revolution for their own purposes. Under his supervision, thousands of security files on Libyan citizens were destroyed. The same month, the Libyan leader traveled to the Tunisian–Libyan borderpost at Ras al-Jadir to help destroy its buildings, arguing that Libyans were now free to travel as they wished. In 1988 alone, 1 million Libyans – referred to disparagingly as "Green Locusts" by their neighbors – visited Tunisia, armed with generous hard currency allowances provided by the Libyan government.

After the difficult years of the country's revolutionary decade, these small but symbolically important measures provided the regime with a breathing space that had not existed before. It reached out, furthermore, to entice Libyan exiles back to the country, making promises of employment and of immunity from prosecution. Confiscated passports were returned to Libyan citizens, and their issuance was now entrusted to Popular Committees rather than to the security sector organizations. The Libyan leader also met with some opposition figures hoping to bring them back to Libya as a show of support for the regime, but largely failed to do so.

In one of his most remarkable declarations since 1969, Qadhafi then adopted a number of further measures that portrayed him as encouraging greater legal guarantees within the country, as promoting a greater degree of freedom, and as as an advocate of human rights. He admitted that Libya's revolutionary legal system had led to abuses. He proposed codifications of legal principles through the GPC, singling out in particular the activities of the security sector organizations and putting them under the GPC's area of responsibility. In May 1988, he called for a halt to arbitrary arrests and insisted on a clear codification of all crimes for which citizens could be arrested. The revolutionary courts were summarily disbanded – except for charges of treason – and replaced by People's Courts. A new Ministry of Justice was created in March 1989 to ensure the implementation of the various decrees and announcements.[3]

The apotheosis of the liberalization campaign was the dramatic announcement in June 1988 of *Al-Wathiqa al-Khadra al-Kubra lil-Huquq
al-Insanfi 'Asr al-Jamahir (The Great Green Charter of Human Rights in
the Era of the Masses).*[4] *The Green Charter*, if fully implemented, would
in effect have put a halt to, and reversed, the arbitrariness and unpredictability of the country's revolutionary decade. Article 2 of the *Great Green
Charter*, for example, recalled the earlier revolutionary directives on private property, and declared it "sacred and protected." There were further
references to accountability for everyone, much in the same vein as the
earlier criticism of the Revolutionary Committees. It also contained the
promise of the right to legal council (Article 9), strengthened in 1989 by
the GPC's adoption of a law that established, in principle, the independence of the judiciary.

The *Great Green Charter*, however, also included major caveats and
clauses that in effect rendered the document much less powerful. The provisions for private property could be overridden by "the public interest" –
leaving unspecified what this encompassed. Under Article 25, every Libyan
was obligated to defend the Jamahiriyya "until death." Article 26 stipulated
that "acts contrary to the principles and rights" expressed in the *Great
Green Charter* were unacceptable. In effect, both provisions extended the
uncertainty that had been created during the early years of the revolution
when any potential political activity could be labeled as treasonous by the
regime – and hence not covered by the stipulations of the *Green Charters*
Article 9. This earlier measure had never been rescinded, and was used
against members of secular and Islamic opposition movements later in the
decade and into the 1990s.

Qadhafi's attempt to bring greater predictability and accountability
must be viewed, therefore, within the larger context of the country's political life, and particularly within its formal and informal power structures.
The *Great Green Charter* did not contain any stipulation that would have
allowed political opposition, nor did it make the expression of such opposition in any public setting possible. As the Libyan leader continued to
argue, Libya was a Jamahiriyya ruled directly by its citizens. Hence, the
rules of opposition and of free expression did not apply. In effect, the *Great
Green Charter* did not provide either the civil or political rights that are
normally provided under international law nor, as one long-term observer noted, "the privileges of citizenship."[5] No free press was allowed, for
example, since, according to official dogma, people had the right to express

themselves freely at the Popular Congress meetings. Similarly, no independent labor unions could be established since the Libyan people were in principle already the owners of their own factories. And no opposition could be tolerated outside the Popular Congress and Committee system since it already represented the people. Finally, there could be no opposition on religious grounds since under Article 10 religion was declared subject to "personal and direct relations with the Creator, without intermediary."

In a distinct sense, therefore, the range of remedies suggested by the *Great Green Charter* further emphasized the longstanding ideological ambiguities of the Libyan leader – as well as his concerns to retain political power. In the end, many of the *Charter's* stipulations and guarantees were eviscerated in the early 1990s as opposition to the regime intensified. The reshuffle of the country's Cabinet – over which the GPC had no control – that followed the announcement of the *Great Green Charter* further heightened existing uncertainties. Two of its newly appointed ministers were long-time "Green Men" – dedicated revolutionaries. Their appointment indicated that the regime was not taking any chances. Furthermore, Qadhafi's reconfirmation at the March 1990 GPC of the separation between formal and revolutionary authority (first adopted in March 1979) was the final confirmation that, for all its promises, the *Great Green Charter* would never be allowed to affect or diminish the control functions of the regime.

PROTECTING THE REGIME: FORMAL AND INFORMAL MEANS OF POWER AND CONTROL

The need to "adjust" the revolution in the face of the economic sanctions and of growing internal discontent posed, nevertheless, a delicate dilemma to the regime. In principle, all authority belonged to the people, expressing their will through the Popular Committee and Congress system. In reality, criticism and grievances were only allowed to be expressed in a highly scripted form that served Qadhafi's intentions to keep the political system unbalanced and unpredictable. Furthermore, as stated above, the earlier law on Revolutionary Authority that labeled opposition as treason had never been rescinded, and prevented individual and organized dissent.

Even in authoritarian systems like the Jamahiriyya, however, rulers often rely on formal political mechanisms that, while essentially powerless, have the ability to serve as listening devices. The Popular Committee system did play this important role for the regime. It allowed the Libyan leader, in a very skillful fashion, to neutralize potential public displays of disagreement. By "taking the pulse of the people," he was then able to appropriate the expressed sentiments for his own political harangues and exhortations. In this fashion, in a way that became a routine feature in Libyan politics, the Leader – who in principle no longer belonged to the decision-making process of the Jamahiriyya – could criticize a wide range of abuses and shortcomings, simultaneously appeasing the population while keeping potential groups of opposition unbalanced and portraying himself as above the fray. Thus, the Libyan leader was often able to appear as the most virulent critic of whatever was ailing Libya's economy and whatever shortcomings the population had to endure, while skillfully deflecting blame on to others.

While the country's oil boom was unfolding in the 1970s and early 1980s, this strategy worked well. Because of their relatively high level of living standards, few Libyans felt inclined to make complaints on economic grounds. But in the late 1980s and 1990s, economic conditions had changed dramatically. The economic legacy left by two decades of a directionless *etatisme*, coupled with a dramatic decline in oil revenues, now found Libyans standing in bread lines, as the state supermarkets – once part and parcel of *The Green Book*'s policies to eliminate private traders and shopkeepers – descended into increasing disarray due to mismanagement and alleged corruption. Not surprisingly in a political system that routinely neglected organization and bureaucratic development, the supermarket scheme (or the state more generally) seldom delivered what citizens needed in their daily lives, and it provoked immense anger and frustration. Although a black market was reluctantly tolerated, and much informal economic activity persisted, neither could compensate for the absence of a retail infrastructure that ensured predictable and reliable deliveries of essential economic goods. The expulsion in the Summer and Fall of 1985 of thousands of expatriate workers – many of them Tunisians who had taken over the menial jobs Libyans no longer wanted to perform – had further added to the already existing chaos.

Beyond the purely economic hardships, however, there were a number of other frustrations that proved equally hard to swallow for the average Libyan and the country's elites alike. The deepening diplomatic isolation prevented large numbers of students from studying overseas, and increasingly made international travel – except to neighboring countries, and even then at enormous loss of time – impossible for virtually everyone. At the same time, the lingering war in Chad was starting to take its toll – physically as the number of casualties mounted, but also psychologically as the regime was forced to order military trials for defectors. The cynicism among the population was heightened when optimistic reports about the war eventually proved untrue. Finally, and despite the revolution's insistence on egalitarianism and solidarity, it became clear that economic differentiation had started to take place in the country. Amid the enforced austerity of public life in the cities, certain groups among the military, the country's diplomatic elite, and other top bureaucrats visibly benefited in ways not available to the average citizen.

The appearance of inequalities – a subject that once constituted one of the cornerstones of Qadhafi's denunciations of the monarchy, and of his rationale for avoiding liberal economic policies – provided a rallying point for a number of Islamist groups, particularly in Cyrenaica where resistance to the regime was in part linked to longstanding reservations about Qadhafi's own political use of Islam. Throughout the early 1990s, a series of uprisings of Islamist groups were harshly put down. Their suppression relied in large part on the Revolutionary Committees – which were rejuvenated for the purpose – rather than the country's regular army. It provided an indication once more of the suspicion with which the regime – much like King Idris during the monarchy – regarded the regular army.

Although Libya's armed services had grown substantially – from 7,000 in 1969 to 85,000 by 1988, after which their size was reduced as a result of Libya's defeat in the war in Chad – they were never allowed to develop a professional ethic that could have created a distinct corporate identity or distinct interests. Despite a lavish procurement program of equipment and hardware throughout the 1970s and early 1980s, Libya's military was never assigned tasks meant to safeguard the regime. Instead, it was carefully located, and its leadership regularly rotated, between garrisons in the country's seven military regions – the most important being Tripoli, Benghazi, Sirt, and Tubruq. As a result of a carefully balanced system of promotions and rotations, the Jamahiriyya's armed forces had been kept de-politicized throughout the 1970s and early 1980s. The growing internal discontent that materialized afterwards was fueled, in part, by the embarrassing debacle in Chad, and by deteriorating economic conditions that often left wages unpaid for months on end. The army's highly inadequate response to the April 1986 bombings had only been a pinprick indicator of a much larger malaise. The dismal performance of the Libyan army at Maaten al-Sarra, its main base in southern Libya – a humiliating defeat by ragtag Chadian forces who overran the local airfield with a few machine-guns mounted on Toyota pickup trucks – starkly revealed its professional incompetence.

To many seasoned observers, Libya's routing in Chad had not been surprising. The country's procurement of weapons, much of it from the former

Soviet Union, had often been haphazard and uncoordinated. Purchases served the whims of the country's leadership, based on the need to keep its top military supporters supplied with new hardware. The fortunes of the Libyan army's procurements, however, waned once the embargoes against shipments of military hardware to Libya by the United States and Europe were imposed in 1978 and 1986 respectively. The collapse of the Soviet Union, which had routinely provided about half of the country's acquisitions, added to the decline. In addition, US pressure on other providing countries, as well as the general condition of the economy, all contributed to the fact that Libyan procurement of arms and assorted military items declined slowly throughout the 1980s, and then, after 1989, in a more precipitous fashion. Until then, Libya consistently increased the proportion of its gross domestic product dedicated to military outlays, and expanded the size of its military forces. In several important ways, the military in Libya, despite its unreliability in the eyes of the regime, became an outlet for employment and for advancement in a country where the alternative most often consisted of working for one of the state's bureaucracies where advancement was unlikely.

In the early 1980s, Libya routinely imported in excess of $3 billion in arms purchases annually. Between 1979 and 1983 alone, it spent an estimated $12 billion, roughly half of that on hardware from the Soviet Union. When its fortunes changed as a result of the collapse of the Soviet Union and the sanctions, the country's military watched uneasily as purchases were drastically curtailed. In 1993 and 1995, the Jamahiriyya imported no arms at all, and only minuscule amounts ($10 million, $20 million, and $5 million, respectively) in 1994,1996, and 1997.[6] By the end of the decade, arms imports into Libya had virtually ended, even as the country attempted to purchase some weapons on the black market. It was only in the wake of suspension of the UN sanctions in 1999 that Libya would once more return to purchasing arms – an estimated $100 million worth of contracts with Russia in an attempt to upgrade and renew some of its antiquated Soviet-era weaponry.[7]

In the Jamahiriyya, as during the monarchy, two separate sets of institutions retained the monopoly over the use of force: the regular armed forces, and a set of praetorian-guard-like organizations that were responsible for the physical survival of each regime. As described above, Libya's Revolutionary Armed Forces after 1969 were carefully kept on the sidelines of the country's political life. Except for one brief period between 8 September and 7 December 1969, Libya since the September 1969 coup has never had a Ministry of Defense. The real control functions of the regime therefore lay elsewhere. Resembling the monarchy's earlier efforts to create a praetorian guard for its protection at the expense of a national army, real power was concentrated in a number of security apparatuses that came to dominate the intimate details of Libyans' lives, and of the country's formal political system, after 1969. The growth of this multi-layered and overlapping system of security organizations within Libya was a clear indication that the regime firmly intended to protect itself as opposition to the regime started to crystallize – and of the extent to which mechanisms of security, controlled directly by the country's leadership, remained the ultimate source of power in the Jamahiriyya.[8]

Certainly, the creation of the Revolutionary Committee system in 1977, and its expansion in the years afterwards, was meant as part and parcel of this security system. Neither its creation, nor the safeguarding role it assumed, had been a part of Qadhafi's *Green Book*. Rather, Qadhafi had developed in *The Green Book* the notion of armed citizens – as opposed both to a standing and professionalized army, and to specialized bodies like the Revolutionary Committees that would act as tripwires for the regime. Since 1974, the Libyan leader had supported the creation of a People's Militia, based on his notion that popular resistance and collective self-defense – as during the resistance to the Italians – was, at least rhetorically, the most efficient way to ensure the country's security. Its existence was formalized in Article 9 of the Proclamation of People's Power of March 1977 which states that "defending the country is the responsibility of every citizen." In effect, however, this militarization of society never went beyond symbolic displays of the People's Militia at carefully staged national events. The creation of the Revolutionary Committee system in a sense therefore constituted an admission that, at least from a security standpoint, the regime judged popular authority to be suspect and unreliable. The temporary curtailment of some of the Revolutionary Committees' power after the mid-1980s in effect did not alter the regime's ability to protect its revolution. Indeed, as the campaign against the Islamists proved, the actions taken against the Committees could, at the pleasure of the Libyan leader, be rescinded when he judged the regime threatened.

By the early 1990s, Libya's current bifurcated system of power and control had been consolidated. Formal political power and authority resided within the GPC. Real power, however, remained within the so-called "revolutionary sector" of the revolution. The country's layer of security organizations was only one element of the informal mechanisms of control. They were never subject to political control by the GPC, but were consistently put at the direct disposal of the Libyan leader, subject only to his own directives. Their rapid growth after 1970 had created a set of security institutions that were deliberately kept in either separate, vertically integrated organizations that reported directly to Qadhafi and his top security advisors, or consisted of an overlapping and integrated network that provided a carefully controlled system of checks and balances. Of these institutions, the most important has been the *maktab ma'lumat al-qa'id* (the Intelligence Bureau of the Leader) that is located within Bab al-Aziziyya, the military compound in Tripoli that serves as a residence for the Libyan leader as well. It was created, in the early 1970s, with the help of the East German Ministry for State Security and coordinates the intelligence for all other security organizations. It organizes as well the activities of the *al-ishtikhbarat al-askariyya* (the Military Secret Service), and has been headed by a close confidant of Qadhafi, Ahmad Ramadan al-Asabiyya, who is also responsible for the Leader's personal security. The Jamahiriyya Security Organization (*hai'at amn al-jamahiriyya*), with its division into internal and external security branches, has been under the control of Abdullah al-Sanusi and includes several of the regime's most trusted supporters. The latter became a leading figure in the *al-mathaba al-alamiyya* (officially known as the "World Center for the Fight Against Imperialism, Racism, and Fascism") that was involved in the persecution of Libyan opposition movements in exile throughout the 1980s.[9] In addition to these, a number of other organizations such as the Revolutionary Guards (*al-Haras al-Thawri*), the People's Guard (*al-Haras al-Sha'bi*), and the Purification Committees (*lijan al-tathir*) were created in the late 1980s and early 1990s to provide additional security.

In addition to these security organizations, the informal mechanisms of power and authority in Libya include a number of organizations that were never constitutionally defined. The first, and most important, of these remains the Free Unionist Officers' Movement (*rabitat al-dubbat al-ahrar al-wahdawiyin*) whose members still occupy central positions within the armed forces, tracing their legitimacy back to the early years of the revolution. Estimated at roughly sixty to eighty members, their backgrounds, rooted in different tribes, have been instrumental in stabilizing the country since the revolution. In addition to the remaining members of the original RCC, the *rabitat* also includes individuals like Ahmed Abu Lifa, Muhammad al-Sadiq, and Yusuf Dibri – an intimate of the Leader's entourage since their enrollment at the Benghazi Military College – and Sayyid Muhammad Qadhaf al-Dam, a nephew of the Leader. As a measure of their importance, several Free Unionist Officers (an estimated sixteen in

2005) are in charge of the *sha'biyat*, with Sayyid Qadhaf al-Dam heading the strategically important *Sirt sha'biyat*.

A second informal circle are the *rabitat rifaq al-Qadhafi* (the Forum of Companions of Qadhafi). Headed by Ibrahim Ibjad, the Forum is estimated to contain roughly 100 members who are routinely tapped for filling important and sensitive civilian posts – such as diplomatic posts, university and research institute directorships, and other executive positions. In addition to Ibjad, the Forum contains individuals like Muhammad Aqil and Muhammad Khalil. Aqil became the first director as well of the Green Book Center – the Jamahiriyya's most privileged institution for the dissemination of the *Green Book* ideology – and was succeeded by Ibjad.

The third informal organization is the *lijan al-qiyada al-sha'biya al-ijtima'iya* (People's Social Leadership Committees). First announced by Qadhafi as a new organization in Darna in 1994, the Leadership Committees have grown in size and importance, and consist of heads of families or prominent individuals within the country's regions. Their purpose is to help maintain social stability within the Jamahiriyya by controlling both family and tribal members. Their role, originally limited to social control, was expanded after 1996 to include the distribution of state subsidies and the provision of legal documents. Headed by a General Coordinator who is normally a high-ranking member of the military, the People's Social Leadership Committee system is an increasingly powerful informal mechanism that can be used by the Leader to balance the political system further when needed.

The last group of informal organizations consists of relatives of the Leader, as well as of members of the Qadhadfa and affiliated tribes. These include Brigadier Ahmed Qadhaf al-Dam and his brother Sayyid, nephews of Qadhafi. The former has been Chief Commander of the Cyrenaica region since 1995 while the latter (since March 2004) has been the General Coordinator of the People's Social Leadership Committees. In this function, Sayyid Qadhaf al-Dam, according to the Leader, is his successor if he should die. Other individuals around Qadhafi include Colonel Khalifa Hanaish and Colonel Abdullah al-Sanusi, head of the country's security since 1992. Finally, a number of individuals from the Qadhafa tribe, as well as from the Warfalla and Maqarha tribes, have obtained high positions within the Revolutionary Committee movement, or have been put in charge of politically insecure areas like Darna. The infiltration of growing numbers of these individuals, particularly into the security organizations, has led some observers to describe the phenomenon as a "re-tribalization" of Libya.[10]

In sum, the bifurcation between the Jamahiriyya's formal and informal mechanisms of control and political power accentuate once more the limited institutional control Libyan citizens have had over their country's ruler and his actions. In effect, unless the country's leadership clearly approves, there is no public control or accountability provided. The GPC, as the embodiment of the country's formal institution for governing, has control neither over the country's security or justice organizations, nor over those (like the General People's Committee – the Cabinet) that represents it. Within the non-formal institutions of the country's security organizations, the Revolutionary Leadership makes all decisions and has no accountability to anyone. Despite the March 1977 Declaration of the Authority of the People, the Revolutionary Leadership since then has been, and remains until today, the supreme authority of the Jamahiriyya. Whatever corrective actions were taken after 1986 did not in any way constitute a retreat from control by the country's Revolutionary Leadership.

THE ECONOMIC SANCTIONS AND THEIR IMPACT

In the years between December 1979 – when Libya had been put on the US State Department's first list of state sponsors of terrorism – and the April 1986 US bombing of Tripoli and Benghazi, several developments in the deteriorating relationship between the United States and the Jamahiriyya had taken place. These included the closure of the US embassy in Tripoli and of the People's Bureau in Washington, the embargo of crude oil and then of refined petroleum products from Libya, and, finally, in January 1986, the comprehensive trade embargo against the Jamahiriyya. Six years later, in April 1992, the United Nations as well would extend an economic embargo after Libya refused to turn over suspects involved in the December 1988 Pan Am 103 bombing over Lockerbie (see below).

In order to understand the impact of both sets of economic sanctions against the Jamahiriyya, several factors of a different nature must be assessed to comprehend their real impact on the decisions Libyan policy-makers took during these years and beyond.[11] An initial point to consider is that, during the period analyzed in this chapter, Libya's overall economic performance steadily worsened. One aspect certainly was the decline of oil prices starting in the early 1980s, made worse by the dramatic plunge in 1986 when the Reagan administration imposed its first set of sanctions. With revenues from oil exports – which still made up 95% of the country's overall revenues – dramatically declining, and with the regime unwilling initially to cut back on military expenditures, the curbs on imports forced Libya to abandon a number of important projects that under the announced *infitah* would have led to a greater diversification of the economy. The country drew down its international reserves, sought to conclude a number of barter deals rather than paying in cash for projects, and committed less money to making payments on its trade debts. A second point to consider is the impact of the economic directives of *The Green Book* during the regime's revolutionary decade, described above. While Libya may have outspent most other oil exporters in the region during the 1986–2001 period, its economic performance consistently lagged behind countries that were exposed to similar oil shocks. The turmoil surrounding *The Green Book*'s economic directives must be blamed to a large extent for that economic downturn.

In light of these two factors, the direct impact of the US unilateral sanctions between 1986 and 1992 was relatively small. Its importance, therefore, was not so much in influencing Libyan economic decisions directly – although it did so on a few occasions – but rather in heightening the country's vulnerability to the multilateral sanctions that were to follow in the 1990s, and in forcing Libya to conclude deals with economic partners, particularly in the oil industry, it would normally have eschewed. Despite the fact that the United States had been the single largest importer of Libyan oil in 1981, the 1982 ban on imports of Libyan crude had been offset by the country's ability to sell to the European market, and by its ability to bring crude onto the US market via the spot market or as a refined product. Even the banning of products from the Ras al-Unuf refinery in late 1985 had not led to significant damage to Libya's oil sales: the country was readily able to market its highly sought-after crude and refined oil to Germany and Italy. Within the first thirteen months after the US ban, Great Britain increased its imports of Libyan crude by 350%, and Libya started to export to new trading partners like Turkey and Brazil.[12]

Greater damage was done, however, by the impact of the US ban on the country's investment pattern. Since the early 1980s, Libya had started to invest considerable amounts of money in downstream activities in Europe, acquiring a network of gasoline stations across western and eastern Europe, Egypt, and Malta, in addition to refineries for its oil. These investments had been made in part in anticipation of, and in part as a reaction to, the US ban, in order to guarantee that the country would be able to find steady outlets for its oil. There was, in addition, a political dimension to these investments as well: Tripoli clearly considered that they would help to solidify closer relations with Europe. Once the US ban had been expanded to all exports to the Jamahiriyya, the impact on Libya became more onerous as the country faced the withholding of aviation technology, airplane parts, and other types of high technology for its oil industry. In 1983 alone, the United States had vetoed almost $600 million worth of large civil aircraft export licenses to the country. Libya proved able to secure most of these embargoed imports from other sources, but at a considerably higher cost.

Similarly, the 1986 freeze of all Libyan foreign assets in the United States was relatively benign since Libya had been careful not to make substantial investments in the country, and had shifted most of its liquid assets to other venues in anticipation of US measures. Overall, it was estimated that less than 2% of Libya's total overseas investments of roughly $5 billion were affected.[13] United States pressure on international lending agencies to avoid extending loans to Libya also proved at best a minor irritant since the Jamahiriyya either was not eligible to borrow from the World Bank because of its relative wealth, or simply refused to do so. In part because of political considerations, but also because of a lack of sophistication in managing its financial fluctuations, Libyan policymakers, rather than increasing the country's foreign debt to offset balance-of-payments deficits, simply ran down its foreign reserves, cut back on imports, temporarily suspended payment of trade debts, or swapped oil for imported goods. Hence, Libya's foreign debt remained quite small throughout the 1980s and into the 1990s. The US sanctions and Libya's unorthodox methods of meeting its financial obligations had further effects on the country's economy. Some western export credit agencies refused to extend further government medium- and long-term credits to the country and some banks, shipping companies, and assorted international companies reviewed their exposure to Libya – wary of the country's reputation for unpredictability and of the chaos brought about by *The Green Book*'s directives.

Until the imposition of the multilateral sanctions in April 1992, Libya's oil production and export levels remained in line with its OPEC quota. The LNOC assumed operation of the oilfields once run by US companies as soon as Washington announced the sanctions. As a result, when US companies were told in 1986 to curtail their operations in producing and marketing almost one-third of Libya's oil for the European market, the LNOC readily took over the responsibility. But most observers agreed that the Libyan oil sector was in urgent need of modernization, in part because some of the fields had been producing since the 1950s and needed new recovery technology.[14] US technology, know-how, and equipment had been instrumental in building and maintaining the Libyan oil industry since the 1950s. The LNOC not only had difficulty acquiring the needed spare parts as the unilateral sanctions were put into place, but simply did not have the needed expertise and technological knowledge to maintain production at a steady level. In addition, many European firms proved reluctant to provide that expertise and manpower, despite a number of "gentlemen's agreements" between them and the US government to watch over claims of American companies in the country.

In fact, the gradually emerging problems in Libya's oil industry were perhaps more due to the fact that some of the older oilfields were inevitably deteriorating, to the fact that Libya had neglected to sufficiently invest in the industry after taking over international oil operations in 1973, to the fact that the EPSA II provisions proved unable to attract much interest for exploration beyond the existing fields (see below), and to Libya's overall reputation. Even the reality that the LNOC had always remained outside the purview of the revolutionary measures advocated by *The Green Book* proved of little assurance to many international companies.

Overall, the US sanctions on Libya's oil sector by themselves had an almost negligible direct impact – Libya would unlikely have had the capability to produce substantially more oil during the 1980s even if the sanctions had not existed. The regulations under the Iran Libya Sanctions Act (ILSA) of 1996 (see below) proved of marginal value in deterring investment. Investment patterns in Libya hardly changed after its passage, due in large part to the fact that the country – except for a major overhaul of some of its infrastructure – was not in need of substantial investment that would have superseded the $40 million limit imposed by ILSA. In addition, companies simply amended old contracts to accommodate new investments, and avoided signing new contracts that could have triggered ILSA regulations. But the combination of ILSA and previous sanctions did create an environment in which the long-term prospects for the country's oil industry became more closely circumscribed, and the earlier set of US sanctions made the country's economy overall more sensitive (if not vulnerable) to additional pressures that would soon materialize in the form of multilateral sanctions. In many ways the US sanctions magnified the overall existing problems in Libya's oil sector, creating greater uncertainty in the process.

The seven-year period of multilateral sanctions (April 1992 to April 1999) against Libya, combined with existing conditions within the country, proved much more damaging than the US sanctions alone had been. Libya's economy grew only 0.8% a year during the period, and the country's per capita GDP fell from $7,311 to $5,896 at the same time.[15] In 1998 alone, the country's export earnings had dropped to roughly $7 billion, the lowest since the oil price crash of 1986. The financial impact of the multilateral sanctions had, as in the case of the US unilateral ones, been mitigated by shifting Libyan assets away from vulnerable locations. But, as a result, Libya's ability to earn income abroad hampered its ability to pay foreign companies. In the more restrictive economic climate of the 1990s this proved a much bigger irritant than it had been in the previous decade, forcing Libya to limit trade further, and making it more difficult to secure short-term credit at a time when oil prices continued to decline.

Undoubtedly, however, the trade restrictions of the multilateral sanctions proved much more difficult to deal with. Adjusting and shifting trade patterns, as Libya had done previously, no longer proved possible under the multilateral sanctions. The ban on imports affected particularly Libya's downstream oil operations and its aviation industry. Its inability to obtain equipment for the maintenance of its refineries forced Libya to search for substitute technology and parts (often on the black market) that were often suboptimal, and were several times more expensive than normal international market prices. It also made it necessary for Libya to forgo upgrading its refineries, making it impossible to produce more gasoline for domestic consumption. It also meant that Libya had to spend increasingly scarce foreign reserves on purchasing lighter fuels abroad rather than being able to use its own best-quality crude for producing more lucrative high-end fuels. The country's airline industry was also dramatically affected: with a halt in passenger traffic, a shortage of spare parts, and a deteriorating technical capability, the damage went far beyond the estimated financial loss of $900 million during the period.[16]

The uncertainty surrounding the sanctions proved, as always, to make matters worse. Subject to review by the Security Council every four months, the fear of additional, more stringent measures, as well as the continued pressure from the United States for such actions, proved a deterrent in several ways. The value of the Libyan dinar declined, and inflationary pressures were exacerbated by the fact that all commodities had to be brought into the country overland or by sea, and by the growing pressure of a burgeoning black market. The sanctions also forced Libya to maintain an unnecessarily high level of reserves, not knowing whether additional sanctions would be imposed. With domestic investment virtually halted, the government was forced to curtail several development projects and the country suffered shortages of foreign exchange throughout the period of the multilateral sanctions. In addition, the continuing uncertainties, the lack of international flights into the country, the sheer inconvenience of gaining access to the country, and the lack of financial resources to devote to it forced Libya to forgo developing several sectors it had marked for that purpose under its *infitah* strategy. Perhaps the most obvious was tourism. With its archaeological treasures and Mediterranean coastline, Libya stood potentially to gain billions of dollars in tourist revenues that had been left untapped – albeit, deliberately – by the Qadhafi government in the past. As one source points out, "the extent to which sanctions helped suppress these numbers [of visitors] is evident when the volume of travelers to Libya in 1995 (85,000) is compared with that in 2001 (190,000), the first full year after the suspension of sanctions."[17]

As a result of the sanctions, international companies grew more reluctant to work in Libya, and the premium required for their services reflected the high price the country paid. As described below, within the energy sector Libya proved able to continue attracting largely western and eastern European investment, but on some occasions it had to rely on companies it would, except for the sanctions, have avoided. Several of these were small- to medium-sized companies, with limited production capabilities or services, which preferred to invest in projects with short-term pay-offs rather than the more complex and long-term agreements the Libyan government hoped to conclude in order to expand exploration beyond the Sirt Basin. As the country's oil infrastructure aged, as the sanctions started to impinge on the ability of the country to get cutting-edge technology, and as production leveled off, Libya's oil industry often relied on second-rate technologies and proved able to attract only a few companies that had sufficient know-how for the kind of enhanced oil recovery techniques it needed.

The oilfields that had been taken over from US companies by the LNOC slowly declined in production as Libya struggled to manage them with increasingly outdated US equipment. Production from LNOC-operated fields declined on average 8% annually after the take-over. Finally, Libya also hoped to exploit its enormous, and largely unexploited, natural gas reserves – primarily for the European market, but also to substitute natural gas for oil on the domestic market. Although several companies expressed an interest, it was clear that interest among international companies remained limited as long as the sanctions were in place. LNOC in 1993 ultimately signed a large $5.5 billion joint venture for development of the Western Libyan Gas Project with one of its oldest customers, Italy's AGIP-ENI. It involved an undersea pipeline – since constructed – to bring the gas, via Sicily, to Italy. Agip-ENI argued that, since the original contract had been signed in 1993, it was exempted from ILSA's regulations. The controversy surrounding the contract, however, ensured that further development of the country's enormous natural gas fields would remain suspended until more propitious times made international investments possible again.

Exports of Libyan oil remained the country's sole economic lifeline. Not surprisingly therefore, the country's leaders went to enormous lengths to try and minimize the impact of the US and multilateral sanctions on its oil industry. During this period of internal turmoil and of open confrontation with the West, Libya's hydrocarbon sector, as always, remained to the largest extent possible insulated from ongoing events. Much as during the monarchy and the years since 1969, petroleum affairs continued to be managed in a technocratic manner by the LNOC. But it was impossible of course that this relative isolation, and the LNOC's traditionally independent decision-making, would not be affected by the larger political turmoil the country found itself in – particularly as a substantial part of the sanctions targeted the oil sector of the country directly.

Between 1974 and 1988, exploration and the granting of concessions in the Libyan oil sector had been subject to the stipulations of EPSA I and EPSA II. During that time, the attractiveness of Libyan oil – to the United States and to Europe – had allowed LNOC to wring concessions from the consortiums and multinational oil companies on terms that were highly favorable to the country, despite the first few years of the US unilateral sanctions. The announcement of EPSA II in 1979 was a sign that the Libyan government had become preoccupied with the depletion of proven reserves, and with the need to make new discoveries of oil. Despite the first six years of the Reagan administration's embargo, until 1988, Libya's production-sharing arrangements differed substantially from those then applicable in most other oil producers throughout the world – and the LNOC remained confident that it could maintain those profitable arrangements in the future.

By 1988, when EPSA III was announced, however, the internal and international conditions that had informed LNOC policies had started to change quite dramatically, not so much as a result of the US sanctions as due to the downturn of oil prices in the international market. As a result of these low prices, and of the multilateral sanctions after mid-1992, for the next decade LNOC directors would be forced to make decisions they clearly considered suboptimal for Libya's oil industry and infrastructure. Elf Aquitaine, the French parastatal, withdrew from its operations in the 1980s as a result of the French–Libyan disagreement over Chad. The admittance of eastern European companies to help discover oil had been one early measure to help remedy the declining reserves in the country, but the decision had clearly been made out of necessity and was highly unpopular at LNOC. Despite this makeshift gesture and the appealing conditions of EPSA II contracts, they failed to solve the country's basic problem of insufficient exploration. Except for the eastern European companies, they also proved unable to attract many new companies despite the known existence of promising acreage.

In 1980, the Libyan government announced that it was negotiating with thirteen foreign consortiums or companies under EPSA II conditions – including Elf Aquitaine, Occidental, the Oasis Consortium, Coastal States (a US company), Deminex, and Wintershall (from Germany). By the end of the decade all of these except the German companies had left Libya. The major factor was of course the US government's decision in 1986 to order all US companies and citizens to leave the Jamahiriyya. The exit of the US companies – which, among others, included the Oasis Consortium, Conoco, Grace Petroleum, and Occidental – had more severe implications. While production was not immediately affected – since the day-to-day operations could be performed by Libyans who had gained production experience while working for western companies – LNOC's real concern was with the US decision's impact on exploration.

Libya was careful to ensure that the US companies that had left retained "suspended rights" to their concessions under so-called "standstill" agreements. Mindful of their early involvement in the development of the country's oil industry and their expertise and knowledge of the country's oilfields, LNOC officials were anxious to leave options open for the eventual return of the US companies. By 1988, all Major and independent US producers had left the country. In addition to the ones that left in 1986, Gulf and Phillips had earlier abandoned operations in 1970, Amoco in 1975, Esso in 1981, Nelson Bunker Hunt (nationalized) in 1973, and Texaco and Socal (the Amoseas partnership) in 1974. Of the non-US Majors, BP had been nationalized in 1973, and Shell would leave in 1991. In the wake of the companies' withdrawals throughout the years, the LNOC had by 1988 created four subsidiaries to manage the acreage of those companies that had left: the Arabian Gulf Corporation, the Sirt Oil Company, the Waha Oil Company, and the Zueitina Oil Company – the latter two to manage the Oasis and Occidental holdings, respectively.

Faced with the collapse of oil prices in the mid-1980s, low internal production, the effect of the economic sanctions, and financial difficulties linked to the considerable expenditures on the Great Man-made River

Project and the Misrata steel works, the government's EPSA III of early 1988 promised attractive conditions for both onshore and offshore acreage. Some of the terms of EPSA II – particularly cost recovery for the oil companies – were amended to entice new investors. The strategy partially paid off: by the end of 1995 there were two dozen foreign oil companies again operating in Libya. Many of the companies, however, were newcomers to the country's oil industry and had neither the experience nor – as the LNOC had pointed out – the capital required for large-scale exploration investments. This was only partly compensated for by the remaining presence of European companies who had been involved in Libya's oil sector for decades, and who increased their participation as the US companies left: AGIP, OMV (Austria's NOC), Wintershall, Veba (the German oil and petrochemical company), and the French company Total. Finally, the adjudication by the International Court of Justice of a dispute between Libya and Tunisia over an offshore boundary line led to a joint exploration company that would eventually open up Libya's only offshore area under EPSA III conditions to investors.[18]

In retrospect, EPSA III suffered also from the more general uncertainties created by the country's confrontation with the West. This had forced the LNOC to diversify its partners for exploration and operation purposes in ways it considered detrimental to the long-term health of the country's oil industry. Because of the nature of the development of its oil infrastructure – with enormous early discoveries in the Sirt Basin which, in 1995, still constituted 72% of the country's reserves – most exploration had remained limited to areas easily accessible to that early infrastructure. But the Libyan government had clearly intended EPSA III as an enticement for further, more remote exploration. This had, except for some small-scale efforts by a handful of eastern European companies, not happened. Throughout the 1990s, and particularly in 1999, there were consistent rumors that Libya would consider offering additional incentives under newly designed EPSA IV arrangements. It was perhaps symptomatic of the existing political and economic constraints until 1999, however, that these new arrangements would not emerge for several more years – until not only after Libya had been rehabilitated by the international community, but also when the United States as well had decided to abandon its sanctions (see Chapter 7).

Libya's economic fortunes, however, changed considerably in 1999. The suspension of the multilateral sanctions in April undoubtedly were one major factor. Not only did they remove actual constraints, but they also had the effect of lessening both the opprobrium for international companies in dealing with Libya and the climate of uncertainty that had prevailed. Equally important, however, was the upswing in international oil prices that took hold soon after the lifting of the sanctions, combined with a growing spare capacity in OPEC countries by the following year. After years of contraction and stagnation, growth returned once more to the Libyan economy, and inflation abated. As international investor confidence and oil prices kept rising, so did interest among non-US companies in returning to the Jamahiriyya. Aware of the changing international conditions, the LNOC strategically organized a number of international oil and gas conferences to entice investors further, and kept hinting at attractive conditions under new EPSA regulations.

ATTEMPTS AT ECONOMIC REFORM

The relaxation of some of the regime's revolutionary measures, particularly the curtailment of the Revolutionary Committees, was matched in the economic arena by an attempt to reduce the hardships of *The Green Book*'s directives regarding the role of the state and of private enterprise in the Jamahiriyya. If Qadhafi throughout 1986 and 1987 skillfully blended populist appeals with his usual blunt criticisms and exhortations for greater personal involvement with the revolution in his announcement of economic liberalization, Ahmad Jalud at the GPC Secretariat meeting of 18 July 1987 dissected the structural origins of Libya's economic difficulties in a more technocratic fashion. He pinpointed the persisting mismanagement of the economy, the difficulties in establishing coherent acquisition programs for the country in light of the growing impact of the economic boycott by the United States, high levels of inflation, and an inability to guarantee distribution of goods for both industrial and consumer purposes.[19]

Jalud's expose had captured the by now familiar dilemmas of development in oil states. Libya's first oil boom during the monarchy, as well as the oil booms of 1973 and 1979, had represented peculiar challenges to the country: how to efficiently use the sudden windfalls for purposes of general economic development. As in other oil exporters in the region, the sudden and massive inflows of wealth had led to the creation of an economic bureaucracy that was more attuned to the distribution of the country's riches rather than to the establishment of institutions meant to manage, arbitrate or regulate the state's use of its sudden revenues. To that extent, Libya's position was not significantly different from the benign neglect of state economic institutions that marked other oil exporters. But in the Jamahiriyya, this process of spending and of forgoing regulation to manage the local economy had gone far beyond simple benign neglect, and had been exacerbated and purposefully extended by Qadhafi's insistence that state institutions were to be smashed. The directives of *The Green Book*, the incessant waves of destabilization, and sometimes the physical destruction of the country's bureaucracies in effect had made Libya an economy where the maintenance of coalitions of supporters necessary for survival – ranging from army elites to Revolutionary Committees, to the country's citizens themselves – assumed a central role in adjudicating the distribution of revenues.

Even more than in other oil exporters of the region, the distribution of the country's revenues in this fashion, and the virtually unlimited spending even as economic clouds gathered on the horizon were meant to achieve political goals. The spending had implicitly imposed upon the country's citizens a social contract during the boom years, which, in return for political quiescence, promised that the state would take care of citizens' daily economic needs. Under those arrangements, a profound economic crisis for the state threatens to become a political one – for if the state can not longer keep its promise, why should citizens keep their end of a bargain foisted upon them during times when revenues run high?

The economic and political reforms in Libya after 1986 were therefore intrinsically linked – for real economic liberalization and reform would have meant the introduction of markets and competitive market processes that inevitably create conflicts between citizens about access to economic resources. Markets also invariably create disparities in income. Indeed, it was to avoid both phenomena – which Qadhafi viewed as detrimental to citizen interaction in a political community – that *The Green Book* had eschewed a reliance on market mechanisms. Economic liberalization efforts in Libya therefore represented a fourfold challenge to the regime: a need to create new institutions to regulate better and make economic transactions more transparent, to reform institutions whose primary goal often focused on simply distributing revenues gathered by the state, to introduce markets and competition for resources, and, finally, to contain whatever political fall-out the three previous sets of measures might entail.

Qadhafi clearly understood the implications of what a sustained economic liberalization effort would mean. In earlier comments on *infitah* (liberalization) strategies in other Arab countries, he had caustically noted that it represented a failure to make local economies work, and would lead to a new form of economic colonialism:

You will see that those who have failed to resolve their economic problems in their countries and who couldn't mobilize popular forces for the development and for the exploitation of the country's resources turn ... toward *infitah*, as in Egypt. They open the gates to foreign exploitative capital, to sumptuous palaces, to American corporations, to multinationals. In this way they compensate for the accumulated defeats by throwing themselves into the arms of economic colonialism.[20]

Despite these reservations, Libya embarked upon its own *infitah* in two distinct waves: a first attempt between 1987 and 1990, followed by a second set of initiatives after 1990. The overall objectives were to reduce state involvement in the country's economy, and to promote greater efficiency by concentrating on two distinct goals. These consisted of encouraging private sector initiatives in all sectors of the economy except heavy industry, and of achieving significant cuts in state spending, in part by reducing the country's traditional heavy outlay for subsidies in all sectors. When the first wave of *infitah* was announced in March 1987, state intervention in the local economy was pervasive. Despite the pretensions of popular management, all manufacturing, foreign and domestic retail trade, agriculture, and service provisions were highly centralized. Roughly two dozen trading companies were in charge of all manufacturing, industrial and agricultural imports, as well as those of foodstuffs and consumer goods. An estimated 70–75% of all Libyans were employees of the state. The creation of state supermarkets – called "popular markets" – in the 1970s had extended state control down to the retail level. As in many centrally managed economies – but exacerbated because of the ready availability of resources – the country's economy was highly inefficient, marked by low productivity, and extremely high labor costs for almost exclusively foreign labor in all sectors. Despite the country's wealth, living standards had steadily declined since the mid-1970s.

The first set of reforms centered around the introduction of *tashrukiyya* (self-management) enterprises that allowed for the creation of cooperatives despite the earlier legislation of "partners, not wage-earners" announced in the 1970s. Within one year, approximately 140 medium- and small-scale enterprises had been created that, at least in principle, no longer enjoyed state subsidies. Simultaneously, the ban against the retail trade was lifted, allowing private shops to re-open. In September 1988, the state's monopoly on imports and exports was abandoned, as well as subsidies on tea, flour, salt, and wheat. Farmers' markets – officially abandoned but reluctantly tolerated during the revolutionary decade – reappeared. Professionals were allowed to resume private practices, even though the government maintained its role in setting fees.

The measures taken after 1990 were meant to reinforce and extend this earlier wave of reforms. Qadhafi now argued publicly for a clear distinction between the private sector and the state, in order to "take the burden off public institutions."[21] He suggested the closing of unprofitable state enterprises, the imposition of higher fees for state-provided services like water and electricity, and a reduction of the number of state employees. In a measure that some Libyans viewed as a means to curtail the growing power of the GPC, Qadhafi proposed a further populist measure: a decentralization of the country that would shift the administrative burdens and expenses away from the major coastal cities into smaller administrative communities responsible for their own budgets. The GPC simultaneously adopted a number of laws that provided for joint-stock companies, creating the ability to open foreign currency accounts and to obtain import permits for private companies. For that purpose, a number of state and commercial banks were created. Hoping to capture some of the capital flows that sustained the informal economy, special laws were passed to offer protection for reinvested capital. The second wave's final directives, in the Spring and Summer of 1993, focused on efforts to promote tourism – hoping to capitalize on the country's desert and archaeological sites – and to provide greater guarantees for foreign investment. Convertibility of the Libyan dinar was taken up by the GPC in January 1994 but remained unaddressed for the time being.[22]

On the surface, the number and range of measures suggested in the adopted legislation would have made the Libyan *infitah* one of the most dramatic in the region's history of economic reform during the 1980s and 1990s. It would also have dramatically recalibrated the position of the state within the economy and, by implication, altered the way in which the regime could use economic patronage for its own political goals and, ultimately, for its survival. Starting in early 1988, the Jamahiriyya's official gazette and the GPC proceedings included a wide array of regulations meant to speed up the reform process. The reality, however, contrasted sharply with the proposed intentions. Most of the adopted laws were never implemented, although some private traders returned, suspicious and reluctantly, to re-open their businesses. Few, however, proved willing to take serious risks amidst the remaining uncertainties and unpredictability of economic and political life in the Jamahiriyya. They opted instead for small-scale economic activities – usually of a service nature – that carried low risks and required little private investment. There was no evidence that the new *tashrukiyya* enterprises ever operated as envisioned, and similarly little evidence that a real retreat of the state took place. Although some subsidies were lowered, the proposals for increased fees for government services were never implemented. Whatever cutbacks took place were often put on the shoulders of the country's foreign labor, in effect protecting the country's own consumers.

From 1987 through 1989 Libya consistently ran trade deficits that were only turned around by rising oil prices in 1989 when the country's current account moved once more into the black, bringing its international reserves to $5.8 billion. Despite the announced changes in the country's banking system, the Jamahiriyya's commercial banks were non-functioning, and would only be revived almost fifteen years later. Banks in general supported public enterprises at the behest of the ministries to which public enterprises were consigned – and thus indirectly at the discretion of the Qadhafi government. In effect, the liberalization waves' impact could perhaps best be described as a subterfuge – where a hesitating, newly created private sector was allowed to provide and distribute what the state through its inefficient distribution system of state supermarkets could not deliver to Libyan citizens, leaving the state in charge of the distribution of welfare provisions. As a result, Libya by the mid-1990s was filled once more with the kind of consumer goods and food supplies it had enjoyed before the revolutionary decade. The lack of confidence in the local economy, however, was demonstrated by the fact that for most everyday purchases the US dollar had become the currency of choice.

THE LESSONS OF FAILED REFORMS

The failure of the country's *infitah* strategies revealed in stark fashion the deleterious impact of the long-term neglect of the economy, and of the impact of the revolutionary measures on the economy and on the country's political system. In addition, as one of the country's top policymakers admitted in retrospect, reform of the economy was unlikely to take place under the difficult circumstances that resulted from the sanc-tions.[23] The Jamahiriyya faced profound obstacles to economic reform not only because of lack of regulation, but also because it simply could not afford to devote the necessary energy under the circumstances to attempt serious reforms. Until the downturn of oil revenues in the mid-1980s, the country's income was primarily distributed to keep a large array of coalitions loyal, and to pursue the development of a few high-profile projects – the Man-made River Project, the Misrata steel works, and the Ras al-Unuf petrochemical complex – and the remainder was spent on military hardware and foreign adventures. By the end of the 1990s, the country's economic concerns were much wider and included what several of the country's own top technocrats, including its reformist-minded prime minister, saw as a possible major downturn in the country's economy unless real reform took place.[24] In desperation, the GPC in 1997 adopted Law #5 that allowed for foreign direct investment in the country. But it was a sign of the times that the measure generated virtually no response.

Libya's economic *dirigisme*, once imposed according to Qadhafi's *Green Book* precisely to avoid the economic differentiation and the intense struggles that regulating private sector activities entails in market economies, could no longer be sustained – as a result of the economy's inefficiencies, the rampant corruption, and the growing impact of the multilateral sanctions. But the challenges to the country's economic and political mechanisms were enormous after decades of centralization and lack of regulation. The very purpose of the country's *infitah* was to introduce market mechanisms. Such a move would have necessitated on the part of the country's rulers an attempt to create functioning regulatory and administrative institutions that could support a market economy. It would have necessitated the creation and maintenance of institutions that could provide economic information and incentives, and a legal system that could efficiently enforce regulations. A sustained *infitah* in Libya would, at least temporarily, have meant a greater involvement by the state to make an economic transition possible – to tax, to collect and disseminate information, to dispense law, and to define and enforce property rights. This "perfection of the state" very clearly was unacceptable to Qadhafi whose basic philosophical tenet focused on the lessening of the state's impact on citizens' lives.

Furthermore, in Libya since independence, the country's rulers had deliberately fostered policies that limited an active, interventionist role for the country's institutions and bureaucracies. The king had done so as a policy of benign laissez-faire; Qadhafi had pursued his concept of statelessness in a more deliberate manner that, ironically and paradoxically, brought all aspects of the economy under state control. Indeed, the 1977 Sabha announcement, *The Green Book*'s stipulations on private property, and the economic exclusion of citizens during the country's revolutionary period had all been meant to destroy the institutions that would now have to be created or re-created to pursue a real *infitah*.

In addition, the *dirigisme* of the country's economy had also become an important mechanism of control for the Qadhafi government. The nature of the economy and the use of the country's resources had in effect made most Libyans superfluous to the daily management of the economy. The Libyan leader had spent considerable effort to maintain the economic fortunes of various groups of supporters – by instituting tariffs, by restrictions on imports and exports, and by licensing procedures that benefited favored groups. This had been done in a careful fashion as Qadhafi remained highly suspicious of any corporate or organized group whose interests could coalesce. By deliberately avoiding a reliance on a market system that had the potential to create groups of individuals with differing economic interests and prowess, Qadhafi's economic strategy had become tightly intertwined with the pursuit of egalitarianism, one of the regime's major political goals. Since egalitarianism had provided such a *Leitmotiv* for the revolution, a sustained liberalization that provoked inequalities could easily be exploited by the opposition, particularly by the Islamists, for their own purposes.

Not surprisingly, local reactions to the country's attempts at reform and liberalization revealed the interests and power of different constituencies in Libya. The initial phase met with little resistance since the liberalization of trade and the end of import regulations benefited consumers and small entrepreneurs who were now free to import food and consumer goods from abroad. This first set of measures also did not affect the fortunes of those groups deemed vital to the Libyan leader's maintenance of power: the country's top technocrats within LNOC and other privileged and protected state institutions, managers of state enterprises, the military and those entrepreneurs with close links to the military. Indeed, the first phase strengthened their fortunes: they could now more easily gain access to credit, engage openly in import and export transactions, and use more readily available foreign currency for major capital goods imports. Paradoxically therefore, the lack of regulation that accompanied the first wave of reform brought about an even greater degree of economic stratification. Small retail merchants and entrepreneurs did not have equal access to capital and, as a result, restricted their operations to food, services that required little capital, and to consumer goods imported from neighboring countries.

The second wave, if implemented, would have hurt virtually all groups in the country – but particularly the one singled out above as the nucleus of the regime's supporters. Real import regulations and free access for everyone to a liberalized banking system, for example, would have ended the economic riches provided to those who could obtain licenses. For the average Libyan the second wave proved unwelcome as well. The loss of wage policies and subsidies that had maintained their standard of living (at a relatively low level) would perhaps disappear. The idea, furthermore, of becoming entrepreneurs in a political system that had been marked for almost two decades by high levels of unpredictability produced little enthusiasm. The Qadhafi government had fostered this unpredictability, and had implicitly, through its distributive policies, fostered citizens' inclinations to avoid personal initiative and risk. In the end, no group in Libya considered the *infitah* strategies in their interest. The average citizen, the small entrepreneurs, and those still working in the agricultural sector were inherently suspicious of a reduction of the elaborate welfare functions of the state that provided a risk-free, albeit limited, existence. To the central supporters of the regime an open market system could only mean the potential loss of privileges.

Finally, the *infitah* strategies came at a time when the regime felt particularly beleaguered. They would have meant loosening some of the tools it had created to manage Libyan citizens and to prevent opposition. The potential development of groups with similar economic interests that they were willing to defend opened up the possibility of opposition. Qadhafi clearly pinpointed the political dangers of economic liberalization in his speeches, as well as its undesirable cultural side effects that would diminish his attempts at egalitarianism. Many of his actions in the wake of the *infitah* announcements showed his clear opposition to those hierarchical institutions a sustained liberalization effort would entail. In a highly publicized event after the announcement of the first liberalization measures, he continued his populist measures, publicly destroying thousands of land records and deeds to private houses in Tripoli, proposing to hand over the country's oil revenues directly to the people, encouraging black-market activities as instruments of popular power, and proposing home education for all children.[25]

CONFRONTATION, TERRORISM, AND SANCTIONS

President Reagan's warning in the wake of his invocation of the International Emergency Economic Powers Act in early 1986 – that the United States would take additional steps to confront the Qadhafi regime if needed – quickly became reality. A bomb explosion on 4 April 1986 at a discotheque in West Berlin frequented by US servicemen was blamed on Libyan operatives. Two weeks later, on 15–16 April the United States bombed Tripoli and Benghazi, leaving one of the Libyan leader's adopted daughters dead at Bab al-Aziziyya. The raid on Libya – codenamed Operation El Dorado Canyon – came within hours after the European Union had reached an agreement to reduce the number of Libyan diplomats in Europe, and to reduce dramatically their own number in the Jamahiriyya. As part of their agreement, they also adopted more restrictive visa requirements for Libyans traveling to Europe. International cooperation to act against Libya came within two weeks after the US bombing when the leaders of the G7 issued a declaration at their Tokyo meeting to fight terrorism, singling out Libya as the main responsible party. The declaration involved as well limits on arms to the Jamahiriyya, further limits on diplomatic activities of countries involved in terrorism, and improved extradition procedures for bringing suspected terrorists to trial. Despite the killing of Yvonne Fletcher in April 1984, however, even Britain's Prime Minister Thatcher, a close ally of the US in its fight against terrorism, resisted economic sanctions on the grounds that an embargo could readily be circumvented by other countries.

The bombing of Tripoli and Benghazi marked the apotheosis of the US–Libyan confrontation. In its wake, the regime seemingly reevaluated its policies. Through a number of diplomatic initiatives, Qadhafi attempted to break the country's diplomatic isolation within the region and vis-à-vis Europe. In 1987, after the humiliating defeat by Chadian forces just north of the Aouzou strip, Libya withdrew from the country and agreed to submit its claim to the contested territory to the International Court of Justice. This brought the long-festering conflict that dated back to the monarchy to an end, temporarily improving French– Libyan relations. At the same time, the Libyan leader participated in the creation of the Arab Maghreb Union in 1989, meant to construct an economic community among the North African countries. In a number of speeches when he finally reappeared in public, Qadhafi announced the country's intention to withdraw from its earlier activism. President Reagan's successor, George H. W. Bush, temporarily shifted toward a less confrontational policy with Libya, maintaining economic pressure on the country nevertheless. After what seemed like a temporary lull, the United States in September 1988, however, accused Libya of manufacturing chemical weapons at Rabta – a charge that soon would be extended to an accusation that Libya was pursuing weapons of mass destruction.

It was, however, the explosion of the Pan Am flight 103 over Lockerbie on 21 December 1988, followed by the 19 September 1989 explosion of the French UTA 772 airliner over Niger, that propelled the antagonism between the West and Libya to a new and more coordinated level.[26] In late 1991, the United States and Great Britain indicted two Libyan security officials, Abdel Basset Ali Muhammad al-Megrahi and Al-Amin Khalifa Fhimah, for their alleged involvement in the bombing. Joined by France, which similarly indicted four Libyan intelligence officers in the UTA flight 772 bombing, the three countries asked for the surrender of those charged with the crime. In January 1992, under the chairmanship of Great Britain, the United Nations Security Council (UNSC)

Figure 6. The Lockerbie bombing in December 1988 marked the apotheosis of the Libyan regime's involvement with international terrorism and, in retrospect, marked a turning point in the regime's use of international adventurism for its political purposes.

unanimously passed Resolution 731, calling on Libya to comply with the three countries' demands for the extradition of suspects. Several weeks later, the UNSC passed Resolution 748 once more requesting the handing over of the suspects, and threatened further sanctions if Libya failed to comply within two weeks. When Libya rejected the demands as a violation of its national sovereignty, the UNSC on 15 April 1992 banned all international flights into the Jamahiriyya, and issued an embargo on all arms sales. Under the resolution, the sanctions could only be lifted if Libya surrendered the Lockerbie suspects, and ceased all forms of support for terrorism. It further called on Libya to pay compensation for the victims if the two suspects were found guilty.

With Libya resolutely refusing to turn over the suspects, the UN sanctions were renewed on a three-monthly basis. In the United States, Congress – urged on by a number of groups, including the Families of Pan Am 103 – exerted pressure on the Clinton administration to strengthen the US sanctions further. In November 1993, finally, the UNSC passed Resolution 883 that included additional bans on the sale of certain oil technology and equipment to Libya. Significantly, however, the United States had not been able to include a total embargo of Libyan oil exports. But in August 1996 the US Congress, in the most damaging measure so far, adopted the Iran and Libya Sanctions Act (ILSA). It further constrained international trade with the Jamahiriyya, and included provisions for sanctions against foreign companies dealing with or investing more than $40 million in Libya's oil industry – leading to a dispute with Europe over the legality of the ILSA provisions.[27]

The unease of the European countries and the gradual violation of the ban on flights into Libya – particularly by African leaders – indicated that by 1998 the international isolation of Libya was slowly starting to crumble. In September 1997, the Arab League asked its members to take measures that would alleviate the sanctions against Libya, and the Organization of African States in June 1998 announced that its members would no longer enforce the UN sanctions unless the United States and Great Britain agreed to hold the trial of the Lockerbie suspects in a neutral country – one of the conditions under which Libya was willing to compromise with the UNSC. In August 1998, the United States and Britain, seeking a compromise as well to stem the erosion of the sanctions, agreed to have the trial take place in The Hague. After some additional wrangling, Libya handed over the two suspects in April 1999 to the Netherlands.

The outcome of the trial on 31 January 2001 – which found al-Megrahi guilty but acquitted Fhimah – opened up a slight rift between the United States and Great Britain on one hand, and between the United States and the remainder of the international community on the other, based on the perception that US policy was in part governed by strong domestic interests. The pressure from the Lockerbie families proved highly effective within the United States, but was viewed as emblematic of, and an extension of, a history of bad US–Libyan relations that far predated the Lockerbie incident. As Libya promised compensation for the victims of UTA flight 722, compensation to the relatives of Yvonne Fletcher, and incentives to international investors, the United States called on Libya to meet the other demands it had put forward, including taking responsibility for its officials' actions in the Lockerbie bombing and providing adequate compensation. The United States acquiesced to the suspension of UN sanctions, but ruled out having the US sanctions officially lifted until all conditions were met. Pressure from Congress led to the renewal of ILSA legislation and, for the time being, rendered any further debate on improving US–Libyan relations moot. In such a state of suspension they remained until after the events of 11 September 2001. By that time, however, events both within and outside Libya had started to alter the interaction between the Jamahiriyya and the international community – in ways that changed the impact US measures had vis-à-vis Libya.

THE REVOLUTION CURTAILED

Three decades after the 1969 military take-over, Qadhafi's attempts at statelessness and popular rule looked increasingly tarnished, if not in outright disarray. Neither the successive waves of mobilization, nor outside military action against the Jamahiriyya, had managed to maintain or rekindle a measurable level of popular support. Despite the regime's attempts to portray itself as a victim of US and international aggression – and to link the country's economic difficulties to the imposed sanctions – none resulted in the hoped-for surge of support and legitimacy for the regime. The Popular Committee and Congress system persisted as the country's sole political institution, but few Libyans had any illusions as to its actual power. As in most other oil states in the region, legitimacy in the Jamahiriyya remained intricately linked to the regime's ability to provide a certain level of economic well-being to local citizens. As the sanctions took hold, inflation soared, and the delivery of goods often became erratic and unpredictable. The everyday lives of Libyans had become measurably more difficult. At the end of the 1990s, wages, often at a dismal 250–300 dinars per month even for highly qualified personnel, had been frozen for almost two decades. Petty bureaucrats and professionals alike were moonlighting to make ends meet. The regime had allowed the re-emergence of some retail trade in the cities, while the state supermarkets stood abandoned, or were transformed into government offices. Despite these palliatives, however, the diplomatic isolation that made travel and education in the West more difficult – and, in the case of the United States, impossible – still imposed a heavy toll.

The "extension of the revolution" after the US bombing in 1986, the two waves of economic liberalization, *The Great Green Charter of Human Rights*, the halting diplomatic attempts to bring Libya back into the international community, the temporary curtailment of the Revolutionary Committees: all were meant to rejuvenate support for the regime at a time it felt besieged. None, however, altered the country's basic political structures that concentrated power at the very top around Qadhafi, protected by a bevy of security apparatuses and informal groups. Although the economic liberalization and the curtailment of the Revolutionary Committee movement fleetingly tempered the confusion and the arbitrariness that had marked daily life in the Jamahiriyya since the early 1970s, there were as yet no signs of any kind of political transparency, accountability, or the rule of law that could have consolidated both sets of reforms on a more permanent basis. In the end, the regime reaped what it had so deliberately sown: unwilling to remove the kinds of unpredictability that made Libyan citizens reluctant to participate either economically or politically in running the country, most had simply become bystanders in a system they had no chance of reforming. So profound was this de-politicization that even opposition groups operating outside Libya confessed their inability to affect events inside the Jamahiriyya until the Qadhafi regime had been removed.[28]

It was ironic therefore that, despite the use of continuous revolutionary exhortations for self-reliance and activism, the Jamahiriyya had become a country where virtually everything – from food to high-technology items – was imported. Libyans absorbed all the benefits bestowed upon them by an oil economy, but politically stood cowed and silent. Opposition was, by the fact that Libyans in principle ruled themselves, impossible. This enduring contradiction between Qadhafi's incessant calls for activism, and the passivity the political system itself engendered, stood starkly revealed as the Jamahiriyya moved toward the new millennium.

The failure of the two waves of economic liberalization provided important indications of the intimate links between the politics and the economic development problems of the country. After three decades of centralization, of poor decision-making, of outright neglect, and of making economic development subject to the whims of revolutionary pursuits, Libya had developed intricate patterns of patronage that in effect constituted major political as well as economic liabilities to serious reform. The state's ability to provide (decreasing levels of) welfare to the general population had – as long as the oil boom lasted – become part and parcel of the regime's populist rhetoric, and of its ability to reward its close supporters handsomely. Both sets of entitlements were under siege by the end of the 1990s.

Such is the resilience to reform in oil exporters like Libya, however, that it would take another two-and-a-half years before the spectacular announcement of Libya's renunciation of weapons of mass destruction in December 2003 opened up the road toward full-fledged international normalization, and toward badly needed economic reconstruction and possible reform. As the new millennium dawned, however, seasoned observers and participants alike realized that – whatever the outside pressures on Libya were – for a number of internal reasons, as well, the Jamahiriyya's Everlasting Revolution had run its course. Qadhafi himself, in a number of adroit speeches, tried to portray Libya's shifting policies – in such sharp contrast to his old rhetoric – as a new beginning: the "liberation stage" of his revolution had successfully ended, and a new page could now be turned. As the daily reading of a fragment of his *Green Book* on Libyan television proclaimed, the world was now ready for its own, international version of the Everlasting Revolution. The Jamahiriyya should take up its historic role in facilitating its adoption everywhere.[29] Except among a handful of the regime's core supporters, the exhortation no longer had the power even to provoke serious debate.[30]

CHAPTER 7

Reconciliation, civil war, and fin de régime, 2003–2011

The period between 2003 and 2011 in Qadhafi's Libya was marked both by continuity in how the regime retained its hold on power and by a set of discontinuities as the country started to adjust to its reintegration into the international community from which it had been excluded for two decades. When the regime decided to give up its weapons of mass destruction (WMD) in December 2003, Qadhafi's self-proclaimed revolution had left indelible patterns on the country's political, social, and economic structures. To many observers, but particularly to Saif al-Islam al-Qadhafi, the Libya's leader's son, it was clear that many of those structures now needed to change if the country were to fully benefit from the opportunities its reintegration into the international economy and community afforded. Western-educated, Saif al-Islam al-Qadhafi argued that to meet the challenges of Libya's emergence from its diplomatic and economic isolation, both political and economic reforms would be needed. The resistance to the ideas and initiatives of Saif al-Islam as self-appointed reformer ensured that his efforts would run into severe difficulties, hinting at the debilitating legacies Libya faced after more than three decades of his father's experiments in statelessness.

By the time the agreement on WMD was signed in December 2003, European and other foreign investors had started to make their way back to Tripoli after the multilateral sanctions were suspended in April 1999. It was clear, however, that only a complete lifting of the U.S. sanctions could deliver the kind of economic resurgence and the necessary international diplomatic imprimatur that both Said al-Islam al-Qadhafi and his father sought. This could only be accomplished if the Jamahiriyya was taken off the U.S. State Department's list of sponsors of state terrorism. The country's economy, beyond the oil sector, remained unproductive and actively involved few of the country's citizens. The infrastructure of the oil sector itself was aging, and Libya needed substantial investment to update it – conservatively estimated between $10 billion and $30 billion in the medium to long term to increase its oil production to 3 million barrels per day within a decade. Although the Libyan National Oil Company (LNOC) had established itself as a capable manager of the country's oil fields, its officials were the first to admit that the country required international technology and know-how that would enable it to expand production, in part by drilling for oil beyond the Sirt Basin, including offshore. Libya needed the kind of expertise and capital investment that could only be provided by some of the Western – including U.S. – companies that had left the country as a result of the sanctions or because of the uncertainty of the investment climate in Libya.

The regime's agreement to allow the Lockerbie suspects to be tried, its willingness to settle the UTA issue, the diplomatic attempt to salvage its international reputation, and the start of back-channel diplomacy in 1999 between Libya, Great Britain, and the United States were all seeming indications that the Qadhafi regime was willing to settle for a more pragmatic and responsible set of policies that would reintegrate the country politically, diplomatically, and economically within the international community. There were, however, still enormous hurdles to be crossed at the beginning of the new millennium. These included a monetary settlement for the Lockerbie victims (whose families had come to constitute a determined lobbying group in Washington), a clear disavowal of terrorism as a foreign policy tool, and, most importantly, transparency on the issue of WMDs. Although a number of technocrats and young intellectuals, some allied to Saif al-Islam al-Qadhafi, were slowly finding their way into a system that had traditionally afforded no opportunities for anyone but those firmly committed to its revolutionary slogans, the lack of institutionalization within the country's political system still left much of that process subject to the vicissitudes of Qadhafi's own decisions. By the end of the decade, most of Saif al-Islam's attempts at reform had been hemmed in substantially by opponents within the regime – a force even someone as privileged as Saif al-Islam had been unable to neutralize.

It indicated that even as the country proceeded on its path to reconciliation with the West and was willing to entertain some economic changes, regime survival remained the paramount concern of Qadhafi and those who were part of his revolution. Every diplomatic, economic, and internal political decision remained carefully weighed against their impact on the fate of the coalitions of supporters – and possible opponents – within the country. How powerful and painful those trade-offs had been in the past was attested to by the two waves of *infitah* in 1987 and after 1990 (see

Chapter 6), which, in effect, constituted a subterfuge. They comprised a selective economic liberalization that relieved some of the internal pressures in light of the hardships Libyan citizens had faced. They also combined the curtailing of some of the revolution's excesses, without, however, affecting the basic power structure of the regime.

Although many Libyans still viewed Qadhafi with some grudging admiration, by the time the WMD agreement was signed, much of the energy of his revolution had dissipated beyond the possibility of rejuvenating it as an active force in the country's political life. Almost two generations of Libyans had grown up since the 1969 coup, many of them well educated, often, as Saif al-Islam al-Qadhafi, in the West. Many were impatient with a political and economic experiment that afforded few opportunities for employment beyond some of the country's enormous and enormously inefficient bureaucracies that promised no real chance for personal advancement or allowed any sense of entrepreneurship for those not intimately connected to the regime.

It was clear that Saif al-Islam al-Qadhafi had read the general mood of the country accurately. While he announced some of his plans publicly at the Davos World Economic Forum in 2005, his father's exhortations for internal political activism continued, but the disappointments of his grander plans for regional unity, the difficulties within the country's oil sector, the lingering effects of the earlier economic boycotts, the unresolved debacle over Lockerbie, and the seeming indifference that remained among the population had started to take their toll.

At that point, Mu'ammar al-Qadhafi had been the country's leader for almost four decades, and a certain personal weariness seemed to have set in. Perhaps it resulted from the satiety of one-man rule in a country where People's Power masqueraded as democracy, or from weariness of the legions of fawning officials who instantly promoted thc Leader's pronouncements to dogma. Increasingly, he started to portray himself simply as the *éminence grise* of the revolution and as a world revolutionary figure – a self-deception that would be fueled by Western consultants and public intellectuals eager, in return for some petrodollars, to burnish the image of Qadhafi internationally. The way in which Saif al-Islam al-Qadhafi went about advocating and tried to implement his own vision for Libya in many ways reflected his father's authoritarianism and self-delusion: As a self-appointed reformer, Saif al-Islam felt little need for consultation beyond those international consulting firms that, he naively argued, would turn Libya into a vibrant economy. His pronouncements and his style of management were yet another indication of the kind of pathology political systems like his father's often create: They were clear indications of the kind of detachment from reality that often comes to mark regimes no longer beholden to their people.

Both for Qadhafi and for his son, oil revenues remained the key to pursuing their different visions – and here Libya proved exceptional once more. Despite the reluctance the economic sanctions had engendered among international firms, the country remained an extremely attractive target for the oil companies. In 2000, 2001, and 2002, executives from international oil and gas companies continued to rank the Jamahiriyya as the top exploration spot anywhere in the world. Part of this enthusiasm was due to the fact that three-quarters of the country's territory remained unexplored, and that its natural gas reserves were known to be enormous and also largely untapped. Few international oil executives therefore doubted that substantial discoveries and profits could be made in the future – but the general uncertainties and unpredictability of working in Libya, together with the effects of the boycott and sanctions, had created an environment where investments, despite the continuing professionalism of the LNOC staff and the fact that the oil sector remained isolated from internal political developments, were held in abeyance. Rumors had circulated throughout the 1990s that Libya would open up new concessions under EPSA IV conditions that would make it attractive for companies to invest or to return to Libya. None of this could take place, however, until the larger political issues surrounding Libya's interaction with the international community had been solved – something Libya had started to devote itself to, quietly and unobtrusively, in a campaign led by a handful of regime intimates and, increasingly, by Saif al-Islam al-Qadhafi, since early 1999.

The result, made public in a spectacular announcement that captured attention worldwide in December 2003, led the country's leadership to announce that it would give up its WMDs. After decades of confrontation with the West, the Libyan decision to cooperate on the WMD issue marked the apotheosis of a process of reappraisal on which the country's leadership had embarked. The agreement came at the end of a period of protracted negotiations and back-channel diplomacy on WMD and other issues that had started – almost exclusively, at first, at the behest of the British government – between Libya, Great Britain, and the United States. In the end, it was a process of careful and sustained diplomatic negotiations, holding out a set of both carrots and sticks to the Libyan side, that produced the agreements.

THE ROAD TO DISARMAMENT

As intractable as the impasse between the Jamahiriyya and the West still appeared in the first two years of the new millennium, relations between the two sides had – albeit at a glacial pace – started to change by that time. A number of pinprick indicators after Libya had turned over the Lockerbie suspects in April 1999, and once the UN sanctions were lifted, hinted at the possibility of a rapprochement between Libya and the West. Back-channel conferences and talks, initially between Great Britain and the Jamahiriyya, were slowly laying out the differing talking points that would form the background to the reconciliation and to the December 2003 agreement. In June 1999, Libyan and U.S. officials met for the first time in eighteen years in an official capacity to discuss the UN sanctions. In March 2000, U.S. State Department officials visited Libya to assess lifting the existing travel restrictions to the Jamahiriyya. As a sign of changing times, perhaps none was as symbolically indicative of the unfolding changes as the appearance of an article in May 2001 in *Foreign Affairs*, one of the United States' most important establishment journals, arguing that a rogue regime had come in from the cold.

Domestic constituencies within the United States – particularly the Pan Am 103 families – continued to press for the marginalization and punishment of Libya, however. As a result, U.S. policy makers saw little urgency in restoring any type of relationship with Libya. The U.S. Congress in April 2000, in a Sense of the Senate resolution, advised the president not to lift travel restrictions and to consult with the Senate on U.S. policy toward Libya. In November 2000, the State Department renewed the travel ban, and the president reauthorized the Iran and Libya Sanctions Act (ILSA) in August 2001. After Libya turned over the Lockerbie suspects, and after the UN sanctions were lifted, however, it became more difficult for the United States to contain Libya by enlisting international cooperation in pursuit of justice for the Lockerbie victims. Although the United States retained its unilateral sanctions in the wake of the Lockerbie verdict, and insisted that Libya meet all UN demands before the suspension of the multilateral sanctions could be extended formally to lifting them, it was clear that the dynamics and the interaction between Libya and the international community was caught in a maelstrom of change – and that the United States, willy-nilly perhaps, needed to reexamine its previous policies as well.

Indeed, viewed from a U.S. perspective, how much sense did unilateral sanctions make when the international community was welcoming Libya back into the fold? Could a sanctions-led policy still retain the purpose it had during the 1990s, when multilateral cooperation was assured and when the threats emanating from Libya were tangible? The answers to these questions had seemingly changed in the wake of the Lockerbie settlement. Washington could encourage the positive changes in Libyan behavior, knowing that retaining the country's isolation looked increasingly problematic and impractical, or insist on keeping the regime isolated and find itself on the margins of the gradual reintegration of the Jamahiriyya into the international community.

Libya's support for U.S. efforts in its campaign against international terrorism in the wake of the September 11, 2001 attacks added to Washington's dilemma. Qadhafi quickly condemned the attacks and described the invasion of Afghanistan as a justified act of self-defense by the United States, labeling the Taliban regime "Godless promoters of political Islam." While the United States kept insisting on the need for Libya to fulfill all its obligations under the UN resolutions and continued to highlight the country's pursuit of WMDs, a number of trilateral talks between Britain, the United States, and Libya, as well as negotiations between American and Libyan lawyers over the details of compensation for the Lockerbie victims, quietly took place.

U.S. officials in early 2000 also acknowledged that the Jamahiriyya had distanced itself from further involvement in terrorism and from supporting groups involved in terrorism. The Abu Nidal organization and several other groups had been asked to leave the Jamahiriyya. Ronald Neumann, at the time Deputy Assistant Secretary of State for Near Eastern Affairs, argued that Libya's actions in regard to the Abu Nidal organization were "not window dressing but a serious, credible step."

Slowly also, Qadhafi's rhetoric regarding a solution to the Arab-Israeli conflict had been altered, in effect questioning both the tactics and the rationale of what had once been one of the Jamahiriyya's ideological cornerstones. His earlier dismissal of the Camp David Accords and of the 1993 Israeli-PLO Oslo Accords had gradually yielded to a previously unknown pragmatism – one admittedly met by some skepticism among those who argued that, here as elsewhere, it represented nothing but a cynical ploy to attract investment to the country and to reshape the country's image internationally. But whereas in February 1996 – following a number of suicide bombings in Israel – the Leader had still praised the attacks and hectored Arab states to help against "Israeli terrorism," within three years, in 1999, he announced to Palestinian militants that Libya would only deal with President Arafat's Palestinian Authority in addressing the lingering crisis in the occupied territories. Although his rhetoric at times remained fiery and

Figure 7. Tripoli, Libyan Arab Jamahiriyya. As part of his efforts toward a greater Libyanrole in Africa, Colonel Qadhafi invited the Sudanese leaders to a conference in Tripoli inMay 2005 regarding the crisis in Darfur.

seemingly uncompromising, Qadhafi cautiously endorsed Saudi Arabia's two-state solution at the Beirut 2002 Arab League summit.

At the same time, many of Libya's foreign policy initiatives – particularly in sub-Saharan Africa – changed considerably in scope and nature. From its earlier destabilizing or confrontational ventures in Uganda, Chad, Tunisia, and Egypt, the regime gradually distanced itself from direct or indirect involvement in most of the regional insurgencies it had supported in the past. After the humiliating military defeat in Chad in 1987, the dispute over the Aouzou strip had been referred to the International Court of Justice. When the court ruled in favor of Chad, Libya acquiesced in the ruling and has abided by the decision ever since. Relations with Egypt turned cordial after years of open hostility. Both countries embarked on a collaborative effort to find a solution for neighboring Sudan's protracted civil war. The effort resulted in Sudan's acceptance of an Egyptian-Libyan peace plan that nevertheless left the conflict festering. In April 1999, Qadhafi brokered a peace accord between Uganda and the Congo, sending Libyan troops to Uganda to help implement it.

The following month, Libya embarked on a quiet round of negotiations with Great Britain in an attempt to break its diplomatic and economic isolation. The talks had been urged on Qadhafi by a bevy of longtime senior advisors. That year, the country's per capita GDP had fallen to its lowest level in more than a decade, despite the adoption of Law #5 of 1997 that had created a formal legal framework for direct foreign investment. Under the circumstances at the time, Law #5 had very few chances of attracting investment beyond the oil sector. At the same time, however, the regime, without officially approving it, allowed small retailers and investors to reopen stores and to reinvigorate the country's small-scale commercial life that had been absent since the revolutionary decade. Almost overnight – and despite periodic efforts by municipal committees to restrict commercial activities – Libya's main streets were filled once more with small restaurants, cafes, and shops selling household goods, groceries, and electronics.

The round of negotiations, informal meetings, and off-the-record conferences initiated by Britain steadily grew in scope, eventually to include Libyan activities in sub-Saharan Africa, issues surrounding the 1984 London shooting of Yvonne Fletcher, Lockerbie, Libyan cooperation in illegal migration toward Europe, and a number of smaller issues. When Libya agreed to settle the Lockerbie issue by promising to adhere to a tiered process of compensation for the victims' families that would eventually, in return, lead to the suspension of U.S. sanctions against Libya and to the removal of the Jamahiriyya from the U.S. State Department's list of sponsors of terrorism, most outstanding issues between Libya and the West had been addressed.

The only major issue that remained of great concern to the United States in particular concerned Libya's attempt to produce unconventional weapons and WMDs. Throughout the 1980s, Washington had watched Libyan efforts to acquire such weapons with increasing concern, devoting considerable attention to gathering intelligence on the country's progress. The ongoing controversy in the 1980s and 1990s over an underground facility at Rabta and an industrial complex in Tarhuna – where the U.S. administration accused Libya of gearing up for chemical weapons production – accelerated U.S. efforts to deny the Libyan government any technology or imports that could be used for such purposes.

In 1997, the CIA had concluded that the Jamahiriyya's efforts to acquire unconventional weapons had started to slow down – a conclusion that was later proven to be true for chemical weapons, but not for Libya's attempts at obtaining further missile and nuclear technology. When the UN sanctions were suspended, however, Washington's concern focused on the fact that Libya would now be able to purchase the technology and components necessary to resume its quest for nonconventional weapons. This concern increased when Chinese Scud missile parts were discovered en route to Libya, as well as by the interception of a ship in Malaysia with parts used for nuclear technology that was also bound for Libya. Although most analysts were skeptical that Libya had the capacity and knowledge to produce nuclear weapons, the CIA in 2001 warned of a renewal of a Russian-Libyan civilian nuclear program that could lead to weapons-related research.

Libya's willingness to consider and adopt reforms resonated in London and Washington. For the West, there were a number of overlapping interests in rehabilitating Libya. First was to convince its leadership to abandon once and for all its support of terrorism, which had marked much of the country's revolutionary decade but which the government had all but abandoned since the late 1990s. Second, both London and Washington were interested in putting a halt to the country's weapons proliferation, particularly WMD. Clearly the U.S. administration viewed an agreement on WMD with Libya as an important gesture that would send the right signals to other proliferating countries. Finally, Great Britain and the Clinton and George W. Bush administrations viewed the Jamahiriyya's policies in sub-Saharan Africa with considerable skepticism and hoped to circumscribe its actions there.

There was as well a realization and understanding in Washington that its policy of isolating Libya was increasingly turning counterproductive as Britain and other European countries were willing to reengage with the country in the wake of the Lockerbie trial and the Libyan government's willingness to settle victims' claims. In April 2003, the Atlantic Council – an organization hardly friendly to Libya – had issued a report entitled "US-Libyan Relations: Toward Cautious Reengagement." The report advocated a "A New Strategy for a New Context" and aptly summarized in its pages the new realities of the U.S.-Libyan relationship at the end of the millennium:

The current US strategy towards Libya – an implicit strategy of isolation – was developed for a very different international context than the one that currently exists. Put in place during the 1980s, the strategy was appropriate for the Cold War context and for dealing with Libya's hostile behavior at the time. Since then, however, both the general context and specific Libyan behavior have changed, rendering the current set of accumulated laws and regulations that govern US relations with Libya outdated and inappropriate. Furthermore, the current strategy provides no vision for US-Libyan relations once the remaining issues surrounding the 1988 bombing of Pan Am flight 103 are resolved. Thus, US strategy needs to be

changed to reflect better the new environment and new opportunities. . . .
Such a strategy would be based on the recognition that a continued effort to
isolate Libya is unlikely to produce results, given that other countries have
reestablished relations with Libya and are actively pursuing commercial
opportunities there. A parallel strategy would be organized around priority US objectives (understanding that some may be more easily achievable
than others). It should also seek opportunities to cooperate with European
countries as these share many interests with the United States.

Once Libya had signed the agreement on the WMD issue, a flurry of
diplomatic and economic activities followed, indicating the eagerness of
both the West and the Jamahiriyya to settle whatever issues were left outstanding. In February 2004, the United States lifted its travel ban to Libya.
The following month, the first U.S. Congressional delegation visited
Tripoli. In April, British Prime Minister Tony Blair paid an official visit
to the country, while the United States lifted most of its economic sanctions against the Jamahiriyya. Later that month, the Libyan leader flew to
Brussels for an official visit to the European Union. In June, the United
States and Libya formalized the emerging new relationship by officially
reestablishing diplomatic relations. The United States formally revoked its
trade embargo against Libya at the end of September, and the European
Union lifted its arms embargo by mid-October. By that time, the United
States had removed all of Libya's nuclear weapons' program equipment
and had started to get rid of the country's chemical weapons. The diplomatic and political initiatives were matched by a flurry of commercial
activities that intensified throughout as oil companies, oil support firms,
tourist agencies, and other service businesses vied for what was widely considered an undeveloped and potentially highly lucrative market.

PRAGMATISM, ECONOMIC REFORM, AND POLITICAL REALITY

Although the WMD announcement captured a dramatic moment in
Libya's political life, its underlying pragmatism was based on a number
of developments that had started to worry Qadhafi over a much longer
period of time – developments that prompted the Jamahiriyya to come
to terms with the lingering and progressively worsening state of its economy. By the time of the publication of the Atlantic Council study, Libya
had already taken a number of corrective measures to break the isolation
due to the sanctions and had started to reform its economy. The country's
economic liberalization and its attempt to settle all outstanding issues with
the West not surprisingly coincided. By the time the WMD agreement was

formally announced, Libya had already embarked for almost two years on economic reforms.

In January 2002, the country announced its intention to open up its economy further and to attract foreign capital to the country. For that purpose, it unified its exchange rate, pegging the Libyan dinar to the IMF's Special Drawing Rights, in effect devaluing the country's official exchange rate by more than half as part of a strategy toward unification of the country's multitiered (official, commercial, black-market) foreign exchange system. The devaluation was also meant to increase the competitiveness of Libyan firms and to help attract foreign investment into the country. The same month, Libya cut its customs duty rate by 50 percent on most imports, hoping to offset the effects of its currency devaluation.

In March 2003, a few months before the WMD agreement, the General People's Congress adopted legislation meant to augur in the country's third attempt at *infitah*. The legislation included an authorization to privatize a large number of the country's state-owned economic enterprises. In June, Qadhafi admitted that the country's public sector had failed and should be abolished, and also called for the privatization of the country's oil sector. Libya's Parliament during the same month selected former Trade and Economy Minister Shukri Muhammad Ghanem, a proponent of liberalization and privatization, as Prime Minister. Ghanem, a technocrat who had been brought back to Libya after a period working at OPEC, clearly saw his task as removing, as much as possible, the inefficiencies the state-controlled economy had created in the previous decades. Determined to implement his reforms, but aware of the enormous resistance this would entail within the country's patronage-driven system, he slowly set about trying to build up a technocratic team around him. The Energy Ministry was restored and Abdallah Badri – a technocrat with long experience in the oil sector – was appointed to head the LNOC in order, in part, to negotiate the return of the Oasis Group (Marathon Oil, ConocoPhillips, and Amerada Hess) to their Waha and Zueitina concessions, a move that was meant to send reassuring signals to other U.S. oil companies.

After decades of avoiding the advice of international financial institutions, the country also accepted its obligations under Article VIII of the IMF's Articles of Agreement and in October 2003 released the details of the IMF's first Article IV consultations, which called, among other issues, for wide structural reforms, improved macroeconomic management, and the removal of trade barriers and price subsidies. The IMF report in part informed the deliberation and adoption of a number of the economic directives taken up by the General People's Congress in March 2004.

As the new millennium dawned, the Jamahiriyya found itself burdened by an accumulation of economic problems the country's leadership found impossible to ignore. In contrast to 1975 when a technocratically inclined faction (centered around Muhayshi) had lost out to the revolutionaries inside Libya, conditions in early 2003 proved infinitely more difficult. For Libya, the reasons for settling the outstanding issues with the West were very clear: After roughly two decades of sanctions, the combination of the country's economic legacy of an inefficiently state-run economy with economic and political hardships engendered by those sanctions, as well as the internal pressures from a burgeoning younger population with scant possibilities of meaningful employment – Libya's unemployment in 2003 was estimated at 30 percent – had made the continuation of the previous three decades' economic experiments impossible. The Jamahiriyya needed outside investment and expertise for new oil and natural gas exploration, and for restoring or updating some of the oil industry's industrial and oil infrastructure that the LNOC readily admitted was outdated. The country was also determined to break out of the physical (until the lifting of the United Nations' travel ban) and diplomatic isolation in which it found itself.

In addition, for reasons that had been noted only by careful Libya observers during the last decade, a process of generational turnover was slowly taking place inside the country, which slowly brought a number of reform-minded, younger intellectuals and technocrats to the fore. Eventually the Leader's own son, Saif al-Islam al-Qadhafi, would emerge as their champion. Their hand was strengthened by the dire condition of the country's economy and by the fact that the lifting of the sanctions acted as a catalyst to push their ideas forward. In contrast to 1975, when revolutionary fervor and ample resources made a disregard for economic efficiency possible, the new millennium no longer offered the Libyan regime such options.

Many of the country's elite had seemingly reached the conclusion that the Al-Fatih revolution as a mobilizational tool had run its course inside Libya. In private conversations and public speeches, Qadhafi and those around him now distinguished between the revolutionary period, when the confrontation with the West had made the strategy of isolation and confrontation necessary, and the changed international context that now made those earlier policies obsolete. Ever attuned to portraying the new changes as the result of Libya's steadfastness in the face of adversity, the Libyan leader noted at the March 2004 General People's Congress that they were an indication of a battle Libya had won. Clearly, although the country's leadership was determined to break the diplomatic isolation in which it found itself, the breakthrough was to be portrayed as a Libyan victory.

Libya's objectives under the economic liberalization strategy were clearly spelled out by Prime Minister Ghanem:

The strategies and initiatives that we are taking ... [are] trying [to create] a new and comprehensive architecture for the national economy ... [which includes] a lot of incentives to foreign investors, such as tax exemptions in the first few years, a major cut in corporate taxes, establishing a free zone in Misurata [Misrata] and opening the capital of public companies for foreign investors ... [and] to cut down mismanagement and corruption and of course bureaucracy."

The practical measures in support of the new strategy were adopted by the General People's Congress at its March 2004 annual meeting. The government envisioned the privatization of 360 of the country's state companies – privatization now euphemistically referred to, in light of The Green Book 's original directives against private ownership, as "the extension of popular ownership." In addition, the reforms included extensive banking-sector reform and the introduction of private banks. The proposals also encompassed tax reform, the creation of a stock exchange, newly relaxed rules for foreign companies investing in the Jamahiriyya, and a plan to promote the country's almost nonexistent tourist sector. The measures in effect amounted to the dismantling of what until now had been a semi-socialist economy, hoping to reduce in the process the stagnation and the stranglehold of the country's bureaucracy.

The dry technical language of the IMF report at the time summarized the challenges Libya would face as it embarked upon Ghanem's reforms:

The key challenge facing the authorities in the medium and long-term is to achieve sustainable high rates of economic growth to generate employment opportunities for a rapidly growing labour force. The authorities agreed that this goal would not be achievable without a drastic reduction in the dominant role of the public sector.... Unemployment, which may be as high as 30 percent, remains one of Libya's greatest problems, with the bloated state sector unable to accommodate the many new job-seekers produced by the fast growing population. Until private sector reform starts delivering tangible results, the problem – compounded by Muammar Qaddafi's 1997 move to open Libya's border to 2 million African immigrants – is only likely to worsen.

The IMF urged the Libyan authorities to move toward greater budget transparency and to cast the country's budget within a coordinated medium-term framework that would take into account the nonrenewable nature of Libya's hydrocarbon resources. From a purely technical economic viewpoint, Libya's economic situation and its attempts to transit toward a market-led development strategy show many similarities to those of centrally controlled economies that have liberalized in the past two decades. Libya is perhaps more favorably located, given that it has ample financial reserves to cushion temporary imbalances, and can look forward to a high sustained income as more oil comes online.

Although the new reforms asked for greater diversification of Libya's economy, the hydrocarbon sector would once more be called on to provide the necessary revenues. By 2003, only one-quarter of the country's territory had been seriously explored for oil and, except for one patch along Libya's western coastal area, only one area has been explored for offshore drilling. Both the Libyan government and international oil companies expected that the country's proven reserves of 30 billion barrels could easily be raised to 130 billion barrels, clearly making Libya one of the top three investment destinations worldwide for oil companies.

Libya in 2003 was exporting roughly 1.5 million barrels per day, significantly less than its 1970 production. LNOC now wanted to increase production to 3 million barrels per day – the equivalent of its 1970 production – but admitted that Libya needs roughly $30 billion in foreign investment to do so, $10 billion alone by 2010.[1] In addition, plans were developed to exploit extensively the country's enormous natural gas deposits – increasing production for export to 40–50 billion cubic meters per year within ten years – and to update the country's Liquefied Natural Gas (LNG) infrastructure, which is limited to one liquefaction plant at Marsa al-Burayqa. To encourage investment in the hydrocarbon sector, Libya carefully designed a new set of Exploration and Production Sharing Agreements (EPSA IV) that, judging by the enthusiasm with which international oil companies flocked to Tripoli, proved once more the attractiveness of Libyan oil.

In August 2004, for the first time in almost two decades, Libya formally announced its intention to open up fifteen new offshore and onshore blocks for exploration and production agreements. Among the more than 120 companies that registered bids or expressed interest in further exploration of oil and natural gas in the country were Occidental, Amerada Hess, ChevronTexaco, ConocoPhillips, Marathon Oil, and Anadarko, as well as a number of European and international companies. The announcement of the winners at the end of January 2005 by the Libyan National Oil Corporation's exploration department and the terms of the contracts clearly revealed Libya's priorities. Beside awarding contracts to Brazil's oil giant Petrobras, Algeria's Sonatrach, the Indian Oil Corporation – all state-owned – and an array of other international companies, eleven of the fifteen oil exploration licenses went to U.S. companies, including

Occidental, Amerada Hess, and ChevronTexaco. Clearly, one of Libya's priorities was to have U.S. firms closely involved once more in the country's oil industry, even if doing so seemingly came at the expense of the European companies – particularly French-owned Total – that had supported the country during the sanctions period. The conditions of the contracts were stringent, with the successful companies required to pay a total of $132.9 million upon the signing of the contracts, and with obligations to spend a further $300 million for exploration. Successful companies would take shares ranging from 10.8 percent to 38.9 percent of production, with the remainder accruing to the government.

That same month, at the Davos World Economic Forum, Saif al-Islam al-Qadhafi announced a vast reform program for the Libyan economy, announcing that "the old times are finished and Libya is ready to move onto a new stage of modernization ... [which] will be conducted in a well organized manner that ensures new ownership and ownership by the people of Libya, not just a small class of oligarchs like Russia or Egypt." With Abd al-Hafid Zlitni, the chairman of Libya's National Planning Council, beside him, Saif al-Islam al-Qadhafi added that Libya had recruited some world experts to help in the effort, and conceded that "[t]here may be some reaction against them in Libya, but they are the best."[2] The world experts were the Monitor Group whose *National Economic Strategy: An Assessment of the Competitiveness of the Libyan Arab Jamahiriyya* was meant to guide Libyan development, and whose director, Michael Porter, eventually delivered a lecture on its contents in front of the General People's Congress in Tripoli.[3]

Perhaps not so surprising, both Monitor's report and Saif al-Islam's statement in Davos left precisely unconsidered those aspects of Libya's three decades of, at best, erratic economic management that would be instrumental in determining how far the country could hope to reform: The fact that the political system, the patronage system on which it crucially hinged, and the lack of any legal guarantees effectively made any real structural economic reforms difficult, if not impossible. Although the Monitor report contained all the customary razzle-dazzle of highly paid international management consultancy reports, and Saif al-Islam's speeches as well were laced with the buzzwords of the powerful international vocabulary officials of transition economies now routinely use – deregulation, transparency, rule of law, property rights, efficiency, markets – neither addressed the link to the country's political management that prevented anything but the usual muddling through.[4] That Saif al-Islam and his brothers soon emerged as young oligarchs themselves, as well as that the major reform

188   *A history of modern Libya*

statement for the country's economy was made by someone who had no official standing within Libyan political life, and did so without consulting the General People's Congress – those facts attested eloquently to the lingering impact of personal politics and to the lack of institutionalization that still surrounded policy formulation in the Jamahiriyya in 2005.

Beyond personal politics, there also remained deeper structural problems in the Jamahiriyya's economy that continued to make reforms problematic. In most Western economies, institutional development in support of economic development took place over relatively long periods of time. Above all, what most efforts at sustained economic reform throughout the world have shown is that moving toward markets under conditions where there is no real history of them requires careful and greater regulation by the state – not simply handing over everything to the market but, at least initially, a greater willingness to involve itself in sustained regulation. As this book has demonstrated, for reasons that closely link economic strategy to regime survival, Libya at several junctures during its revolutionary phase deliberately stepped back from regulation and from creating or maintaining state institutions that could have established such regulation.

In light of its history of statelessness enshrined in the Green Book and pursued so assiduously since 1969, it was worth asking how well Libya would deal with professed attempts to develop Libya's ability to fine-tune its ability to regulate. A second question necessarily followed: Qui bono? Who would benefit from the reforms? If, as both Saif al-Islam al-Qadhafi and Prime Minister Ghanem suggested at the time, this transition was for the benefit of all Libyans and about restructuring social entitlements, were they willing to allow what is almost always inevitably linked to deep economic reform: the changing of a peculiar social contract – the way the state and its citizens interact – that has become part and parcel of how the regime operates and survives since 1969?

It was in part this more essential question that informed the remarkable – by Libyan standards – debates during the January 2005 GPC meeting in Sirte. The debate within the GPC over the economic reforms – pitting Prime Minister Ghanem and his supporters (including his patron Saif al-Islam al-Qadhafi) against a coalition of opponents headed by Ahmed Ibrahim, the Assistant Secretary of the GPC with close links to the "revolutionary" part of the regime, and by Abd al-Qadr al-Baghdadi – was both uncommonly vigorous and acrimonious.[5] Above all, the debate perhaps for the first time also showed how clearly Ghanem had come to realize that what was at stake was not simply economic reform, but also a number of surrounding political and institutional reforms that would be needed if the former were to succeed – issues that had been considered off-limits until then.

Ghanem argued for the right of the prime minister to make his own cabinet appointments and for substantially increased power to push the reforms through. He also insisted on a clear separation of power between the legislature and the executive to ensure that proposed legislation would not be hostage to what he described as "invisible" forces, and for greater power for the judiciary. To those requests Ahmad Ibrahim and al-Baghdadi responded that there is no need for separation of power or for a constitution because Law #1 and Colonel Qadhafi constituted the only political references in Libya. When Qadhafi attended the meeting toward its conclusion, he cautiously supported Ghanem in his reform efforts but left the larger questions the prime minister had raised untouched. What Ghanem in effect had asked for – in words that would have been unimaginable a few years earlier – was for a constitution for the country, a project for which Saif al-Islam al-Qadhafi had started to garner support. In a speech at the time he pointed out, in language that mirrored Ghanem's strong endorsement of a more democratic Libya, that "the democratic system that we dreamed of does not exist in the realm of reality ... the existing system has its equivocation and misuse of the term 'democracy.' It has a sense of hidden corridors."[6] The "constitution project" would eventually, much like many important aspects of the proposed economic reforms, be curtailed by the "revolutionaries" inside Libya and abandoned.[7]

Certainly after 2003, the economic and political climate in Libya was substantially different from that of the 1980s and 1990s when, as a result of anemic oil prices, bad management, and the economic sanctions, previous sets of reform faltered. The times were more auspicious for the country's latest wave of reforms. The continued visibility of reformers like Prime Minister Ghanem and Saif al-Islam al-Qadhafi augured well for the implementation of the reforms. As events were soon to demonstrate, however, their positions remained precarious. At the same time there was an appreciation among the Libyan leadership that the international threat environment in the wake of the Lockerbie settlement and the lifting of UN sanctions had changed substantially, making reforms perhaps less formidable. This realization added to the pragmatism Libya adopted, realizing also that the newfound opening toward the West raised a number of internal and external expectations the country would need to respond to adequately. Finally, high oil prices – and the promise of sustained income – meant that the country's economic fortunes after 2003 were substantially better than those it faced in the 1980s and 1990s, matched by the knowledge that the government had fewer economic options but to embark on serious reforms.

In light of what subsequently happened, it is worth repeating that Libya had attempted to liberalize its economy twice before: from 1987 to 1990, and then in a second wave after 1990. At the time, state intervention in the economy was pervasive: The state dominated all manufacturing, agriculture, foreign and domestic retail trade, banking, insurance, as well as major services. State trading companies were in charge of all industrial, manufacturing, and agricultural imports. The government furthermore intervened indirectly through interest-free credit, state spending, subsidies, and price manipulation of goods. By 1987, an estimated 70–75 percent of all Libyans were government employees. In 2004, according to Prime Minister Ghanem, 862,000 Libyans still depended on the state for their livelihood.[8] Particularly the "deepening" liberalization wave after 1990 had been meant to extend cuts in state spending, gradually withdraw subsidies, promote private sector initiatives in the industrial, trade, and agricultural sectors, remove state import and export monopolies, further diversify the economy (including the promotion of tourism), and create a viable banking system that would support these new initiatives.

Many of these earlier advocated measures now reappeared in the economic strategy outlined by Prime Minister Ghanem. Most outside observers at the time of the earlier liberalization waves agreed that they did not really accomplish much in terms of recalibrating the role of the state in the economy, except for bringing about a relatively easy to implement and maintain "consumer infitah."

In the years following the Davos speech by Saif al-Islam and the publication of the Monitor report, the Libyan government embarked on a seemingly ambitious set of further initiatives to reform the country's economy. Salaries for government employees and those working in state-owned companies, after being frozen for decades, were raised substantially. Several major companies, including banks and the country's mobile phone sector, had been selected for privatization. Many of the onerous requirements for business visitors were eased, and custom tariffs on a whole range of goods and commodities reduced or abolished. Local technocrats investigated the possibilities for increasing the efficiency and attractiveness of free economic zones along the coast. Domestic fuel prices were allowed to rise, and traditional subsidies for water and electricity were reduced. Under the aegis of the country's National Economic Strategy Project, the National Council of Economic Development was established in early 2007, meant to coordinate, speed up, and oversee the different privatization and liberalization initiatives. As always in the past, the oil and gas sector had been the recipient of the most prudent, independent advice, further indicating the privileged position it enjoyed in the country's economy.

But even though the debate at the spring 2005 GPC meeting had seemingly indicated a willingness of the country's reformers to publicly tackle a number of economic and political issues crucial to expand and solidify the liberalization and reform measures at the expense of regime stalwarts, subsequent developments provided indications of how sensitive the reforms were once more viewed by the regime itself. A cabinet reshuffle in March 2006 replaced reform-minded Prime Minister Ghanem with Ali Baghdadi Al-Mahmudi. Mahmudi's new cabinet was largely seen as a setback for the reformers, and Mahmudi himself was much less outspoken than Ghanem and less inclined to challenge those opposing the economic reforms. This further slowed down what was already problematic progress in the non-hydrocarbon sector.

The Libyan leader's own pronouncements on the country's economic strategy proved, as always, more in tune with political and security considerations than economic ones. In his speeches in the years following his son's announcements at Davos he continued to show his personal suspicion of the country's new economic strategy, even though he demonstrated once more that he perfectly understood what the failures of the Libya economy were, in a speech delivered a few months after Ghanem's dismissal as prime minister: "We don't produce anything.... We sell only oil and consume everything.... The kind of trade in which you produce nothing and import goods in exchange for oil – it's a catastrophe.... To explore for oil, to export it and earn money which you use to pay for imports, and to then sell those imports locally: This isn't prosperity. It doesn't lead to the nation's progress."[9]

Shortly before, and despite the fact that the National Economic Strategy Project had urged diversification into health, tourism, construction, and other non-oil projects, Qadhafi in a speech in July 2006 derided the presence of foreigners in the country, arguing that they drained Libya of its resources. This was followed soon afterward by a barrage of speeches, as the one cited previously, in which he took his own citizens to task for their dependence on oil revenues, expatriate labor, and massive imports. In a somewhat surreal fashion he then urged Libyans to start manufacturing the goods they needed, seemingly oblivious to what his own policies – or lack thereof – had meant for the productive capacities of Libya in any economic sector. In March 2008, Qadhafi argued for dissolving the country's cabinet because it had failed to distribute the country's revenues adequately to Libyan citizens.

He then reintroduced one of his favorite solutions to Libya's economic problems: distribute oil money directly to all Libyans.[10] Finally, in a move that augured badly for the new economic approach, he had several businessmen arrested on the grounds that they had violated the principles of the Green Book's people's socialism. By now, however, these pronouncements of the Leader were unlikely to derail the larger initiatives on which the country had embarked. Still, they reinforced the uncertainty that had long prevailed in Libya and that made individuals suspicious of becoming entrepreneurs. As a result, they further slowed down the needed changes in the five clusters identified in the Monitor's National Economic Strategy plan within the non-hydrocarbon sectors. In many ways, the differing pronouncements of the Libyan leader and of Saif al-Islam on Libyan economic reforms were good indicators of the larger, more structural issues at hand.

Despite this slowdown, Libya's economy continued to show slow and incremental improvements toward greater efficiency in its regulatory capacities. By the end of 2010, the country had, at least in principle, made some progress in creating the statutes necessary to implement some of these reforms. A plethora of stipulations regarding Commercial Law, Customs Law, Income Tax Law, Stock Market Law, Labor Law, Communications Law, Land Registry Law, and laws regulating the activities of the Libyan Investment Authority had been adopted. The IMF's 2010 Article IV Consultation's preliminary conclusions that year reflected the positive side of these developments, but also once more underscored the persisting lack of reliable data and the continued overreliance on hydrocarbon revenues, and it hinted at the broader governance issues that persisted.[11]

In retrospect, the years between 2003 and 2011 were perhaps the last chance Libya had to seriously deal with the disastrous legacy of the Qadhafi years – short of an actual uprising against the regime. In light of the interwoven structures of Libya's political economy and of its weak institutional architecture, economic reform would inevitably had necessitated political changes as well – something both Shukri Ghanem and Saif al-Islam al-Qadhafi had clearly come to realize. But the proposed strategy by Ghanem and Saif al-Islam also entailed a substantial upgrading of the state's ability to regulate in order to, down the road, augur in a more deregulated economy. It was clear from unfolding events during the period that the process of doing so would be painfully slow and full of obstacles at the powerful hands of those with economic interests in retaining the old structures. Nothing in Libya's history since 1969 – or indeed during the monarchy – had suggested their willingness to let the country's citizens be involved in such choices in a more democratic political system.

The fact that the country's political structures – the pretensions of People's Power notwithstanding – were effectively off-limits to reform was therefore particularly problematic. It remained equally worrisome that much of the impetus for economic (and political) reform had largely come about – as most other political or economic initiatives in Libya's modern history – in a noninstitutionalized fashion. Its major public supporter, Saif al-Islam al-Qadhafi, had no official standing in the country's political or economic hierarchy, yet his plans and announcements trumped those of even the country's reformist prime minister, Shukri Ghanem. His ambitions for a more liberal economy and for a more open political system met with enormous resistance. Even though some of his proposals for a more efficient economy undoubtedly resonated among the more technocratically minded managers of the country's ministries and planning institutes, real structural reforms proved as yet not feasible.

Libya's historical dilemmas had put the country at a particularly important fork in the road. It could have pursued a type of state-led market reform – as in neighboring Tunisia or Egypt – that entailed a highly authoritarian state that relies on close cooperation between the state and a number of business coalitions, guarded by the country's own security organizations and fueled once more by oil in the Libyan case, that would have kept the current economic structures in place while maintaining circumscribed social contracts that continued to deliver political quiescence. Alternatively, the Jamahiriyya could have pursued the more incisive changes suggested by its reformers, realizing that such a pursuit would inevitably have led to further demands for accountability, transparency, and political voice – while moving away from the patronage-driven and patrimonial system of the past.

As a result of a combination of interlocking reasons that were both historical and institutional, Libya faced a set of peculiar problems in addressing the economic and political reform measures during the 2003–2011 period. The development of good state institutions that allow for sustained reform – those that provide incentives for generating market-promoting public goods while minimizing rent seeking into the hands of the government – had traditionally been abandoned in favor of a social contract that carefully subscribed the role of the individual vis-à-vis the revolution. Both Ghanem and Saif al-Islam realized that reforming such social contracts by creating finely-tuned regulatory and legal institutions in effect opens up their creation and pursuit subject to real public discussion and debate – something the Qadhafi government was unwilling to address.

The presence of the security sector and informal institutions without real accountability except to the Leader himself, much like the wholesale state management of the economy until the recent reforms, had always been a management shortcut, indicative of an inability to construct over time complex layers of regulatory, stabilizing, and legitimating state institutions. The two issues Libya faced after 2003 – neither of which was inherently easier than the other – was to either create viable institutions beyond the coercive and distributive ones or to reform and adapt existing institutions to reduce powerful coalitional and patronage systems. The latter would in effect have meant the demise of the regime.

The structural legacies of Libya's past – centralized control of virtually all economic resources and political energy without actual regulation – continued to cast a very heavy shadow over the reform efforts in the years after 2003 because, like previous efforts, they threatened to upset patronage networks that had since 1969 deliberately been created and maintained to ensure regime survival.

FROM ARAB SOCIALISM TO PAN-AFRICAN UNITY

For the first decade after the 1969 coup, Qadhafi had spent much political energy on regional foreign policy initiatives to bring about some kind of unity and coherence to Arab socialism. His self-perception as the ideological heir to Gamal Abdul Nasser had never been shared by the region's leaders. They viewed his activism, his blunt assessments of friend and foe alike, with suspicion and, more often than not, disdain. The seven unification schemes the Jamahiriyya had concluded since 1969 with a variety of regional partners all withered away, some of them almost as soon as the ink on the agreements was dry. At the same time, Qadhafi's long-simmering anger at the inability of the Arab world to present a unified front against Israel and the West, and at its impotence in trying to turn the Arab League into a viable organization that could adopt his own vision of Arab solidarity, had led to a number of verbal skirmishes during Arab summits that resulted in further mutual alienation. When the Libyan leader finally walked out of the May 2004 meeting of the Arab League in Tunis – after once more calling for a dismantling of the organization and after repeating his populist assertion that "[t]here is one agenda laid out by the Arab people and another by the Arab governments" – it marked the end of a process of reevaluation and reorientation that reached back almost fifteen years.

Throughout the 1970s and 1980s, Libya had also maintained a steady presence in sub-Saharan Africa, combining the country's financial resources with a rhetorical anti-imperialism that supported a number of local coups and insurgencies throughout the region. Symptomatic of the relationship between Libya and several of the sub-Saharan African countries had been the country's interactions with the Organization of African Unity (OAU), which, except for the three years after the 1969 coup, were tumultuous and confrontational. Between 1979 and 1986, the Jamahiriyya had steadily become ostracized from the organization. Instrumental to the country's isolation had been its full-scale intervention in Chad in December 1980, with a so-called Islamic Legion made up of African and Arab volunteers that had been trained and supplied by Libya. Concerned, in addition, with Qadhafi's efforts to destabilize local governments and by his persistent meddling – including an open call to Zaire's Muslims to engage in a *jihad* against the Mobutu regime in 1985 – the OAU slowly but effectively put a halt to the Libyan leader's sub-Saharan ambitions.

This isolation, and Libya's crushing defeat at Fada and Wadi Dum in Chad in the spring of 1987, marked the beginning of a new relationship between the Jamahiriyya and sub-Saharan Africa. At the twentieth anniversary celebrations of the revolution on 1 September 1989, Qadhafi announced his willingness to bring the long-festering Aouzou strip debacle before the International Court of Justice. Some questioned whether this represented more than a tactical move on Libya's part – an effort to deal more effectively with the economic hardships the country faced, or a tacit acknowledgment that French and U.S. open or covert support for Chad now presented insurmountable obstacles in light of the other difficulties the country faced. Others interpreted it simply as an attempt to put an end to persisting internal criticism of the war, which had reached previously unknown levels inside the Jamahiriyya. When the International Court in February 1994 ruled in favor of Chad's claim, however, remaining Libyan troops left the country, and officials from both countries signed a formal communique in Tripoli that assigned the territory to Ndjamena.

By that time, much of the African continent's own revolutionary rhetoric had dimmed in the wake of the collapse of the Soviet Union and the emergence of an international political climate where the old-time orthodoxy and rhetoric of revolution and anti-Westernism had become suspect. From his previous role as spoiler in sub-Saharan African politics, Qadhafi now wanted to turn to mainstream, more conventional politics that would yield the leadership role he craved. Under such circumstances, the earlier maverick role of the Libyan leader no longer held much promise. Although the occasional flashes of rhetoric still punctuated, almost ritually, his speeches to the sub-Saharan African leaders, Libya quietly began a diplomatic and economic campaign throughout the region, directed by the Secretariat of International Cooperation. The country's "Voice of the Greater Arab Homeland" radio station was renamed the "Voice of Africa." In his speeches, the Libyan leader continued his condemnation of the Arab regimes. Africans, not Arabs, were now portrayed as Libya's real supporters.

In subtle ways, the multilateral sanctions to which the country was subjected had had an impact on the brittle and deteriorating relationship between Libya and its regional Arab partners. The Arab world's reaction during the diplomatic maneuvering leading up to the UN sanctions, and then the countries' reluctance to contravene them once they were put into place, heightened Qadhafi's perception that the Jamahiriyya's role in inter-Arab politics had been substantially degraded. The rationale for the Arab leaders' reluctance to contravene the sanctions – based in part on the realization that doing so would undermine their own insistence for the implementation of UN Resolution 242 of 1967 that called on Israel to trade land for peace – was considered self-serving and hypocritical in Tripoli. When the Arab League leaders instead opted for mediating between Tripoli and Washington, Qadhafi in response threatened to withdraw from the organization.

In June 1994, the Ministers of Foreign Affairs of the OAU member-states had furthermore passed a resolution asking the UN Security Council to revoke the organization's sanctions against Libya, noting at a subsequent meeting that the "obnoxious sanctions" affected not only the Libyan people, but African workers from neighboring countries as well. Qadhafi was now welcomed in a number of African countries, and several of the continent's leaders, including Nelson Mandela in October 1997, visited Tripoli. In June 1998, finally, at a meeting of the Organization of African Unity in Burkina Faso, its delegates endorsed a decision to defy the UN sanctions. When Qadhafi requested the same of the Arab League meeting in Cairo in September 1998, the request was met with a rebuff. The Libyan leader turned more resolutely toward Africa, calling in August 1999 for the creation of what he termed "the historic solution for the [African] continent ... a United States of Africa."

At the same time, several African countries proved willing to break the ban on international flights into Tripoli. In 1998 alone, the heads of state of Burkina Faso – then acting chairman of the OAU – Niger, Mali, Chad, the Central African Republic, Gambia, Eritrea, Uganda, and Zimbabwe arrived at Tripoli's airport in violation of the UN sanctions. To the West, it seemed as if Libya deliberately used its improving relations with Africa to exert pressure to remove the multilateral sanctions – particularly when the OAU the same year openly stated that it would defy the air embargo if

Great Britain and the United States did not accept the trial of the Lockerbie suspects in a neutral country, one of Libya's demands. Nelson Mandela simultaneously mediated between the two sides to break the deadlock over the Lockerbie issue. It was also rumored at the time that the Arab League would, after all, fall in line with the OAU's position. Although it remained unclear whether these developments had a real influence in London and Washington, both governments on 24 August agreed to try the Lockerbie suspects in the Netherlands under Scottish law.

In the end, a number of developments coincided to make Libya's new-found Africa policy possible. There was Qadhafi's personal disappointment with the continued isolation of Libya, offset by a potential new leadership role that would burnish his personal and the Jamahiriyya's reputation. In addition, the Chad debacle, and the more general aspects of the country's outcast image internationally, slowly reoriented and refocused the Libyan leader's vision of his new Africa policy. No longer, however, would the old patterns of subversion and abruptly shifting, opportunistic alliances of the 1970s and 1980s be maintained. Qadhafi clearly aimed for a new kind of statesmanship that had previously been unknown. By the time of the special OAU summit organized by Qadhafi in Sirt in September 1999, the new policies had started to bear some fruit.

Libyan trade missions, financial assistance, the establishment of health clinics, and efforts to contain Islamic radicalism and unregulated migration from Africa toward Europe led to a number of agreements that slowly insinuated Libya back into the continent's political and economic life. Despite the remaining skepticism among many leaders in sub-Saharan Africa, Libya pushed forward suggestions for the creation of a number of bilateral and multilateral organizations – including COMESSA, the Community of Sahel and Saharan States – that would bring about regional economic and security arrangements and, eventually, according to Qadhafi, lead to a United States of Africa. If Libya's rapprochement to sub-Saharan Africa was meant originally to help put pressure on the countries imposing the multilateral sanctions, the lifting of those sanctions in 1999 introduced a new dynamic in Libyan-African relations. For, as Libya sought to curry favor with Europe, its geographical location as an important transit route for illegal African immigration to the European Union forced the Qadhafi regime to make unpopular choices vis-à-vis its African partners, and to subject itself to numerous rounds of negotiations with the European countries.

Once the sanctions were removed, the Qadhafi government eagerly moved forward with a number of initiatives to help create a "United States

Figure 8. Female soldier during the 34th anniversary of the revolution
in September 2003.

of Africa" with a continent-wide government that would eventually have
at its disposal a single African military force, as well as unified currencies
and passports. Although his plans for further initiatives were stymied at
the time, Qadhafi was appointed as chairman of the African Union in
February 2009. As during his earlier pursuit of Arab unity, his plans for
African unity were met regionally with mixed reactions. Whereas some
African governments applauded his efforts and the financial aid the Libyan
government had provided in the past for a wide range of economic and
training projects, others urged caution.[12] Perhaps nowhere would this lingering ambivalence be expressed more vividly than in the reactions the
African Union expressed toward Libya's civil war after February 2011.
Despite a number of diplomatic initiatives, and despite the repeated intervention from South Africa to reach a compromise, the regional organization would pursue essentially a hands-off approach rather than articulate
a robust intervention.

THE DELUSIONS OF QADHAFI AND OF THE WEST

As Libya embarked on its process of reintegration into the international
community after 2003, the Jamahiriyya faced an unprecedented opportunity to chart a new economic and political future, as well as to rebuild

its economy for long-term growth and development in ways that could benefit all Libyan citizens. Certainly the actions of the Libyan government had shown that, when necessary, the regime was not averse to making pragmatic choices. The slowly emerging class of technocrats and intellectuals, united around Saif al-Islam al-Qadhafi, had become both emboldened and empowered by the growing challenges the country faces, and were pressing for reform. Institutions such as the Green Book Center, which had once been the mouthpieces of the regime's ideological diktats, seemed to have lost their prestige, their focus, and much of their funding as the economic crisis deepened in the late 1980s and the 1990s.[13] Qadhafi's visits to the EU headquarters in Brussels, the visit of U.S. Secretary of State Condoleeza Rice to Tripoli in September 2008, Libya's election to the UN Security Council, the warm receptions given by Prime Minister Berlusconi of Italy to the Libyan leader on several visits – all seemed to indicate that the Leader had turned a page. At a Council on Foreign Relations gathering following his UN visit in September 2009, Qadhafi almost nostalgically recalled his earlier, confrontational policies by noting that "We were young people, we were very revolutionary, we were very excited, and we were part of the times.... A dramatic shift has taken place in the world."[14]

But his performance the day before at the UN General Assembly – during which he demanded a seat on the Security Council for Africa – belied this image of a former revolutionary seemingly at peace with his new role. In a long speech that repeated virtually all of his long-standing grievances against the West and against an unjust international order, the Leader tore up the preamble to the UN charter as a symbol of his anger. Being introduced to the General Assembly as the "leader of the revolution, the president of the African Union, the king of kings of Africa" provided another quick glimpse of the kind of sycophantic adulation that surrounded him. His welcome of Louis Farrakhan of the Nation of Islam to the Libyan mission for many undoubtedly rekindled much less happy memories of his earlier support of groups to which he felt ideologically close.

To some in Washington, the juxtaposition of Qadhafi's two performances in New York came as no surprise. During all his years in power, his speeches had always deliberately been calibrated to address different audiences, even if that meant some internal inconsistencies. To many Western policy makers, but particularly those in Washington, the agreement on WMD in December 2003 had always raised a large number of critical questions. If Qadhafi had appeared increasingly pragmatic in the years leading up to the WMD announcement, how much of that pragmatism had been forced on him by the impact of the sanctions and by the general isolation in which Libya found itself during most of the 1990s? How genuine therefore was Libya's newfound willingness to play by internationally accepted norms of state behavior? Was the pragmatism part of a process of adjustments to a number of economic and political realities that could be reversed in the future? Or was it simply a means to ensure a return of international investment, and of U.S. technology, to the country's decaying oil infrastructure?

The years since the WMD agreement and since Libya had settled the outstanding issues in its wake had provided contradictory evidence. On the one hand, there were signs that some measures of efficiency in the management of the country's economy had very slowly started to take hold. The 2010 IMF consultancy had accurately pinpointed that at least at some of the country's most important regulatory institutions – including the Central Bank – a more technocratic approach was slowly emerging and that political interference had somewhat diminished. The flurry of laws that had been passed by 2010 to make this more technocratic regulation possible certainly had been a positive sign. On the other hand, however, there were still clearly visible elements of constant political interference present. Shukri Ghanem's removal as prime minister effectively meant the end of the broader reform agenda he had advocated – an agenda that for the first time had linked economic and political reform.

The demise of the country's would-be reformers clearly indicated the resilience of the country's "revolutionary structures." Saif al-Islam al-Qadhafi's eventual withdrawal from further attempts at reform provided eloquent testimony to the fact that his own attempts had been stymied. The constitutional project, once started under his imprimatur, had been waylaid. It was very clear that in Libya, where large-scale patronage had skillfully been used to keep the political system stabilized, any attempt to either change the mechanisms of patronage or to threaten the economic fates of those intermediaries who had profited from its maintenance for four decades was bound to fail without any alteration of the very principles of the political system that had helped create it. Even the power of a privileged player like Saif al-Islam al-Qadhafi had proven incapable of altering its structures in any significant way.

Libya was once more muddling through. One of the underlying factors that took considerable wind out of the reformist sails was, as always, the presence of oil revenues. As described previously, the lifting of the economic sanctions after Qadhafi's agreement to abandon his WMD program had brought back the international oil companies after 2003, and it increased Libya's oil revenues in ways unimagined even a few years earlier. The disparity between piecemeal reforms in the country's economy and the stagnation in its political system continued unabated and, after the attempted reforms by Saif al-Islam al-Qadhafi and Shukri Ghanem, became more visible than ever. It was difficult to imagine anything else in a political system where extensive patronage had been part and parcel of political survival for so long. Close observers wondered how far Libya, after four decades of Qadhafi's rule, had moved forward toward becoming a true political community, and how the enforced stability within this inherently unstable system would resolve itself as the need for further reform of the country's economy would proceed.[15] Many among them argued – much like the Libyan opposition movements in earlier decades – that it seemed unlikely that any meaningful political reform would be possible as long as Muammar al-Qadhafi remained in power.

An added complication was that the Qadhafi government in the wake of the WMD agreement had become a valuable ally of the United States in its fight against Islamic radicalism in North Africa and beyond. From once being labeled one of the masterminds of global terrorism, Qadhafi now found himself in the unfamiliar role of providing intelligence to the United States and, on at least one occasion, participating in the rendition program that brought an arrested Islamist, Ibn al-Shaykh al-Libi, via Egypt to Libya.[16] The Libyan cooperation with the United States in the global war on terrorism predated 9/11. The Qadhafi government strongly condemned the attacks and expressed support for the U.S. decision to attack Afghanistan. Most tellingly, it voiced no opposition to the creation of the Africa Command (AFRICOM) by the United States, meant to create a U.S. military command to make Africa "into another front in its global war on terrorism, maintaining and extending access to energy supplies and other strategic raw material, and competing with China and other rising economic powers for control over the continent's resources."[17] Particularly in light of his own ambitions for Africa, Qadhafi's silence on the issue was highly unusual.

But there were at least a couple of warning signs that in some fundamental ways, little had changed about the regime's behavior. The first concerned the undue pressure the regime exerted on Great Britain for the release of al-Megrahi, the convicted Lockerbie bomber, and his hero's welcome in Tripoli – with Saif al-Islam personally accompanying al-Megrahi from Scotland. The second was the growing cult of personality around Qadhafi that came to dwarf the already considerable efforts since the early 1970s to portray the Libyan revolution as an epoch-making event, guided by a philosophy worthy of serious study. This had always required some suspension of disbelief, which Libyans had had no choice but to submit to. In the aftermath of the lifting of the sanctions, however, this new wave of burnishing the image of Qadhafi was no longer aimed purely at a local audience, but was meant to appeal to an international audience as a part of integrating Libya closer into the international community.

To anyone who had read the Green Book closely or followed Qadhafi's public announcements across the years, this attempt to portray his ideology as someone worthy of contemplation by some of the world's greatest public intellectuals and academics would have required an extraordinary leap of faith. Still, it was one that several international consultants were all too ready to make. After having written Libya's *National Economic Strategy* plan, the Monitor group submitted *A Proposal for Expanding the Dialogue around the Ideas of Muammar Qadhafi*, a $2.9 million "campaign to enhance the quality of the communication about Qadhafi's political and philosophical views ... in concert with a number of independent academics and intellectuals ... [to bring] renowned academics to Libya for direct conversations with Muammar Qadhafi ... [culminating in] a plan to research, write and publish a book about Muammar Qadhafi, the man and his ideas ... [to] present Qadhafi's authentic voice on issues of genuine world importance, in particular the challenge of building a democratic, egalitarian and prosperous society in post-colonial Africa and the Middle East."[18]

Eventually a bevy of public intellectuals and academics wound their way to Tripoli to engage with the Libyan leader: David Frost, Bernard Lewis, Fareed Zakaria, Joseph Nye, Francis Fukuyama, Benjamin Barber, Anthony Giddens, Anne Marie Slaughter, and Richard Perle.[19] Reading some of the invitees' observations, they could at best be charitably described as naive. When asked in an interview whether he considered the Qadhafi family control over the Libyan economy an obstacle to economic reform, Michael Porter, the head of the Monitor group, while in Tripoli in February 2007 to help inaugurate the country's Libyan Economic Development Board, responded that "in a sense, decision-making is widely distributed in this country. People [consider Libya] a dictatorship, but it really doesn't work that way. That is another reason for optimism."[20] And Benjamin Barber, the main subcontractor for *A Proposal for Expanding the Dialogue around the Ideas of Muammar Qadhafi* observed that:

Libya under Gaddafi has embarked on a journey that could make it the first Arab state to transition peacefully and without overt Western intervention to a stable, non-autocratic government and, in time, to an indigenous mixed constitution favoring direct democracy locally and efficient government centrally.... Completely off the radar, without spending a dollar or posting a single soldier, the United States has a potential partner in what could become an emerging Arab democracy smack in the middle of Africa's north coast. This partner possesses vital sulfur-free gas and oil resources, a pristine Mediterranean shoreline, a non-Islamist Muslim population, and intelligence capacities crucial to the war on terrorism.[21]

Inadvertently, the concluding sentence in a nutshell perfectly encapsulated all the self-interested reasons for which, as Qadhafi himself had constantly argued, the West and some of its international consultants had come to take such a renewed interest in Libya. There was furthermore little doubt that what Qadhafi saw as the validation for his ideas by these Western public figures and intellectuals further reinforced the by now somewhat surreal image he had of himself and of his self-styled revolution as being of world importance. His visits to Europe and to the United Nations, the assumption of the chairmanship of the African Union, the visits of U.S. and European dignitaries to Libya, and the visits to Tripoli to come and discuss his philosophy by well-known public figures and intellectuals – all of these helped cement the conviction that, as Qadhafi himself proclaimed on several occasions, Libya had stood up to the West and, in the end, had won: His revolution was now complete.

THE UPRISING IN CYRENAICA AND THE CIVIL WAR

Perhaps, in several ways, Qadhafi's self-styled revolution had indeed been completed – but hardly in the ways the Leader could have envisioned in 1969. It had become self-reverential, beyond criticism, focused exclusively around Qadhafi and his supporters, protected by its highly effective coercive institutions. It had been able to suppress all opposition for more than four decades, eviscerating systematically any expression of organized social, political, or economic interests. It had successfully maintained the fiction of popular participation while its political system made any real participation impossible. But the economic situation in the country had improved for the average Libyan. Businessmen flocked to Tripoli in increasingly large droves, and Libya was being reintegrated into the international community. With its recent economic fortunes dramatically enhanced, and its traditional coercive mechanisms solidly in place, the regime looked as invincible and unassailable as it had ever been. Most observers argued that real change in Libya would not take place as long as the Leader was in power. At the same time, however, the revolution had also become totally irrelevant to most Libyans beyond the patronage it provided. It certainly had not created a sense of identification or of nationhood. It had, except for some small pockets of support, not provided the mobilization the regime craved. People lived with the revolution and could not escape it, but they ignored it whenever possible. As so much in Arab society, what was private and what was public were kept perfectly separated.

The uprising that started on 15 February revealed, within its first few hours already, the depth of lingering resentment against the regime. Started in Benghazi after the arrest of Fathi Tarbil, a human rights lawyer who had represented some of the families of prisoners killed at the Abu Salim prison in 1996, the revolt quickly spread throughout the eastern part of the country – an area Qadhafi had to some degree economically deliberately neglected. It soon became clear, however, that despite their enormous political energy, the rebels had little chance of succeeding in the long term against the onslaught of the regime that could bring loyal brigades, its air force, as well as bands of foreign soldiers to bear down on rebel-held territory. While the battles between the two sides raged back and forth along the coastal area and more sporadically in Tripolitania, loyalist troups steadily advanced toward Benghazi. By the morning of 16 March, they were set to start encircling the capital of Cyrenaica. Already by that time, several of the country's top diplomats had started to defect, and both the United Nations and Europe had implemented a number of sanctions that targeted Qadhafi and his family, and once more imposed arms embargoes and travel bans reminiscent of the 1980s and 1990s.

In Cyrenaica, a Transitional National Council (TNC) emerged that declared itself the sole representative of the Libyan people. It was soon recognized by France, then later by Great Britain and Qatar, and eventually in Istanbul in July 2011 by the United States and other members of the Libya Contact Group – a group of both individual countries and international organizations (including the European Union, the Arab League, individual European countries, the United States, and the United Nations) that gathered in monthly meetings to discuss matters and resolve problems related to the conflict and to the future of Libya. In the United States, the Obama administration had initially proven highly reluctant to enter the fray, arguing that the United States had no real national interests in Libya. But forced to take a position by the consensus within the Arab League, and within the UN Security Council, by growing internal pressures, and by the dire situation of the rebels in Cyrenaica and particularly in Benghazi, the U.S. administration agreed to assume a leading initial role in enforcing the no-fly zone over Libya once the UN Security Council adopted Resolution 1973 on 17 March 2011.

From the beginning, the Resolution proved problematic: It had authorized not only a no-fly zone, but also additional measures to protect civilian lives – a somewhat vague clause that would leave room to expand NATO's mission if judged necessary. Although particularly the United States had made it clear that it did not want to commit ground forces to the conflict, the rhetoric of many of the Western leaders suggested as well from the beginning that anything less than the removal of the regime was unacceptable. The confusion worsened when NATO's help became a sine qua non for the rebels just to be able to maintain their positions, and when it became clear that greater and more decisive NATO intervention would be needed to defeat the loyalist side – an expansion of its mission that South Africa in particular vociferously objected to. At that point, for all practical purposes, the international coalition through NATO had become the arbiter of whether or not Libya's civil war would continue.

By early to mid-July 2011, it appeared that despite the intensification of NATO's campaign, a military solution to the Libya conflict looked increasingly impossible. As a result, diplomatic initiatives to settle the conflict that harked back to the immediate aftermath of the conflict in February increased and intensified, both bilaterally and through the auspices of the UN Special Envoy Abdul Ilah Khatib who had been appointed by the UN Secretary-General for the purpose of finding a possible diplomatic solution to the crisis. The profusion of these road maps, as the different proposals were invariable referred to, despite their contradictions and self-interests, clearly indicated the extent to which the Libyan civil war had become a vexing international concern that was now discussed in monthly international fora.

One of the issues central to the discussions of the Libya Contact Group at the time was the way in which Libya's civil war could be settled and the Qadhafi regime replaced. As the stalemate inside the country continued, a number of plausible scenarios had emerged.[22] In light of the country's tortured history, none appeared likely to resolve the country's long-standing divisions and fissures that had been kept unaddressed during the Qadhafi period. The first involved, as described earlier, a more intense support for the rebels who, aided by NATO air power, could steadily move westward and unify the country by overpowering the western province of Tripolitania. In light of the checkered history between Tripolitiania and Cyrenaica described in Chapter 3, this scenario would undoubtedly have opened up old wounds. When the Kingdom of Libya was created in 1951, Tripolitiania resentfully agreed to be pushed by the Great Powers into a single political entity ruled by a monarchy with its roots in Cyrenaica. The

resentment within Tripolitania, where support for Qadhafi was traditionally strongest, would be enormous if once more a government were foisted
on it either by a Cyrenaican-led rebel movement or through the support of
the international community. By mid-July, it appeared as if this essentially
military scenario was no longer likely.

A second scenario had been to simply allow Libya to separate into two
smaller states, focused around Tripolitania in the west and Cyrenaica in
the east. This would have necessitated a long-standing commitment from
the international coalition to protect Cyrenaica – certainly not a prospect
with which either the United States or the European Union were enam-
ored, and not a scenario any of the warring parties were considering either.
This scenario also appeared increasingly unlikely as none of the local and
international parties involved expressed any interest in letting Libya break
up into separate territories.

Another possible scenario involved the somewhat patient process of
gradually undermining the credibility and prospects of the Qadhafi government over time. This meant systematically undercutting the regime's
traditional methods of using patronage for its survival as the international
sanctions took hold and the regime's financial resources were depleted,
hoping that eventually internal desertions and perhaps a palace coup or
more general revolt would take place within the inner circles of the regime.
As individuals around Qadhafi and his remaining supporters started to
make calculations, much hinged on the perception of his staying power.
In a somewhat crude form of psychological warfare fought with leaflets,
through the Internet, and through personal appearances by the Libyan
leader, both he and the coalition against him attempted to portray their
cause as likely to prevail. The language Qadhafi used still resonated among
his supporters, and was not to be cavalierly dismissed. It was this resilience of the regime, together with the possibility of a long, drawn-out conflict that could expose further fault lines among the rebels in Benghazi,
that made this third scenario also increasingly problematic as the civil war
continued.

Almost by default then, a final scenario emerged that, until July 2011,
had been labeled utterly unacceptable by both sides in the conflict: a diplomatic solution for the crisis that would involve negotiations between
Tripoli and Benghazi. Although perhaps the least attractive scenario for
both sides, a negotiated settlement emerged as the most feasible one to
the many local and outside parties by now involved in the conflict by
early August. For it had become clear that a military victory for the rebels
would perhaps prove elusive and, simultaneously, that the loyalists' options

were being increasingly degraded. A negotiated settlement in a sense also represented perhaps the most promising path for the future of the country, and certainly would minimize – but not eliminate – the dislocations and potential infighting some of the other scenarios entailed.

Despite what many on both sides of the conflict and within the international community would undoubtedly have considered a repugnant solution to the Libyan conflict, it would have kept the country unified without having to worry about the existing differences between its two most powerful provinces. It would have put a halt to further destruction of the country's economy and its oil infrastructure. It would have offered the possibility of a kind of psychological closure for all Libyan citizens that other scenarios did not. Libyans would still face the daunting task of creating a new government, of elaborating the institutions for a new state, and of trying to instill a sense of nationhood. They would also need to design the new arrangements that would allow the different provinces and groups within Libya to work together in a post-Qadhafi world, and to generally engage in a process of state building that would be extremely difficult. But they would be able to do so knowing that they had avoided an even longer civil war and the attending deep and lasting cleavages that could perhaps never be healed.

One of the central issues of this negotiated settlement at the time was the sensitive question of the future of Mu'ammar al-Qadhafi, his family, and the circle of close confidants who remained loyal to him. For the TNC, the removal of Qadhafi from Libya had initially represented a red line they would not cross; vice versa, for the loyalist side, this was a solution they would not consider. The decision of the International Criminal Court to indict Qadhafi and his son for human rights violations further complicated the issue for it meant that the possibility of exile for the Libyan leader had become more problematic.

By early August, after several months of a stalemate, it looked as if this negotiated settlement scenario was slowly gaining traction. It had become evident that the resources and options of the Qadhafi government were steadily diminishing, but that the regime still possessed some power and strength in Tripolitania. And even though the rebels in the east and in the western Nafusa mountains gradually gathered more diplomatic support and weapons for their cause, the fact remained that even a more muscular NATO mission seemingly proved insufficient to reunify the country.[23]

In addition, although the rebels in Cyrenaica continued to cast their movement in glowing terms and their victory as inevitable, a number of fault lines had started to emerge as the conflict dragged on – disagreements that became particularly glaring in the wake of the killing of Abdel Fateh Younes, the rebels' military commander.[24] In the heat of the struggle, criticism of the TNC had been held in abeyance. The fact remained, however, that despite its acceptance by much of the international community, it had been a self-appointed institution whose legitimacy was less robust inside Libya. Additional fault lines appeared between, on the one hand, the rebels fighting the Qadhafi forces and on the other hand the "politicians" in Benghazi and the professional military figures that had once been a part of Qadhafi's army; between those inside and outside Libya[25]; between the young technocrats working at the temporary ministries the TNC had created and some of the older political leadership; between Islamist representatives and some of the more secular figures on the Council; and, finally, between those who wanted to negotiate and those who opposed negotiations.

An assault on Tripoli on 15 August by rebels in western Libya, aided by NATO support and logistical expertise, however, brought all these speculations about different scenarios to an end. Within a few days, the western rebels had not only managed to conquer Tripoli, but had penetrated into Bab al-Azziziya, the logistical and symbolic heart of the Qadhafi regime. The end of the Qadhafi regime was now suddenly inevitable – and the challenges of the TNC to put their planning into practice was about to become reality. The battles of Bani Walid and Sirt – the last strongholds of the regime – would take almost another month to resolve. On 20 October Sirt was finally taken by the rebels and Mu'ammar al-Qadhafi was killed.

For Libya's transitional authorities, a number of even larger conundrums now loomed ahead: the eventual incorporation of Tripoli and Tripolitania into a new political formula for the country, proceeding on a process of reconciliation, creating a set of governing institutions for the country that will be seen as both legitimate and equitable, trying to control the proliferation of weapons in private and militia hands, and, finally but fundamentally, resisting the urge to use oil revenues for political convenience and control – all of this in a country where political dialogue and compromise have been virtually unknown or unwanted since its creation in 1951.

Although historical analogies are always fraught with danger, some of the challenges the monarchy faced in 1951 – and then the Qadhafi regime after 1969 – were left unresolved and continue to persist today. They will constitute the challenges of Libya's new rulers in the months and years ahead: to create the institutions of a modern state out of the chaos of competing interests, especially when faced with large inflows of oil revenues that make such institution building difficult. In addition, the Transitional National

Council and its successors will need to make such a state attractive enough to capture the consensus and allegiance of a wide variety of groups and individuals. Against this background, against unpromising beginnings, the new Libyan authorities will now have to embark on a process of state and nation building the country has never experienced before.

Epilogue: Whither Libya?

By the time the uprising in 2011 took place, Tripoli had been a boom town for several years, reminiscent of the 1960s and 1970s. A string of luxury hotels appeared along the corniche, their lobbies filled with foreign businessmen and local intermediaries pursuing each other in search of opportunities that the lifting of sanctions and the burgeoning revenues from oil sales once more made possible. To anyone who had known the country during the austere years of its revolution, when virtually all private businesses had been abolished or withered away for lack of provisions, the city's streets had been transformed beyond recognition. Many of the revolutionary slogans that had once punctuated urban and rural landscapes alike were giving way to commercial advertising signs. The once ubiquitous portraits of the Leader now vied for attention alongside commercial dioramas that touted an array of products Libyans once could only dream about – most dramatically, advertisements for airline destinations outside the Jamahiriyya. Small shops lined the main streets of the city selling imported food, appliances and furniture. Glittering malls in Tripoli's Hay al-Andalus were now filled with brand-name electronics and other expensive foreign luxuries. Prices for real estate in the area skyrocketed, and private supermarkets now stocked international foods Libyans could only dream of a few years earlier.

But in the wake of the civil war the essential questions that have dogged Libya since its creation as an independent state in 1951 are still left unresolved: the creation of an institutionalized state, and the incorporation of the country's citizens into a meaningful nation. When the uprising started in February 2011, the territories that formed the independent United Kingdom of Libya and then the Jamahiriyya had existed for six decades. During that time, Libya had been changed beyond recognition – from a desert-strewn backwaters to a modern oil economy with intricate links to the international economy. A tribal, impoverished, and barely self-sustaining society had endured the Sanusi monarchy with its confused sense of what political community it represented, and then four decades of the diktats of a revolutionary regime that seemed determined to destroy whatever institutions could create any sense of political community.

Until the discovery of oil in 1959, the country had seemed destined to retain those social and economic features it possessed since time immemorial. Very few Libyans at the time it seemed – except for some small clusters of urban elites – had a real interest in the United Kingdom of Libya as a political community. This was partly due to the colonial legacy, partly to the fact that the comforting and familiar sense of kinship and local – or at best regional – political allegiance could be maintained during the first few years of the monarchy but, importantly, also to the fact that there were few economic prospects for the country that could spark interest and struggles for economic goods that would make the construction of a national community worthwhile.

This changed, literally almost overnight, when oil started coursing through the veins of a barely existing economy that could suddenly produce great riches. Oil riches also sparked, however, a level of social and economic differentiation the country had never witnessed before – and created economic interests that made it worthwhile integrating a country for. Unfortunately for Libya, during the remainder of the monarchy and during the years since, these interests were never nurtured and exploited for the purpose of creating a truly national community. Oil revenues allowed Idris al-Sanusi and Mu'ammar al-Qadhafi to create and maintain social contracts with their subjects that relied overwhelmingly on distributive largesse rather than on perfecting the state.

This remains partly to blame for the low sense of political community Libya faces even today – and for the *sauve-qui-peut* attitude many of its citizens exhibit – a phenomenon Libya's current rulers will need to keep in mind. Oil revenues alone are not to blame for this. Those who were in charge of the country carry an equal burden of guilt. Both Idris al-Sanusi and Mu'ammar al-Qadhafi – in different styles and by different means, but both conveying the same meaning – consistently projected a sense of community for their citizens in various combinations below or above the level of the state and in lieu of the state: kinship, family, tribe, Islam, Arab nationalism, African unity. Under both systems of government – laissez faire or activist – Libyan citizens remained largely bystanders. Both King Idris and Qadhafi lamented the impact of oil on their societies and on its traditional values, but both failed to understand how their policies – or lack thereof – created those outcomes.

Ever since 1969, Qadhafi has pursued a policy of statelessness that, at least in theory, puts all power in the hands of the people. Ironically, as statelessness was pursued, virtually all economic activity within the country came under state control. As opposed to non-oil economies where over time the state develops and finetunes a set of regulatory, extractive, and distributive mechanisms to calibrate the interactions between the state and local society, in Libya this evolutionary process of state and institution building was curtailed and abandoned.

In Libya, the questions that are at the heart of every political system were less pressing to the monarchy and then the Qadhafi government: how revenues are gathered, what compromises the ruler must make with his subjects to obtain them, which institutional capabilities the state needed to develop this task, and how those institutional arrangements reflected the interests of both ruled and ruler. The challenge to the state was not to extract wealth but to spend it. Economic growth could, during prolonged periods, simply be "bought" by increasing the sale of the revenue-gathering resource. Distributive policies become the most common method to meet social contracts, to stimulate domestic economic sectors, and to keep citizens voiceless.

State institutions under Qadhafi became intricate channels for economic largesse and distributive purposes, while their regulatory and legal capacities – already weak by the initial state-building processes described above – tended to remain inefficient and underdeveloped. The lack of economic data in Libya, the occasional physical destruction of state bureaucratic offices and records, and the state's sporadic and ineffective direct intervention in issues ranging from employment, to price setting, to property rights issues were all signs of regulatory weakness. In effect, the country's relative stability until the uprising in 2011 was, more than anything, due to the fact that Libya had not yet been forced to flex its institutional capacity for economic activity beyond distribution. The country had become a prime example of the by now familiar litany of the "too much state, too little state" phenomenon: pervasiveness and lingering control by those in charge of the state that has not translated into efficiency, capability, or capacity.

Under such circumstances, social stratification in Libya resulted overwhelmingly from the distributive and spending patterns of the state, forcing the Qadhafi government to assiduously promote its clients. Much of this maneuvering was concealed by the way in which the country's revenues were carefully shielded from public scrutiny – and much of it would not be revealed until the 2011 uprising had started. Decisions concerning economic policies, distribution, and investments were traditionally kept to the purview of small coalitions rather than assigned to the market. Not surprisingly, this distributive largesse was augmented with reliance on informal mechanisms linked to history, religion, or culture. The enormous bifurcation between formal and informal politics remained a pronounced feature of Libya's political life until the 2011 uprising started – expressed in the supremacy of the revolutionary instruments of rule in the country.

These enduring legacies of the revolutionary period will continue to cast long shadows in the wake of the civil war. Obviously Qadhafi's idea of statelessness and its expression through the Popular Committee and Congress system as a guideline for Libya is finished. In the wake of Qadhafi's death, the economic, social, and political challenges the country faces are enormous. With virtually all modern state institutions having been eviscerated or neglected by the Qadhafi government, Libya now confronts a simultaneous need to restructure its economy away from excessive reliance on the state and on hydrocarbon revenues and to come up with a political formula acceptable to a number of different players that have traditionally been antagonistic but that were held together artificially by the authoritarian policies of the Qadhafi government. In light of the many opportunities that will exist for the different Libyans players in the country's provinces to pursue their individuals interests at the expense of whatever new Libya emerges, the country's future looks clouded.

Despite its rhetoric of internationalism, pan-Arabism, and pan-Africanism, Qadhafi's revolution was a powerful nationalist one, but one that, ironically, did not allow for the creation of a modern Libyan nation or state. It was also a revolution pursued in part in antagonism to the West. It is not yet clear how much of that ideology will survive. Libyans will undoubtedly want to jettison most of it. However, some of what Qadhafi once stood for – his suspicions of the West, his wish to renew Arab grandeur, his initial quest for dignity and self-determination – will continue to resonate within the Libyan political imagination as a new Libya gets constructed. The combination of economic reality, generational turnover, and reintegration into the global economy and community once more will dramatically change Libya's political and economic life, and some form of coherent vision will be needed that equally resonates among its citizens. The *jamahiriyya*'s revolution has ended. The process of creating a new sense of identity and of community out of its ashes started with the uprising of February 2011 and has been passed on to the Transitional National Council and its successors. As Libya now stands poised for its new rulers and a new form of government, it is not clear yet if in this new Libya its rulers can construct this new state and a sense of political community while avoiding the internal turmoil of the Qadhafi years that was propagated by the liberal use (and misuse) of the country's oil revenues. Let us hope so.

Notes

INTRODUCTION: LIBYA, THE ENIGMATIC OIL STATE

1. See, for example, the contributions of Taoufik Monastiri, François Burgat, Hanspeter Mattes, and Moncef Djaziri in Dirk Vandewalle, ed., *Qadhafi's Libya, 1969–1994* (New York: St. Martin's Press, 1995).
2. For a promising start, see the contributions of several Libyan scholars in Anna Baldinetti, ed., *Modern and Contemporary Libya: Sources and Historiographies* (Rome: Istituto Italiano Per L'Africa e L'Oriente, 2003).

1 "A TRACT WHICH IS WHOLLY SAND ..." HERODOTUS

1. Gustav Nachtigal, *Sahara and Sudan. Volume I: Tripoli and Fezzan, Tibesti or Tu* (London: C. Hurst & Company, 1974), p. 34.
2. International Bank of Reconstruction and Development, *The Economic Development of Libya* (Baltimore: The Johns Hopkins University Press, 1960), p. 29.
3. See Pierre Marthelot, "La Libye: aperçu ge´ographique," in Gianni Albergoni *et al., La Libye nouvelle: rupture et continuite´* (Paris: Editions du Centre National de Recherche Scientifique, 1975).
4. An account of the wide variation in population estimates can be found in Nicolah Ziadeh, *Sanusiyah: A Study of a Revivalist Movement in Islam* (Leiden: Brill, 1968), p. 19.
5. All estimates should be used with great caution. A more descriptive report of physical conditions around Tripoli at the time can be found in Miss Tully [Lady Montague], *Narrative of Ten Years' Residence at Tripoli in Africa* (London: Colburn, 2nd edn., 1817).
6. General figures for Cyrenaica in Enrico De Agostini, *Le popolazioni della Cirenaica* (Bengasi: Governo della Cirenaica, 1923).
7. At the end of World War II, an estimated 28,000 Jews remained in Libya. By the mid-1960s this had dwindled down to 6,400, of whom 90% lived in Tripoli. In the wake of the 1967 war between Israel and its Arab neighbors, most Jews still living in Libya left the country. The few that remained saw their properties expropriated by the Qadhafi government in 1970.

8. The classic work on the Sanusiyya remains E. E. Evans-Pritchard, *The Sanusi of Cyrenaica* (London: Oxford at Clarendon Press, 1949). See also Ziadeh, *Sanusiyah.*

9. A. M. Hassanein Bey, The Lost Oases (London: Thornton Butterworth, 1925), p. 60, cited in John Wright, *Libya: A Modern History* (Baltimore: The Johns Hopkins University Press, 1981), p. 13, fn. 6.

10. For greater information on this, and on the value of the trans-Saharan trade, consult A. A. Boahen, *Britain, the Sahara and the Western Sudan, 1788–1861* (London: Clarendon Press, 1964), p. 128.

11. Adrian Pelt, *Libyan Independence and the United Nations: A Case of Planned Decolonization* (New Haven: Yale University Press, 1970), p. 6.

12. For the diplomatic record and sources, see J. C. Hurewitz, *The Middle East and North Africa in World Politics. Volume I* (New Haven: Yale University Press, 1975), especially pp. 552–553.

2 ITALY'S FOURTH SHORE AND DECOLONIZATION, 1911–1950

1. The documentary record can be found in Francesco Malgeri, *La guerra libica (1911–1912)* (Roma: Edizioni de Storia e Letteratura, 1970). For figures on troops, see J. C. Hurewitz, *The Middle East and North Africa in World Politics. Volume I* (New Haven: Yale University Press, 1975), p. 553.

2. John Wright, *Libya: A Modern History* (Baltimore: The Johns Hopkins University Press, 1981), p. 28.

3. For the complications surrounding Ahmad al-Shariff's decision to go to war against the Italians, see Sergio Romano, *La Quarta Sponda: la guerra di Libia, 1911–1912* (Milan: Bompiani, 1977).

4. For a good discussion of these issues, see Lisa S. Anderson, *The State and Social Transformation in Tunisia and Libya, 1830–1980* (Princeton: Princeton University Press, 1986), pp. 117–121.

5. The best account can be found in Makzoum Attia Gaber, "Le mouvement du 'jihad' en Libye face à la colonization italienne de 1911 a 1919." Ph.D. dissertation, University of Provence, 1983.

6. E. E. Evans-Pritchard, *The Sanusi of Cyrenaica* (London: Oxford at Clarendon Press, 1949), p. 122.

7. Lisa S. Anderson, "The Tripoli Republic 1918–1922," in E. G. H. Joffe´ and K. S. Maclachlan, eds., *Social and Economic Development of Libya* (London: MENAS Press, 1982), pp. 43–66. See also John Wright's account, pp. 30–31.

8. Adrian Pelt, *Libyan Independence and the United Nations: A Case of Planned Decolonization* (New Haven: Yale University Press, 1970), p. 18. Evans-Pritchard, 147, mentions November 1921. See Pelt, 18, footnote 23 for further accounts. Pelt's magisterial *Libyan Independence and the United Nations* remains the most detailed and insightful report surrounding the country's creation.

9. Text of the agreement can be found in Al-Tahar Ahmad Al-Zawi, *Jihad al-Abtal fi Tarabulus al-Gharb* (The Holy War of the Heroes in Tripoli)

(Cairo: Imprimerie Tajella al-Jadida, 1950), a partisan source that must be read with considerable caution.

10. The campaigns are recalled by Grazianni, known among the Libyans as "the butcher of Tripoli," in his *Cirenaica pacificata* (Milan: Mondadori, 1934) and Pace romana in Libia (Milan: Mondadori, 1937).

11. Pelt, p. 500, footnote 89. See also J. Wright, p. 42, footnote 10, for some cautionary remarks. After the 1969 revolution, the regime routinely claimed that half of the Libyan population had been killed by the Italians, and Qadhafi at one point mentioned 750,000 Libyans killed.

12. Knud Holmboe, *Desert Encounter: An Adventurous Journey Through Italian Africa* (London: George Harrup & Co., 1936), p. 203; cited in J. Wright, p. 35.

13. A good description of this incident can be found in Saul Kelly, *The Last Oasis. The Desert War and the Hunt for Zerzura* (Boulder: Westview Press, 2002).

14. J. Wright, p. 37.

15. Pelt, p. 31.

16. Claudio G. Segrè, *Fourth Shore: The Italian Colonization of Libya* (Chicago: The University of Chicago, 1974), p. 161.

17. J. Wright, p. 36.

18. For a varnished, laudatory account of Italian policies, see G. L. Steer's somewhat unfortunately titled *Date in the Desert* (London: Hodder and Stoughton, 1939).

19. Among a plethora of sources, see J. L. Miege, *L'imperialismo coloniale dal 1870 ai giorni nostri* (Milan: Rizzoli, 1976), and the unrivaled Segrè.

20. Pelt, p. 31.

21. The official history of the BMA can be found in Lord Rennell of Rodd, *British Military Administration of Occupied Territories in Africa during the Years 1941–1947* (London: His Majesty's Stationery Office, 1948).

22. For a description of the Libyan Arab Forces' involvement in the war, see W. B. Kennedy Shaw, *Long Range Desert Group. The Story of its Work in Libya, 1940–1943* (London: Collins, 1945), p. 150.

23. A good synopsis of the interests and programs of the different parties – as well as those of the international actors – can be found in J. Wright, pp. 50–58 and, in great detail, in Pelt, chapters 1 and 2.

24. Henry Serrano Villard, *Libya: The New Arab Kingdom of North Africa* (Ithaca, N.Y.: Cornell University Press, 1956); Majid Khadduri, *Modern Libya: A Study in Political Development* (Baltimore: The Johns Hopkins University Press, 1963).

25. Pelt, 100.

26. In an interview with the author in London in January 2005, Mustafa Ben Halim, a former Prime Minister of Libya during the monarchy, still expressed considerable consternation about the change of heart.

27. Interview with Ben Halim, London. 20 January 2005.

28. Villard, pp. 23–33.

29. Pelt, 34.

30. Details of the grim economic situation can be found inter alia in several sources: Rawle Farley, *Planning for Development in Libya: The Exceptional Economy in the Developing World* (New York: Praeger Publishers, 1971); International Bank of Reconstruction and Development, *The Economic Development of Libya* (Baltimore: The Johns Hopkins University Press, 1960); Pelt. Figures cited from J. Wright, p. 48.

3 THE SANUSI MONARCHY AS ACCIDENTAL STATE, 1951–1969

1. *The New York Times*, 13 December 1959.
2. Majid Khadduri, *Modern Libya: A Study in Political Development* (Baltimore: The Johns Hopkins University Press, 1963), p. 9.
3. The difficulties of these preliminary negotiations can be grasped from Adrian Pelt, *Libyan Independence and the United Nations: A Case Study of Planned Decolonization* (New Haven: Yale University Press, 1970), and Khadduri, ch. 6.
4. A sentiment shared by former Prime Minister Ben Halim. Interview, London. 20 January 2005.
5. Consult Henry Serrano Villard, *Libya: The New Arab Kingdom of North Africa* (Ithaca: Cornell University Press, 1956).
6. Elizabeth Hayford, "The Politics of the Kingdom of Libya in Historical Perspective." Ph.D. dissertation, Tufts University, 1970, p. 196.
7. Khadduri, p. 204.
8. Villard, p. 42.
9. Khadduri, p. 319.
10. Villard, p. 42
11. Benjamin Howard Higgins, *The Economic and Social Development of Libya* (New York: United Nations Technical Assistance Programme, 1953), p. 37.
12. Four Power Commission of Investigation, Former Italian Colonies, *Report on Libya* (London: Government Publishing Company, 1948).
13. International Bank of Reconstruction and Development (IBRD), *The Economic Development of Libya* (Baltimore: The Johns Hopkins University Press, 1960), p. 8.
14. For background, see ibid., ch. 3.
15. Judith Gurney, *Libya. The Political Economy of Oil* (Oxford: Oxford University Press, 1996), p. 23.
16. Ibid.
17. *JR*, 19/6/55, 8/2/56.
18. IBRD, pp. 60–63.
19. Gurney, p. 39.
20. Cited by ibid., p. 45.
21. Rawle Farley, *Planning for Development in Libya: The Exceptional Economy in the Developing World* (New York: Praeger, 1971), ch. 8; and Frank Waddams, *The Libyan Oil Industry* (Baltimore: The Johns Hopkins University Press, 1980), pp. 177–180.

22. Khadduri, ch. 9.

23. Interview with Mustafa Ben Halim, London. 20 January 2005.

24. Higgins, p. 11.

25. In 1954, Libya had invaded the Aouzou strip for the first time, in an attempt to claim the area. For a more detailed account of Libya's involvement in Chad, including Qadhafi's similar attempts in the 1970s and 1980s, consult Benjamin Neuberger, *Involvement, Invasion, and Withdrawal: Qadhdhafi's Libya and Chad 1969–1981* (Syracuse: Syracuse University Press, 1982).

26. For an analysis of the development and composition of Libya's elites during the monarchy, see in particular Salaheddin Salem Hassan, "The Genesis of Political Leadership in Libya, 1952–1969." Ph.D. dissertation, George Washington University, 1973.

27. Khadduri, pp. 264–267.

28. *JR*, 1966, pp. 2183–2192.

29. In effect, the Qadhafi regime, recognizing the nefarious impact it had would attempt to do away with the system of sweeteners through its Exploration and Production Sharing Agreements (EPSAs).

30. *JR*, 1964, pp. 808–812; 1965, pp. 205–217.

31. Salaheddin Hasan Sury [Salaheddin Salem Hassan], "A New System for a New State: The Libyan Experiment in Statehood, 1951–1969," in Anna Baldinetti, ed., *Modern and Contemporary Libya: Sources and Historiographies* (Rome: Istituto Italiano Per L'Africa et L'Oriente, 2003), p. 183.

32. Ibid.

33. Cited in Khadduri, p. 299.

34. Ibid., p. 298.

35. The same sentiments would come to preoccupy his successor, Mu'ammar al-Qadhafi, whose own trips to the desert – complete with traditional tents and camels – and his often-expressed aversion to city life were part and parcel of the Libyan revolution.

36. Mustafa Ahmad Ben Halim, *Libya: The Years of Hope* (London: AAS Publishers, 1998), p. 328.

37. John Davis, *Libyan Politics: Tribe and Revolution. (An Account of the Zuwaya and Their Government)* (Berkeley: University of California Press, 1987), p. 258.

4 A LIBYAN SANDSTORM: FROM MONARCHY TO REPUBLIC, 1969–1973

1. Ruth First, *Libya: The Elusive Revolution* (Harmondsworth: Penguin, 1974), pp. 110–116.

2. Mu'ammar al-Qadhafi in Hamid Barrada, Mark Kravetz, and Mark Whitaker, *Kadhafi: "Je suis un opposant à l'échelon mondial"* (Lausanne: Editions Pierre-Marcel Favre, 1984).

3. Mohammed Heikal, *The Road to Ramadan* (New York: Quadrangle / New York Times Book Co., 1975), p. 70.

4. Mu'ammar Al-Qadhafi, *As-Sijil al-qawmi bayanat wa ahadith al-aqid Mu'ammar al-Qadhdhafi* (Tripoli: Marakiz ath-thaqafiya al-qawmiya, 1969–1970).

5. John Davis, *Libyan Politics: Tribe and Revolution. (An Account of the Zuwaya and Their Government)* (Berkeley: University of California Press, 1987), p. 38.

6. *JR*, 1972, pp. 1338–1341.

7. See Omar El-Fathaly, Monte Palmer, and Richard Chackerian, *Political Development and Bureaucracy in Libya* (Lexington, Mass.: Lexington Books, 1977), for details on the regime's recruitment attempts.

8. *JR*, 2 September 1973.

9. Qadhafi, cited by First, p. 101.

10. Interview with David Mack, 12 November 2004. Mack was a junior political officer at the US Embassy in Libya in 1969.

11. See Omar El-Fathaly and Monte Palmer, *Political Development and Social Change in Libya* (Lexington, Mass.: Lexington Books, 1980).

12. On Qadhafi's ideas about Islam and its role in modern politics, see Mahmoud M. Ayoub, *Islam and the Third Universal Theory: The Religious Thought of Mu'ammar al-Qadhdhafi* (London: KPI Limited, 1987).

13. El-Fathaly and Palmer.

14. See Judith Gurney, *Libya. The Political Economy of Oil* (Oxford: Oxford University Press, 1996), pp. 48–49, for details.

15. *Middle East Economic Digest*, 31 August 1979.

16. *AAN, 1970*, p. 453.

17. John Anthony Allan, *Libya: The Experience of Oil* (Boulder: Westview Press, 1981), p. 179.

5 *THE GREEN BOOK'S* STATELESS SOCIETY, 1973–1986

1. A good overview of the history of US–Libyan relations can be found in Ronald Bruce St. John, *Libya and the United States. Two Centuries of Strife* (Philadelphia: University of Pennsylvania Press, 2002).

2. *Al-Fajr Al-Jadid*, 12/9/74; 13/9/74.

3. Herve' Bleuchot, *Chroniques et documents libyens, 1969–1980* (Paris: Editions du Centre National de la Recherche Scientifique, 1983), pp. 86–89.

4. Among secondary sources on Qadhafi's *Green Book*, see *International Colloquium in Benghazi: The Green Book. Volume II* (1–3 October 1979) (Tripoli: Foreign Liaison Office, General Secretariat of the General People's Congress, 1981).

5. *SQ*, 1/9/75, pp. 245–248.

6. *SQ*, 1974–1975, p. 688.

7. Mu'ammar al-Qadhafi, *The Green Book. Volume I* (Tripoli: The Green Book Center, 1980), p. 12.

8. *SQ*, 1976–1977, pp. 470–478.

9. Mu'ammar al-Qadhafi, *The Green Book. Volume III: The Social Basis of the Third Universal Theory* (Tripoli: The Green Book Center, 1980), p. 4.

10. *JR*, 8/5/78, p. 491
11. Mimeo, GPC Tripoli, 12/12/89.
12. John Anthony Allan, *Libya: The Experience of Oil* (Boulder: Westview Press, 1981), p. 241.
13. By 1975, according to the government's own statistics, 25% of all Libyan children were being educated, a rise from 16% in 1969.
14. Libyan Arab Jamahiriyya, *Libya. Economic and Social Transformation Plan (1976–1980)* (Tripoli: Secretariat of Planning, 1976), pp. 4–21.
15. Figures from Nicolas Sarkis, "Les Arabes pauvres et les Arabes riches," *Le Monde Diplomatique, August* 1978; *also cited in AAN, 16* (1977), p. 569.
16. Libyan Arab Jamahiriyya, Secretariat of Planning, *Long-term Development Prospects, Issues and Policies, 1980–2000* (Tripoli: Secretariat of Planning, 1979).
17. *FBIS*, 9/9/93, pp. 19–20.
18. On the Revolutionary Committees, see Habib al-Hesnawi, *The Revolutionary Committees and Their Role in the Confirmation and Consolidation of the People's Authority* (Tripoli: Green Book Center, 1987); *Al-Lijan ath-Thawriya* (in Arabic) (Tripoli: al-Markaz al-ʿalami li-dirasat wa-abhath al-kitab al-akhdar, 1985); and the relevant chapters in Hanspeter Mattes, *Die Volksrevolution in der Sozialistischen Libyschen Arabischen Volksgamahiriyya* (Heidelberg: Kivouvou Verlag, 1982).
19. *SQ*, 1979–1980, p. 432.
20. *SQ*, 1978–1979, p. 21.
21. Cited in Mattes, *Die Volksrevolution*, p. 97.
22. *SQ*, 1980–1981, pp. 567–581; see also Ahmad Ibrahim, *Revolutionary Organization* (Tripoli: Green Book Center, 1983). Ibrahim specifically condones violence as a tactic. He later became Secretary (Minister) for Education and Scientific Research and remains (in 2005) Assistant Secretary of the General People's Congress.
23. Ann Elizabeth Mayer, "In Search of Sacred Law: The Meandering Course of Qadhafi's Legal Policy," in Dirk Vandewalle, ed., *Qadhafi's Libya, 1969 to 1994* (New York: St. Martin's Press, 1995), pp. 114–115.
24. *JR*, 29/5/81, p. 1124.
25. *SQ*, 1980–1981, p. 1207.
26. *FBIS*, 20/10/93, pp. 21–23.
27. For more information, consult Dirk Vandewalle, "The Failure of Liberalization in the Jamahiriyya," in Dirk Vandewalle, ed., *Qadhafi's Libya.*
28. For a flavor of the continuing infighting among the groups, see *FBIS*, 3/11/93, p. 21, and *FBIS*, 17/11/93, pp. 26–27.
29. *Middle East Economic Digest*, 3/11/80, p. 1.
30. *Middle East Economic Survey (MEES)*, 15/4/85, B1–2.
31. For Libya's involvement in terrorism, see the annual volumes of the US Department of State's *Patterns of Global Terrorism.*
32. *Public Papers of Presidents: Ronald Reagan, 1986, Volume 1, 18* (Washington: Government Printing Office, 1988).
33. "CIA Anti-Qaddafi Plan Backed: Reagan Authorizes Covert Operation to Undermine Libyan Regime," *Washington Post*, 3 November 1985, A1.

34. *ZA*, 22/8/81; *AAN, 1981*, p. 561.
35. See *AAN, 1981*, p. 558, for more details on the January 1981 Congress.
36. Alain Frachon, "Les de'fauts de l'armure du colonel," *Le Monde*, 30/4/86.
37. For more details, consult *MEES*, 25 #41 (26 July 1982), pp. 3–4; 25 #42 (2 August 1982), p. 3.
38. Jacques Roumani, "From Republic to Jamahiriya: Libya's Search for Political Community," *Middle East Journal*, 37, no. 2 (Spring 1983), p. 166.
39. Based on the only sampling survey ever performed in Libya until now, Amal Obeidi's *Political Culture in Libya* (Richmond: Curzon Press, 2001) details the lingering apathy among Libyan students for many of Qadhafi's ideological constructs.

6 THE LIMITS OF THE REVOLUTION, 1986–2000

1. ZA, 15 February 1987, 17 February 1987.
2. The most complete analysis of the fortunes of the Revolutionary Committees can be found in Hanspeter Mattes, "The Rise and Fall of the Revolutionary Committees," in Dirk Vandewalle, ed., Qadhafi's Libya, 1969–1994 (New York: St. Martin's Press, 1995), pp. 89–112.
3. FBIS, 29 March 1988, 3 May 1988, 5 May 1988.
4. See Ann Elizabeth Mayer, "In Search of Sacred Law: The Meandering Course of Qadhafi's Legal Policy," in Dirk Vandewalle, ed., Qadhafi's Libya, pp. 113–138 for a detailed analysis of the Great Green Charter's provisions and shortcomings from a legal viewpoint.
5. Moncef Djaziri, "Creating a New State: Libya's Political Institutions," in Dirk Vandewalle, ed., Qadhafi's Libya, p. 197.
6. Department of State, Bureau of Arms Control, World Military Expenditures and Arms Transfers (Washington, D.C.: Department of State, 1988), p. 144.
7. Anton Chernik, "Russia Retains a Constant Partner," Defense and Security, 8 May 2001, p. 2.
8. The best summary and analysis of Libya's multiple security organizations can be found in Hanspeter Mattes, "Challenges to Security Sector Governance in the Middle East: The Libyan Case," conference paper for the workshop on the Challenges of Security Sector Governance in the Middle East, Geneva Center for the Democratic Control of Armed Forces, Geneva, 11–13 July 2004.
9. The mathaba was officially disbanded as an independent security organization in October 1992 and folded into different institutions. It retains a political branch inside the Jamahiriyya.
10. See Mansour O. El-Kikhia, Libya's Qaddafi. The Politics of Contradiction (Gainesville: University of Florida Press, 1997).
11. The best overall analysis of the multi-level impact of the sanctions can be found in Meghan L. O'Sullivan, Shrewd Sanctions: Statecraft and State Sponsors of Terrorism (Washington, D.C.: Brookings Institution Press, 2003), pp. 186–223, and in Tim Niblock, Pariah States and Economic Sanctions in the Middle East: Iraq, Libya, Sudan (Boulder, Colo.: Lynne Riener, 2001).

12. Economist Intelligence Unit (EIU), Country Report: Libya, (London: EIU, Third Quarter, 1983), p. 15.
13. EIU, Country Report: Libya (First Quarter 1986), p. 13. Also cited in O'Sullivan, p. 192.
14. See Judith Gurney, Libya. The Political Economy of Oil (Oxford: Oxford University Press, 1996), p. 97.
15. EIU, Country Profile: Libya 2001, p. 25.
16. An estimate by the chairman of Libyan Arab Airlines. See EIU, Country Report: Libya (Third Quarter 1997), p. 15. Also cited by O'Sullivan, p. 381, fn. 89.
17. O'Sullivan, p. 199.
18. See Middle East Economic Digest (MEED), 3 September 1984, A3, for details on the dispute. Also, consult Gurney for further information on EPSA III.
19. Al-Fajr Al-Jadid, 20 July 1987.
20. Hamid Barrada, Mark Kravetz, and Mark Whitaker, Kadhafi: "Je suis un opposant à l'échelon mondial" (Lausanne: Editions Pierre-Marcel Favre, 1984).
21. FBIS, 2 September 1992, p. 19, and FBIS, 1 September 1988, for the earlier reforms.
22. MEED, 18 September 1992; FBIS, 24 March 1993; JR, 27 March 1993; FBIS, 10 May 1993; FBIS, 13 July 1993; FBIS, 2 February 1994.
23. Interview of author with Abu Zayed Dorda, Tripoli, 17/1/05.
24. Interview of author with Prime Minister Shukri Ghanem, Tripoli, 16/1/05.
25. FBIS, 10 March 1993, p. 18; FBIS, 9 September 1993, p. 21.
26. See Chris C. Joyner and Wayne P. Rothbaum, "Libya and the Aerial Incident at Lockerbie: What Lessons for International Extradition Law?" Michigan Journal of International Law, 14 (1993), no. 2, pp. 222–261, for details on the legal issues involved.
27. New York Times, 24 July 1996.
28. A comprehensive anthology of articles and statements published by the National Front for the Salvation of Libya can be found in Libya Under Gaddafi And the NFSL Challenge (n.p.: National Front for the Salvation of Libya, 1992).
29. Among a plethora of articles and speeches, see Douglas Jehl, "30 Years Later, Is It Really Qadhafi?" International Herald Tribune, 7 September 1999.
30. It did require, however, a revisionist account of The Green Book's economic and political directives. See the articles by Saleh Ibrahim on "Rereading the Green Book" (Tripoli, mimeo, 2004 and 2005 – in Arabic).

7 RECONCILIATION, CIVIL WAR, AND
FIN DE RÉGIME, 2003–2011

1. The most recent statement by Shukri Ghanem can be found in Ivo Bozon and Giorgio Bresciani, "The outlook for Libya's oil sector: An interview with the chairman of the National Oil Corporation," McKinsey & Company, November 2010.

2. Saif al-Islam al-Qadhafi, quoted in *The Daily Star*, 29 January 2005.

3. Monitor Group, *National Economic Strategy: An Assessment of the Competitiveness of the Libyan Arab Jamahiriyya* (The General PLanning Council of Libya, 2006).

4. Monitor Group would soon engage on a very different sort of consultancy: a contract to help burnish the international image of Libya's leader by bringing public intellectuals and academics to Libya for conversations with the Leader about his Green Book and ideas about democracy (see later in the chapter).

5. Ibrahim was the author of a book specifically endorsing violence during the revolutionary decade. See his *Revolutionary Organization* (Tripoli: Green Book Center, 1983).

6. Saif al-Islam al-Qaddafi, "The Speech of Saif al-Islam Al Gaddafi, President of Gaddafi Development Foundation, in the First Forum of the National Organization of Libyan Youth," Sirte, 20 August 2006, www.gdf.org.ly).

7. See Amal Obeidi, "The 2009 Constitution Project," paper delivered at the Oxford University conference on "Libya Legacy of the Past, Prospects for the Future." Oxford University, 25–27 September 2009.

8. Interview with Shukri Ghanem, 16 January 2005.

9. "Qadhafi calls for self-reliance," *AlJazeera.net*, 28 August 2006.

10. Reuters, "Gaddafi says cabinet fails to enrich Libya, must go," 2 March 2008.

11. International Monetary Fund, *The Socialist People's Libyan Arab Jamahiriya – 2010 Article IV Consultation, Preliminary Conclusions of the Mission* (Washington, DC: International Monetary Fund, October 2010)

12. For an appreciation of popular support among some of sub-Saharan Africa's young population for Qadhafi and about the complexities surrounding Libyan aid in sub-Saharan Africa, see Jeffrey Gettleman, "Libyan Oil Buys Allies for Qaddafi," *The New York Times*, 15 March 2011.

13. See, for example, a description of the fate of the Green Book Center in Craig Smith, "Looking Upon Qaddafi's Works, Half-Sunk in the Sands," *The New York Times*, 4 January 2005.

14. Mark Lander, "After Fireworks, Qaddafi Shows His Milder Side," *The New York Times*, 24 September 2009.

15. See the papers by Dirk Vandewalle, Ronald Bruce St. John, Amal Obeidi, and Zahi Mogherbi delivered at the 25–27 September 2009 conference, "Libya: Legacy of the Past, Prospects for the Future," at Oxford University. Particularly Obeidi's paper on the failed "constitutional project" and Mogherbi's on the possibility of political restructuring pointed out the dilemmas of implementing serious political reforms in Libya.

16. Andy Worthington, "The Death of Rendition Victim Ibn al-Shaykh al-Libi," *Commentaries*, The Future of Freedom Foundation, 11 May 2009.

17. Daniel Volman, "AFRICOM: What Is It and What Will It Do?" *Review of African Political Economy*, Vol. 34, No. 114, (December 2007), pp. 737–744.

18. Monitor Group, *A Proposal for Expanding the Dialogue around the Ideas of Muammar Qadhafi*, (2007). A copy of the report and other various documents

that were leaked to the Libyan opposition can be found at http://www.libya-nclo.com/DocinEnglish/tabid/598/language/en-US/Default.aspx

19. In the aftermath of the uprising, Zakaria and Slaughter would strenuously argue for a no-fly zone and a more robust military intervention against the Qadhafi regime.

20. Stanley Reed, "Michael Porter on Libya's Potential," *Bloomberg Businessweek*, 23 February 2007.

21. Benjamin R. Barber, "Gaddafi's Libya: An Ally for America?" *The Washington Post*, 15 August 2007. As late as April 2011, Barber kept insisting the West should "engage" Saif al-Islam al-Qadhafi so that he could take on a "transitional, caretaking [role] while his father steps down … others must open the door so Saif can, if he chooses, walk through it and re-embrace the reformer he abandoned at such terrible cost to himself and his country." See Benjamin Barber, "Yes, Saif is a Gaddafi. But there's still a real reformer inside," *The Guardian*, 13 April 2011. See also Paul A. Rahe, "The Vanity of the Intellectual," *Ricochet.com*, 28 February 2011.

22. An earlier version of this more speculative appraisal of the Qadhafi regime's future appeared as "Libya's Divisions" in *Newsweek*, 17 April 2011. See also my "After Gaddafi," *Newsweek*, 7 March 2011, "The Reconstruction of Libya: Local and International Constraints and Opportunities," testimony before the Senate Foreign Relations Committee, 6 April 2011; "To The Shores of Tripoli," *Foreign Affairs*, March 2011. Republished in Council on Foreign Relations, *The New Arab Revolt* (New York: May 2011); and "How Not to Intervene in Libya," *Foreign Policy*, March 2011.

23. For a good analysis of the complexities involved, see Anthony Cordesman, "Libya: Will the Farce Be with Us (and France and Britain)?" *CSIS Report*, 20 April 2011, and Mahmoud Gebril ElWarfally, "What the Libyan Resistance Needs," *The New York Times*, 12 May 2011.

24. For details and repercussions of the Younes killing, see Dirk Vandewalle, "Rebel Rivalries in Libya: Division and Disorder Undermine Libya's Opposition," *Foreign Affairs*, August 2011.

25. The absence of Mahmoud Jibril (Mahmoud Gebril ElWarfally), the titular head of the TNC, from Benghazi for extended periods of time was the subject of much gossip and criticism during a visit by the author to Benghazi in mid-July.

Bibliography

Ahmida, Ali Abdullatif. *The Making of Modern Libya: State Formation, Colonization, and Resistance, 1830–1932. 2nd Edition.* (Albany, NY: State University of New York Press, 2011).

Albergoni, Gianni, et al. *La Libye nouvelle: rupture et continuité* (Paris: Editions du Centre National de Recherche Scientifique, 1975).

Alexander, Nathan. "Libya: The Continuous Revolution," *Middle Eastern Studies,* 17, no. 2 (April 1981): 210–227.

Alghariani, Saad A. "Water Transfer versus Desalination in North Africa: Sustainability and Cost Comparison," *School of Oriental and African Studies, Occasional Paper 49* (London: March 2003).

Allan, John Anthony. *Libya: The Experience of Oil* (Boulder, CO: Westview Press, 1981).

"Libya Accommodates to Lower Oil Revenues: Economic and Political Adjustments," *International Journal of Middle East Studies,* 15, no. 3 (August 1983): 377–385.

Libya Since Independence: Economic and Social Development (New York: St. Martin's Press, 1982).

Allan, John Anthony, M. M. Buru, and Keith S. McLachlan, eds., *Libya: State and Region* (London: Centre for Near and Middle Eastern Studies, School of Oriental and African Studies, 1989).

Anderson, Lisa S. *The State and Social Transformation in Tunisia and Libya, 1830–1980* (Princeton, NJ: Princeton University Press, 1986).

Anderson, Lisa. "Rogue Libya's Long Road." *Middle East Report,* no. 241 (Winter 2006): 42–47.

"The Tripoli Republic 1918–1922," in E. G. H. Joffé and K. S. McLachlan, eds., *Social and Economic Development of Libya* (London: MENAS Press, 1982), pp. 43–66.

Annuaire de l'Afrique du Nord (North African Yearbook). Vols. I–XXX (Paris: Editions du Centre National de la Recherche Scientifique, 1962–2004).

Atlantic Council of the United States. *US–Libyan Relations: Toward Cautious Reengagement* (Washington, DC: The Atlantic Council, 2003).

Ayoub, Mahmoud M. *Islam and the Third Universal Theory: The Religious Thought of Mu'ammar al-Qadhdhafi* (London: KPI Limited, 1987).

Baldinetti, Anna, ed. *Modern and Contemporary Libya: Sources and Historiographies* (Rome: Istituto Italiano Per L'Africa e L'Oriente, 2003).

Barrada, Hamid, Mark Kravetz, and Mark Whitaker. *Kadhafi: "Je suis unopposant à l'échelon mondial"* (Lausanne: Editions Pierre-Marcel Favre, 1984).

Beblawi, Hazem, and Giacomo Luciani, eds. *The Rentier State: Essays in the Political Economy of Arab Countries* (London: Croom Helm, 1987).

Behnke, Roy H., Jr. *The Herders of Cyrenaica: Ecology, Economy, and Kinship Among the Bedouin of Eastern Libya*. Illinois Series in Anthropology, no. 12 (Urbana, IL: University of Illinois Press, 1980).

Ben Halim, Mustafa Ahmad. *Libya: The Years of Hope* (London: AAS Publishers, 1998).

Bianco, Mirella. *Gadafi: Voice from the Desert* (London: Longman, 1974).

Birks, Stace, and Clive Sinclair. "Libya: Problems of a 'Rentier' State," in Richard Lawless and Allan Findlay, eds., *North Africa: Contemporary Politics and Economic Development* (New York: St. Martin's Press, 1984), pp. 241–275.

Blanchard, Christopher M. *Libya: Background and U.S. Relations. CRS Report, Congressional Research Service* (Washington, DC: Congressional Research Service, 2010).

Bleuchot, Hervé. *Chroniques et documents libyens, 1969–1980* (Paris: Editions du Centre National de la Recherche Scientifique, 1983).

Bleuchot, Hervé, and Taoufik Monastiri. "L'Islam de M. El-Qaddhafi," in Ernest Gellner and Jean-Claude Vatin, eds., *Islam et politique au Maghreb* (Paris: Editions du Centre National de la Recherche Scientifique, 1981).

Boahen, A. A. *Britain, the Sahara and the Western Sudan, 1788–1861* (London: Clarendon Press, 1964).

Buru, Mukhtar, John Anthony Allan, and Keith S. McLachlan, eds., *Libya: State and Region* (London: School of Oriental and African Studies, 1989).

Buru, Mukhtar, Shukri Ghanem, and Keith S. McLachlan, eds., *Planning and Development in Modern Libya* (London: Middle East and North African Studies Press, 1985).

Committee for Middle East Trade (COMET). *Libya: The Five Year Development Plan, 1981–1985* (London: Committee for Middle East Trade, 1981).

Cooley, John K. *Libyan Sandstorm: The Complete Account of Qaddafi's Revolution* (London: Sidgwick and Jackson, 1982).

Davis, John. *Libyan Politics: Tribe and Revolution (An Account of the Zuwaya and Their Government)* (Berkeley: University of California Press, 1987).

"Qadhafi's Theory and Practise of Non-Representative Government," *Government and Opposition*, 17, no. 1 (1982).

De Agostini, Enrico. *Le popolazioni della Cirenaica* (Bengasi: Governo della Cirenaica, 1923).

Deeb, Mary Jane. *Libya's Foreign Policy in North Africa. Westview Special Studies on the Middle East* (Boulder, CO: Westview Press, 1991).

Delacroix, Jacques. "The Distributive State in the World System," *Studies in Comparative International Development*, 15, no. 3 (Fall 1980).

Djaziri, Moncef. "La Libye: incertitudes et limites du processus de 'démocratisa-tion' et dynamique de 'l'infiraj,'" in *Annuaire de l'Afrique du Nord* (Paris: Editions du Centre Nationale de la Recherche Scientifique, 1988).

"Le systéme politique libyen 1969–1984." PhD dissertation, University of Lausanne, 1988.

Economist Intelligence Unit. *Libya: Quarterly Report* (London: Economist Intelligence Unit, 1981–2004).

Evans-Pritchard, E. E. *The Sanusi of Cyrenaica* (London: Oxford at Clarendon Press, 1949).

Farley, Rawle. *Planning for Development in Libya: The Exceptional Economy in the Developing World* (New York: Praeger Publishers, 1971).

El-Fathaly, Omar, and Monte Palmer. *Political Development and Social Change in Libya* (Lexington, MA: Lexington Books, 1980).

El-Fathaly, Omar, Monte Palmer, and Richard Chackerian. *Political Development and Bureaucracy in Libya* (Lexington, MA: Lexington Books, 1977).

"The Transformation of Mass Political Institutions in Revolutionary Libya: Structural Solutions to a Behavioural Problem," in George Joffé and Keith S. McLachlan, eds., *Social and Economic Development of Libya* (Wisbech: MENAS Press, 1982; distributed in the United States by Westview Press).

First, Ruth. *Libya: The Elusive Revolution* (Harmondsworth: Penguin, 1974).

Four Power Commission of Investigation. *Former Italian Colonies. Report on Libya* (London: Government Publishing Company, 1948).

Frachon, Alain. "Les défauts de l'armure du colonel," *Le Monde*, 30/4/86.

Gaber, Makzoum Attia. "Le mouvement du 'jihad' en Libye face à la colonization italienne de 1911 à 1919." PhD dissertation, University of Provence, 1983.

Ghanem, Shukri. *The Libyan Economy before Oil* (in Arabic) (Tripoli: National Center for Scientific Research, n.d.).

Graziani, Rodolfo. *Cirenaica pacificata* (Milan: Mondadori, 1934).

Pace romana in Libia (Milan: Mondadori, 1937).

Gurney, Judith. *Libya. The Political Economy of Oil* (Oxford: Oxford University Press, 1996).

Hablutzel, Rudolf. *Development Prospects of Capital Surplus Oil-Exporting Countries: Iraq, Kuwait, Libya, Qatar, Saudi Arabia, UAE* (Washington, DC: The World Bank, 1981).

Hajjaji, Salem. *The Agricultural Development Plans in the Socialist People's Libyan Arab Jamahiriya and the Five-Year Agricultural Transformation Plan (1976–1980)* (in Arabic) (Tripoli: The People's Establishment for Publishing, Advertising, and Printing, 1981).

Hajjar, Sami G. "The Jamahiriya Experiment in Libya: Qadhafi and Rousseau," *Journal of Modern African Studies*, 18 (1980): 181–200.

"The Marxist Origins of Qadhafi's Economic Thought," *Journal of Modern African Studies*, 20 (1982): 361–375.

"Qadhafi's Social Theory as the Basis of the Third Universal Theory," *Journal of Asian and African Studies*, 17, nos. 3–4 (1982): 177–188.

Hassan, Salaheddin Salem. "The Genesis of Political Leadership in Libya, 1952–1969." PhD dissertation, George Washington University, 1973.

Hassanein Bey, A. M. *The Lost Oases* (London: Thornton Butterworth, 1925).

Hayford, Elizabeth. "The Politics of the Kingdom of Libya in Historical Perspective." PhD dissertation, Tufts University, 1970.

Heikal, Mohammed. *The Road to Ramadan* (New York: Quadrangle/New York Times Book Co., 1975).

al-Hesnawi, Habib. *Al-Lijan ath-Thawriya* (in Arabic) (Tripoli: al-Markaz al-ʿalami li-dirasat wa-abhath al-kitab al-akhdar, 1985).

The Revolutionary Committees and Their Role in the Conformation and Consolidation of the People's Authority (Tripoli: Green Book Center, 1987).

Higgins, Benjamin Howard. *The Economic and Social Development of Libya* (New York: United Nations Technical Assistance Programme, 1953).

Hinnebusch, Raymond A. "Charisma, Revolution and State Formation: Qaddafi and Libya," *Third World Quarterly*, 6, no. 1 (1984): 59–73.

Holmboe, Knud. *Desert Encounter: An Adventurous Journey Through Italian Africa* (London: George Harrup & Co., 1936).

El-Horair, A. S. "Social and Economic Transformations in the Libyan Hinterland during the Second Half of the Nineteenth Century: The Role of Sayyid Ahmad al-Sharif al-Sanussi." PhD dissertation, University of California, 1981.

Hulerias, Asteris. "Qadhafi's Comeback: Libya and Sub-Saharan Africa in the 1990s," *African Affairs*, 100 (2001): 5–25.

Hurd, Ian. "The Strategic Use of Liberal Internationalism: Libya and the UN Sanctions, 1992–2003." *International Organization*, 59, no. 3 (Summer 2005): 495–526.

Hurewitz, Jacob Coleman. *The Middle East and North Africa in World Politics, Volumes I and II* (New Haven, CT: Yale University Press, 1975 and 1979).

Ibrahim, Ahmad. *Revolutionary Organization* (Tripoli: Green Book Center, 1983).

International Bank of Reconstruction and Development. *The Economic Development of Libya* (Baltimore: The Johns Hopkins University Press, 1960).

International Colloquium in Benghazi. The Green Book, Volume II (October 1–3, 1979) (Tripoli: Foreign Liaison Office, General Secretariat of the General People's Congress, 1981).

International Colloquium on Muʾammar Quathafi's Thought. The Green Book, Part I (November 12–15, 1981) (Tripoli: World Center for Study and Research of the Green Book, n.d.).

International Monetary Fund. *The Socialist People's Libyan Arab Jamahiriya: 2003. Article IV Consultation – Staff Report; Staff Statement; and Public Information Notice on the Executive Board Discussion* (Washington, DC: IMF Country Report No. 03/327), October 2003, 1–52.

Jentleson, Bruce W., and Christopher A. Whytock. "Who "Won" Libya?: The Force-Diplomacy Debate and Its Implications for Theory and Policy." *International Security*, 30, no. 3 (Winter 2006): 47–86.

Joffé, George, and Keith S. McLachlan, eds. *Social and Economic Development of Libya* (Wisbech: MENAS Press, 1982).

Joseph, Robert. *Countering WMD: The Libyan Experience* (Fairfax, VA: National Institute Press, 2009).

Kelly, Saul. *The Last Oasis. The Desert War and the Hunt for Zerzura* (Boulder, CO: Westview Press, 2002).

Kennedy Shaw, W. B. *Long Range Desert Group. The Story of Its Work in Libya, 1940–1943* (London: Collins, 1945).

Khadduri, Majid. *Modern Libya: A Study in Political Development* (Baltimore: The Johns Hopkins University Press, 1963).

El-Khawas, Mohamed. *Qaddafi: His Ideology in Theory and Practice* (Brattleboro, VT: Amana Books, 1986).

"Qadaffi and Islam in Libya," *American Journal of Islamic Studies*, 1, no. 1 (Spring 1984).

El-Kikhia, Mansour O. *Libya's Qaddafi. The Politics of Contradiction* (Gainesville: University of Florida Press, 1997).

Laham, Nicholas. *The American Bombing of Libya: A Study of the Force of Miscalculation in Reagan Foreign Policy* (Jefferson, NC: McFarland & Co, 2008).

Lemarchand, René, ed. *The Green and the Black: Qadhafi's Policies in Africa. Indiana Series in Arab and Islamic Studies* (Bloomington: Indiana University Press, 1988).

Libyan Arab Jamahiriyya. *Libya. Economic and Social Transformation Plan (1976–1980)* (Tripoli: Secretariat of Planning, 1976).

Libyan Arab Jamahiriyya, Secretariat of Planning. *Long-Term Development Prospects, Issues and Policies, 1980–2000* (Tripoli: Secretariat of Planning, 1979).

Libyan Arab Republic. *The Three Year Economic and Social Development Plan in Brief, 1973–1975* (Tripoli: Ministry of Planning, 1973).

Mahdavy, Hossein. "The Patterns and Problems of Economic Development in Rentier States: The Case of Iran," in M. A. Cook, ed., *Studies in the Economic History of the Middle East from the Rise of Islam to the Present Day* (Oxford: Oxford University Press, 1970).

Al-Maiar, Salem. "The Great Man-Made River Project," *European Desalination Society Newsletter*, 21 (October 2004): 6–8.

Malgeri, Francesco. *La guerra libica (1911–1912)* (Roma: Edizioni de Storia e Letteratura, 1970).

Martel, André. *La Libye 1835–1990: essai de géopolitique historique* (Paris: Presses Universitaires de France, 1991).

Martínez, Luis. *The Libyan Paradox* (New York: Columbia University Press, 2007).

Mason, John Paul. *Island of the Blest: Islam in a Libyan Oasis Community*. Papers in International Studies, Africa Series, no. 3 (Athens: Ohio University, Center for International Studies, 1977).

"Petroleum Development and the Reactivation of Traditional Structure in a Libyan Oasis Community," *Economic Development and Cultural Change*, 26 (July 1978): 763–776.

"Qadhdhafi's 'Revolution' and Change in a Libyan Oasis Community," *Middle East Journal*, 36 (Summer 1982): 319–335.

Mattes, Hanspeter. *Die Innere und Aussere Islamische Mission Libyens* (Hamburg: Kaiser/Grünenwald, 1986).

"Islam und Staatsaufbau: Das theoretische Konzept und das Beispiel der Sozialistischen Libyschen Arabischen Volksgamahiriyya." MA thesis, University of Heidelberg, 1982.

Die Volksrevolution in der Sozialistischen Libyschen Arabischen Volksgamahiriyya (Heidelberg: Kivouvou Verlag, 1982).

Mayer, Ann Elizabeth. "Developments in the Law of Marriage and Divorce in Libya," *Journal of African Law*, 22 (1978): 30–49.

"Le droit musulman en Libye à l'âge du 'Livre Vert,'" *Maghreb-Machrek*, 33, no. 93 (July–August 1981).

Islamic Law in Libya: Analyses of Selected Laws Enacted since the 1969 Revolution (London: School of Oriental and African Studies, 1977).

"Islamicizing Laws Affecting the Regulation of Interest Charges and Risk Contracts: Some Problems of Recent Libyan Legislation," *International and Comparative Law Quarterly*, 28 (1979): 541–559.

Mezoughi, A. A. *Mafhum al-Idara ash-sha'biya (The Principles of Administration)* (Tripoli: Green Book Center, 1984).

Miège, E. L. *L'imperialismo coloniale dal 1870 ai giorni nostri* (Milan: Rizzoli, 1976).

Mogherbi, Mohamed Zahi. "The Socialization of School Children in the Socialist People's Libyan Arab Jamahiriya." PhD dissertation, University of Missouri, 1978.

Monitor Group. *A Proposal for Expanding the Dialogue around the Ideas of Muammar Qadhafi* (Monitor Company Group, L.P., 2007).

Mugharyif, Muhammad [Mohamed Yousef Al-Magariaf]. *Libya between the Past and the Present (in Arabic), Volumes I, II and III* (Oxford: Centre for Libyan Studies, 2004).

Neuberger, Benjamin. *Involvement, Invasion and Withdrawal: Qadhdhafi's Libya and Chad 1969–1981* (Syracuse, NY: Syracuse University Press, 1982).

Niblock, Tim. *Pariah States and Economic Sanctions in the Middle East: Iraq, Libya, Sudan* (Boulder, CO: Lynne Riener, 2001).

Obeidi, Amal. *Political Culture in Libya* (Richmond: Curzon, 2001).

O'Sullivan, Meghan L. *Shrewd Sanctions: Statecraft and State Sponsors of Terrorism* (Washington, DC: Brookings Institution Press, 2003).

Otayek, René. *La politique africaine de la Libye* (Paris: Karthala, 1987).

Otman, Waniss, and Erling Karlberg. *The Libyan Economy: Economic Diversification and International Repositioning* (Berlin: Springer, 2010).

Pargeter, Alison. "Libya: Reforming the Impossible?" *Review of African Political Economy*, 33, no. 108 (June 2006): 219–235.

Pelt, Adrian. *Libyan Independence and the United Nations: A Case of Planned Decolonization* (New Haven, CT: Yale University Press, 1970).

Peters, Emry L. *The Bedouin of Cyrenaica: Studies in Personal and Corporate Power*, ed. Jack Goody and Emanuel Marx (Cambridge: Cambridge University Press, 1990).

al-Qadhafi, Mu'ammar. *As-Sijil Al-Qawmi bayanat wa ahadith al-aqid Mu'ammar al-Qadhdhafi. Vols. I–XXV* (Tripoli: Marakiz ath-thaqafiya al-qawmiya, 1969–2005).

The Green Book. 3 vols. (Tripoli: The Green Book Center, 1980).

"Intervention at the First World Symposium on the Green Book," in *International Colloquium in Benghazi: The Green Book* (Tripoli: Foreign Liaison Office, 1981).

"The Revolutionary Declaration of Brother Col. M. al-Qadhafi, September 1, 1978" (Tripoli: Secretariat of Foreign Affairs, 1978).

Alqadhafi, Saif Aleslam. *Libya and the XXI Century* (Editar Spa, 2002).

Rennell of Rodd, Lord. *British Military Administration of Occupied Territories in Africa during the Years 1941–1947* (London: His Majesty's Stationery Office, 1948).

Romano, Sergio. *La Quarta Sponda: La guerra di Libia, 1911–1912* (Milan: Bompiani, 1977).

Ronen, Yehudit. *Qaddafi's Libya in World Politics* (Boulder, CO: Lynne Rienner Publishers, 2008).

Roumani, Jacques. "From Republic to Jamahiriya: Libya's Search for Political Community," *Middle East Journal*, 37, no. 2 (Spring 1983): 151–168.

Roumani, Maurice. *The Jews of Libya: Coexistence, Persecution, Resettlement* (Portland, OR: Sussex Academic Press, 2008).

Said, Rif'at. *Tatawir al-Ta'lim fi Libiyya (The Evolution of Education in Libya)* (Benghazi: Dar al-Haqiqa, 1972).

Sarkis, Nicolas. "Les Arabes pauvres et les Arabes riches," *Le Monde Diplomatique*, August 1978.

Schwartz, Jonathan B. "Dealing with a 'Rogue State': The Libya Precedent," *The American Journal of International Law*, 101, no. 3 (July 2007): 553–580.

Segré, Claudio G. Fourth Shore. *The Italian Colonization of Libya* (Chicago: The University of Chicago Press, 1974).

Simons, Geoff. *Libya and the West: From Independence to Lockerbie* (Oxford: Centre for Libyan Studies, 2003).

Soudan, François. *Kadhafi, la CIA et les marchands de mort* (Paris: Groupe Jeune Afrique, 1977).

Souriau, Christiane. *Libye: l'économie des femmes* (Paris: L'Harmattan, 1986).

St. John, Ronald Bruce. *Historical Dictionary of Libya, 2nd ed.* (Metuchen, NJ: Scarecrow Press, 1991).

Historical Dictionary of Libya (Lanham, MD: Scarecrow Press, 2006).

"The Ideology of Mu'ammar al-Qadhdhafi: Theory and Practise," *International Journal of Middle East Studies*, 15, no. 4 (November 1983): 471–490.

Libya and the United States: Two Centuries of Strife (Philadelphia: University of Pennsylvania Press, 2002).

Libya: From Colony to Independence (Oxford: Oneworld, 2008).

Qaddafi's World Design; Libyan Foreign Policy 1969–1987 (London: Saqi Books, 1987).

Stanik, Joseph T. *El Dorado Canyon: Reagan's Undeclared War with Qaddafi* (Annapolis, MD: Naval Institute Press, 2003).

Steer, G. L. *Date in the Desert* (London: Hodder and Stoughton, 1939).

Sury, Salaheddin Hasan [Salaheddin Salem Hassan]. "A New System for a New State: The Libyan Experiment in Statehood, 1951–1969," in Anna Baldinetti, ed., *Modern and Contemporary Libya: Sources and Historiographies* (Rome: Istituto Italiano Per L'Africa et L'Oriente, 2003), p. 183.

Tully, Miss [Lady Montague]. *Narrative of Ten Years' Residence at Tripoli in Africa, 2nd ed.* (London: Colburn, 1817).

Vandewalle, Diederik. "The Origins and Parameters of Libya's Recent Actions," *Arab Reform Bulletin*, 2, no. 3 (March 2004): 3–5.

Vandewalle, Dirk. "After Gaddafi." *Newsweek*, March 7, 2011.

"Good Riddance, Gaddafi." *Newsweek*, August 29, 2011.

"L'économie libyenne: un développement trés lent malgré des revenus pétroliers considérables," in Camille Lacoste and Yves Lacoste, eds., *L'état du Maghreb* (Paris: Editions La Découverte, 1991), pp. 454–456.

How Not to Intervene in Libya. 2011 10-March.

"Libya's Divisions." *Newsweek*, April 17, 2011.

Libya since 1969: Qadhafi's Revolution Revisited (New York: Palgrave Macmillan, 2008).

Libya since Independence: Oil and State-Building (Ithaca, NY: Cornell University Press, 1998).

"Libya's Revolution Revisited," *Middle East Report*, no. 143 (November–December 1986): 30–35, 43.

"Political Aspects of State Building in Rentier Economies: Algeria and Libya Compared," in Hazem Beblawi and Giacomo Luciani, eds., *The Rentier State* (London: Croom Helm, 1987).

"Qadhafi's 'Perestroika': Economic and Political Liberalization in Libya," *Middle East Journal* (Spring 1991).

"Qadhafi's Unfinished Revolution," *Mediterranean Quarterly* (Winter 1990).

"The Many Qaddafis." *The New York Times*, February 23, 2011.

"The Reconstruction of Libya Local and International Constraints and Opportunities." Testimony, Senate Foreign Affairs Committee, U.S. Senate, March 2011.

"To the Shores of Tripoli." *Foreign Affairs*, March 1, 2011.

"Rebel Rivalries in Libya: Division and Disorder Undermine Libya's Opposition." *Foreign Affairs*, August 16, 2011

Villard, Henry Serrano. *Libya: The New Arab Kingdom of North Africa* (Ithaca, NY: Cornell University Press, 1956).

Waddams, Frank C. *The Libyan Oil Industry* (Baltimore: The Johns Hopkins University Press, 1980).

El-Warfally, Mahmoud G. *Imagery and Ideology in US Policy Toward Libya, 1969–1982* (Pittsburgh, PA: University of Pittsburgh Press, 1988).

Wright, Claudia. "Libya and the West: Headlong into Confrontation?" *International Affairs* (London) 58, no. 1 (Winter 1981–1982): 13–41.

Wright, John. *Libya: A Modern History* (Baltimore: The Johns Hopkins University Press, 1981).

Al-Zawi, Al-Tahar Ahmad. *Jihad al-Abtal fi Tarabulus al-Gharb (The Holy War of the Heroes in Tripoli)* (Cairo: Imprimerie Tajella al-Jadida, 1950).

Ziadeh, Nicolah. *Sanusiyah: A Study of a Revivalist Movement in Islam* (Leiden: Brill, 1968).

Index

Arabian Gulf Corporation, 157
Arab–Israeli conflict, 76, 98, 108, 130, 137, 178, 215
Arafat, Yasser, 77
Armistice agreements (1918), xviii, 27
Army Day, 71
Asabaa, battle of, xviii
al-Asabiyya, Ahmad Ramadan, 148
assassination, 62, 120, 128, 130, 131
assets, 154
    distribution of, 108
    economic, 106
    freezing of, xxix, 131
As-Sijil Al-Qawmi bayanat wa ahadith al-aqid Mu'ammar al-Qadhafi, 220
ASU, *see* Arab Socialist Union
Atlantic Council of the United States, 181, 182
Atlantic Ocean, 20
Austria, 21, 157
Awjila, 28
Awlad Sulayman tribe, 18
Axis Powers, 36
Ayoub, Mahmoud M., 220
Aziendi Generale Italiana Petroliche, 53

Bab al-Aziziyya, 119, 134, 148, 166, 208
Bablo, Marshal Italo, 32
back-channel diplomacy, 174
Badri, Abdallah, 183
al-Baghdadi, Abd al-Qadr, 188, 189
Baladiyyat, *see* municipality
balance-of-payments, 112, 152
balance-of-trade, 109
Baldinetti, Anna, 215, 219
Banco di Roma, 21, 22
Bandung Conference, 79
Bani Walid, 27, 208
Banking, 47, 51, 64, 87, 107, 108, 152, 162, 165
Banu Hilal, 16
Banu Sulaym, 16
al-Baradei, Muhammad, xxx
Barbary Coast, 16
    see also North Africa
Barber, Benjamin, 202
Barce-Tukra plain, 92
Barrada, Hamid, 219, 223
barter, 151
Al-Baruni, Sulayman, xviii, 26, 27, 28, 29
Basic People's Committee, 103
Basic People's Congress (BPC), xxiv, 103, 119, 120
Basic Production Committee, 106
Al-Bayda, 48, 71
bayt li sakinihi policy, xxv
Bedouin, 26, 27, 29, 31

Ben Halim, Mustafa, 66
Benghazi, xxiv, 14, 15, 20, 21, 24, 26, 36, 44, 48, 52, 62, 69, 71, 83, 145
    see also United States
Benghazi Military College, 148
Benghazi Treaty, 86
Berber, xviii, 16, 18, 26, 29, 30
Berlusconi, Silvio, 199
Bevin-Sforza plan, xx, 39
Bey, A. M. Hassanein, 216
Bey, Abd al-Rahman Azzam, 27
Bilkhayr, Abd al-Nabi, 27
Bin Halim, Mustafa, 49, 62, 66, 69, 70, 71, 217, 218, 219
Bin Uthman, Muhammad, 49
birth rate, 51
black market, 144, 146, 154, 166
Blair, Tony, xxxi, 182
Bleuchot, Herve, 220
BMA, *see* British Military Administration
Boahen, A. A., 216
Bornu, 11, 19
boundary, 40
    administrative, xxii
    dispute, xxv, xxviii, xxix, 65, 158
    geographic, xix, xvii,
    provincial, 48, 55, 82
    see also Aouzou dispute; Chad; Libya–Tunisia
bourgeoisie, 41, 80, 125
Boycott, *see* sanctions; United States
BP, *see* British Petroleum
BPC, *see* Basic People's Congress
Brak, 14
Braspetro, 108
Brazil, 151
Brega, *see* Marsa al-Burayqa
bribery, 70
brinkmanship, 1
British Military Administration (BMA), xix, 34, 37, 46, 217
British Petroleum, xxiii, 53, 58, 157
Brussels, xxxi
budget, xxvii, 57, 67, 104, 110, 111, 129, 162
    deficit, 51–52
    development, 112, 113
    planning, 61
bureaucracy, 8, 18, 50, 68, 93, 102, 105, 110, 111, 145, 146, 164
    economic, 45, 68, 159
    federal, 50
    provincial, 64, 73
    state, 72
bureaucratization, 73
Burgat, Francois, 215
Burkina Faso, 196